Other Books and Series by Jeff Bowen

Cherokee Intermarried White 1906 Volume I thru *X*

Applications for Enrollment of Creek Newborn Act of 1905
Volumes I thru *XIV*

Applications for Enrollment of Choctaw Newborn Act of 1905 Volumes I thru *XX*

Choctaw By Blood Enrollment Cards 1898-1914 Volumes I thru *XX*

Oglala Sioux Indians Pine Ridge Reservation 1932 Census Book I
Oglala Sioux Indians Pine Ridge Reservation Birth and Death Rolls 1924-1932
Book II

Census of the Sioux and Cheyenne Indians of Pine Ridge Agency
1896 - 1897   Book I
Census of the Sioux and Cheyenne Indians of Pine Ridge Agency
1898 - 1899 Book II

Northern Cheyenne Tongue River, Montana 1904 - 1932 Census
1904-1916 Volume I

Northern Cheyenne Tongue River, Montana 1904 - 1932 Census
1917-1926 Volume II

Identified Mississippi Choctaw Enrollment Cards 1902-1909   Volumes I, II & III

Sac & Fox - Shawnee Estates 1885-1910 (Under Sac & Fox Agency)
Volumes I-VIII

I0222746

Visit our website at **www.nativestudy.com** to learn more about these
and other books and series by Jeff Bowen

Portrait of Tecumseh from Lossing's
The Pictorial Field-Book of the War of 1812
is a pencil sketch drawn by Pierre Le Dru,
a young French trader at Vincennes, circa 1808.

SAC & FOX - SHAWNEE

ESTATES 1920-1924

(UNDER SAC & FOX AGENCY, OKLAHOMA)

& WILLS 1889-1924

VOLUME IX

TRANSCRIBED BY

JEFF BOWEN

NATIVE STUDY
Gallipolis, Ohio
USA

Originally published:
Santa Maria, California
2019

Reprinted by:

Native Study LLC
Gallipolis, OH
www.nativestudy.com

Library of Congress Control Number: 2022900261

ISBN: 978-1-64968-138-6

Made in the United States of America.

This series is dedicated to
Tanner Tackett
the Constant Gardner
and Friend
and
In memory of
Raina Mae Fulks.

Ab·sen·tee

noun: **absentee**; plural noun: **absentees**

> 1. a person who is expected or required to be present at a place or event but is not.

(According to Webster)

Shawnee

noun, plural Shaw-nees, (especially collectively) Shaw-nee.

> 1. a member of an Algonquian-speaking tribe formerly in the east-central U.S., now in Oklahoma.

(According to Dictionary.com)

Shawnee Teaching

"Tagi nsi walr mvci-lutvwi mr-pvyaci-grlahkv, xvga mytv inv gi mvci-lutvwv, gi mvci-ludr-geiv. Walv uwas-panvsi inv, wa-ciganv-hi gi gol-utvwv u kvgesakv-namv manwi-lanvwawewa yasi golutv-mvni geyrgi.

"Tagi bemi-lutvwi walr segalami mr-pvyaci-grlahkv, xvga mvtv inv gi bemi-lutvwv, gi bemi-ludr-geiv gelv. Wakv vhqalami inv, xvga nahfrpi Moneto ut vhqalamrli nili yasi vhqalamahgi gelv!"

Translation:

"Do not kill or injure your neighbor, for it is not him that you injure, you injure yourself. But do good to him, therefore add to his days of happiness as you add to your own.

"Do not wrong or hate your neighbor, for it is not him that you wrong, you wrong yourself. But love him, for Moneto loves him also as He loves you!"

Thomas Wildcat Alford
circa 1936

v

Special Note

You will notice throughout these volumes the author has attempted to duplicate from the original documents places on the page that were destroyed due to water damage. Whole sections of a page could be missing or torn into multiple pieces. In order to duplicate the damage you will find various shapes with a white format to try to represent the damage and the loss of the ability to completely transcribe many of the pages.

INTRODUCTION

The history of the Shawnee is fascinating. Naturally the most famous Shawnee known would be Tecumseh, born circa. 1768, after four other siblings before him. His father was Puckeshinwa, a Shawnee war chief from Ohio. Puckeshinwa crossed the Ohio close to what is now Gallipolis with his fourteen year son Chiksika by his side. As they followed the lead of Chief Cornstalk during the fall of 1774. Tecumseh's famous father was mortally wounded during the fight they would soon encounter. The Shawnees were unexpectedly discovered by a couple of early morning turkey hunters from the settlement called Point Pleasant. These hunters ran as fast as possible back to where the Ohio and Kanawha Rivers meet and sounded the alarm that the Shawnees were coming, the fight lasted most of the day but not without loss to both sides. The Shawnees were badly outnumbered. Pucheshinwa was carried back across the Ohio or as the Shawnees called it the *Spaylaywitheepi*, with the intention to take him back to his village. He must have known his time was short as he laid there telling Chiksika to make sure he devoted his time not only to Tecumseh's but also his younger brothers training in becoming warriors. Pucheshinwa succumbed to his wounds shortly after that request and was secretly buried deep in the forest that day. Chiksika saw his father mortally wounded while defending their home. He had a reverence for his father as a great warrior. He wanted to follow his father's path and not die an average death. In his heart, it had to be on the battlefield as a warrior. Tecumseh followed his brother's every step and planned to die defending his land as his father and brother had. There was no surrendering or giving in to the Americans.

There are several descriptions out there of Tecumseh from his contemporaries, but David Edmunds found one during his research that seems to be the most commanding of any found. "Captain John B. Glegg, Brock's aide-de-camp, who was present at the meetings between Brock and Tecumseh, recorded one of the most vivid descriptions of the Shawnee. According to Glegg, in August 1812 Tecumseh still was in the prime of his life, giving the impression of a man ten years younger. Tecumseh's appearance was very prepossessing; his figure light and finely proportioned; his age I imagined to be about five and thirty [he actually was forty four]; in height, five feet nine or ten inches; his complexion, light copper; countenance, oval, with bright hazle eyes, beaming cheerfulness, energy, and decision. Three small silver crowns, or coronets were suspended from the lower cartilage of his aquiline nose; and a large silver medallion of George the Third, which I believe his ancestor had received from Lord Dorchester, when governor-general of Canada, was attached to a mixed coloured wampum string, and hung around his neck. His dress consisted of a plain, neat uniform, tanned deer-skin jacket, with long trousers of the same material, the seams of both being covered with neatly cut fringe; and he had on his feet leather moccasins, much ornamented with work made from the dyed quills of the porcupine."[1]

There were approximately 39 years that passed between Tecumseh's and his father's deaths. It is hard to believe that the Shawnee's history being as extensive as it was during the early stages of the United States that their descendants' records were so closely guarded under the care of a vegetable bind in an leaky attic. Not only the Shawnee's but also the Sac & Fox, the Pottawatomie and the Kickapoo. There are also many other tribal affiliates to be found in this series, not to mention someone like Jim Thorpe and his family members of the Sac and Fox tribe. Not only was he a gold metal Olympian and multiple sport competitor, but at the time one of America's favorite sons. Thank goodness someone was finally conscious of the situation. The description in the next paragraph explains the neglect of these important documents as given by the Oklahoma Historical Societies Microfilm Catalog.

"In 1933 a survey of Indian tribal records in Oklahoma revealed that the files of the Shawnee and the old Sac and Fox agencies had been sadly neglected, and the lack of space for storing them properly had resulted in much loss. Charles Eggers, Superintendent of the Shawnee Agency, reported that most of the non-current records of his agency were boxed in a storehouse. The papers of the old Sac and Fox Agency were in the loft of a warehouse which was also used for storing vegetables. The roof of the building leaked and the papers were in danger of destruction from moisture. Following the passage of the Congressional Act of March 27, 1934 (H.R. 5631 Public No. 133) which placed the tribal records in the custody of the Oklahoma Historical Society."

As described above the history of the Shawnee people isn't an ordinary history but an extraordinary time in all of our ancestors' lives. Reading Allen W. Eckert's extensive studies taken from what is known as the Draper Papers, a historical record meticulously documented beginning circa 1830. Though Draper covered an approximate time between the 1740's to the 1810's, his collection covered documents and transcriptions concerning Boone, Kenton, Rogers Clark and Joseph Brant, not to mention a considerable amount of Shawnee history from the entirety of the Ohio and Mississippi Valley's. Other authors such as Colin G. Calloway and R. David Edmunds provide an in depth study of the Shawnee people as well as Tecumseh and his life leaving no rock unturned in their research.

As you read different references you find diverse opinions on Tecumseh's mother as to what tribe she came from. Eckert through Draper's work says, "This was

---

[1] Tecumseh, R. David Edmunds Pg. 162-163, Para. 3-4

when Pucksinwah, then twenty-six, led the war party against the Cherokees that had resulted in the capture of Methotasa."[2] Indicating Tecumseh's mother might have been Cherokee. Yet, R. David Edmunds writes, "In 1768, while the Iroquois were selling Shawnee lands at the Treaty of Fort Stanwix, a Creek woman married to a Shawnee man gave birth to a son at Old Piqua, a Shawnee village on the Mad River in Western Ohio. The woman had a difficult labor before giving birth in the small lodge especially constructed for that purpose, some distance from the family's wigwam. The mother, Methoataske (Turtle Laying Its Eggs), had grown up among the Creek villages in Alabama and had met her husband when some of the Shawnee sought refuge among the Creeks during the 1750s. The father Puckeshinwa, remained with his wife's people until about 1760, when the family left Alabama and migrated to Ohio."[3]

You also will find different opinions on how they dressed back then or wore their hair. In Edmunds' book *Tecumseh*, his brother the Prophet Tenskwatawa states, "Warriors should again shave their heads and wear the scalp locks worn by their ancestors." And yet in Thomas Wildcat Alford's *Civilization,* he says, "We boys wore our hair short, very much as the girls of today wear their hair bobbed. This is the way Shawnee men always have worn their hair. Never did they braid it, as some other tribes do."

Alford's book *Civilization* out of the many resources read was likely one of the most informative and enjoyable references in the study. Thomas Wildcat Alford was born in 1860 and belonged to the Absentee Shawnee tribe. He states that he was a descendant of Tecumseh. He spoke about when his family slept under the stars each night and that he never had an English name until his father had him go to school at a Quaker mission. Mr. Alford also talks about two things with real clarity. Alford educates us about clans in the sixth chapter, expounding upon the active history of the Shawnees and the different responsibilities of each as well as divisions among the clans that created tribal changes. These dissensions were nothing new. Anyone that has read extensively about the Shawnee will realize that Alford understood his people and their history. When he wrote about tribal clashes or divisions during the early days, he managed to translate on paper their strength and character. He showed for generations they literally believed they were given an ability to make themselves self-reliant when it came to survival. They traveled far and wide following their own path while installing their own way of life that made them powerful adversaries whether it be against the British, the French or the Americans moving west. Other tribes found them to be awful enemies or potent allies. Then he compares their tribal government

---

[2] A Sorrow in Our Heart, Allen W. Eckert Pg. 22, Para. 3
[3] Tecumseh, R. David Edmunds, Pg. 17 Para. 1

and the clan leaders to being quite similar to the U.S. Presidency and the different government entities. Alford also brings up business committees for the tribe.

He starts with a concise description of the clans, "Originally there were five clans composing the Shawnee tribe, including the two principle clans, Tha-we-gi-la and Cha-lah-kaw-tha, from one of which came the national or principal chief. The remaining three, the Pec-ku-we, the Kis-pu-go, and the May-ku-jay, each had its own chief who was subordinate to the principal chief in national matters, but independent in matters pertaining to the duties of his clan. Each clan had a certain duty to perform for the whole tribe. For instance the Pec-ku-we clan, or its chief, had charge of the maintenance of order and looked after the celebration of things pertaining to religion or faith; the Kis-pu-go clan had charge of matters pertaining to war and the preparation and training of warriors; the May-ku-jay clan had charge of things relating to health and medicine and food for the whole tribe. But the two powerful clans, the Tha-we-gi-la and the Cha-lah-kaw-tha, had charge of political affairs and all matters that affected the tribe as a whole. Indeed, the tribal government may be likened to the government of the United States, in which each state (clan), with it governor (chief), is sovereign in local matters, but subordinate to the president of the United States (principal chief) in national matters. The difference is that the president of the United States must be elected, and may be changed with each election, while the principal chief came to his office by heritage and held it for life, or during good behavior.

At the time of which I write the Shawnee tribe had been divided for many years, and only the Tha-we-gi-la, the Pec-ku-we, and the Kis-pu-go clans were represented in the Absentee Shawnee band. These three clans always had been closely related, while the Cha-lah-kaw-tha and the May-ku-jay had always stood together, and were represented in the group that I have mentioned as living in Kansas at the time of the Civil War."[4]

As referenced earlier Thomas Wildcat Alford brought up their present Indian agent, Thomas, on September 13, 1893, wanting him to present a list of prominent men in their tribe to hold positions on a business committee. This presented a whole new world for the tribe with new pressures through white change so to speak. The government was instilling in their world the destruction of their heritage in tribal customs and culture all to control Indian land through allotment. When he was being told to help form this committee, he was actually being told, what we are doing is we are wiping out your way of life forever. The Congress of the United States was presenting the abolition of all tribal governments so the land could be manipulated through the Curtis Act of 1898. They said, we are splitting the land up. They were allotting so many acres to each tribal member. How much they got depended on

---

[4] Civilization, Alford; Pg. 44, Para. 1-2

whether they planned to farm or raise cattle. If they were building herds they were given double the land for grazing. Alford said, "It was on the thirteenth day of September, 1893 that Agent Thomas informed the Shawnees that he had been directed by the Commissioner of Indian Affairs to submit for approval the names of seven of the most prominent men of the tribe who would constitute a Business Committee to supersede the chiefs and councilors of the old tribal government. The Business Committee was to represent the Absentee Shawnees as a tribe in all dealings with the United States and to act in an advisory capacity to the individual members of the tribe. They were to certify to the identity of grantors of sales of land and to act for the tribe in other matters.[5]

During the study it was noticed that the Curtis Act being enacted on June 28, 1898 and Alford's mentioning its initiation during 1893 became a point of interest or at least premature. It was found that Congress had actually started working in this area of seizure approximately five years prior to the agent's notification, "In 1893 Congress began a special allotment process for the Five Tribes, enacting a number of laws that affect the governmental powers of the tribes. Some of these laws, like the 1889 and 1890 Acts, extended certain Arkansas laws over Indian Territory and expanded federal court jurisdiction; they are relevant today only insofar as they may indirectly affect tribal judicial powers."[6]

Their mention of these laws only being relevant today, though actually not spoken, plead plausible deniability while coinciding with the Indian Reorganization Act of 1934. The government was on a mission. Land and control. The allotment had to take place. They were wanting statehood. They were wanting the Native people to be under one umbrella with everyone else. Tribes were nations. Just like a foreign nation, they were their own government. Originally our constitution was modeled after the Iroquois model, had to start somewhere? So what we did was split up the land among the people that already owned it. Then we took what was left, approximately 90 million acres and sold it at a profit. Who got the money? Only the politicians at the time know? But years after taking the chiefs and councils away there was likely mass chaos like a town hall today. So the government likely was wanting out of the tribal control business. At least enough that they could just control it without being in the bullseye so to speak. Congress and the state had already achieved its goals. So this act was written with the statement that it was a model to make all think we do this for you. "The IRA was intended to provide a mechanism for the tribe as a governmental unit to interact with and adapt to a modern society, rather than to force the assimilation of individual Indians.

---

[5] Civilization, Alford; Pg. 161, Para. 2
[6] Federal Indian Law, Cohen; Pg. 781, Para. 3

The IRA was also an attempt to improve the economic situation of Indians. The Act was intended to stop the alienation of tribal land needed to support Indians, and to provide for acquisition of additional acreage for tribes. Tribes were encouraged to organize along the lines of modern business corporations; a system of financial credit was included to reach this economic objective."[7] Interestingly enough Cohen and Alford both mention this same organizational technique, only one as law and another as a tribal member.

It is disconcerting just in reading a reference from Senator Charles Curtis as he mentioned in his biography that by the time Congress finished rewriting the bill he had submitted he hardly recognized it. "Officially titled the "Act for the Protection of the People of Indian Territory", the Act is named for Charles Curtis, congressman from Kansas and its author. He was of mixed Native American and European descent: on his mother's side -Kansa, Osage, Potawatomi, and French; and on his father's - three ethnic lines of British Isles ancestry. Curtis was raised in part on the Kaw Reservation of his maternal grandparents, but also lived with his paternal grandparents and attended Topeka High School. He read law, became an attorney, and later was elected to the United States House of Representatives and Senate. He served as Vice-President under Herbert Hoover. In the usual fashion, by the time the bill HR 8581 had gone through five revisions in committees in both the House of Representatives and the Senate, there was little left of Curtis' original draft. In his hand-written autobiography, Curtis noted having been unhappy with the final version of the Curtis Act. He believed that the Five Civilized Tribes needed to make changes. He thought that the way ahead for Native Americans was through education and use of both their and the majority cultures, but he also had hoped to give more support to Native American transitions."[8]

The records within this series concern The Absentee Shawnee as well as many other people with different tribal affiliations. Also within these pages are closely related tribes that were under the same agency (The Sac & Fox Agency, Oklahoma) for many years like the Sac & Fox, the Pottawatomie and the Kickapoo. There are likely state recognized Shawnee tribes in the United States, but, "The Absentee Shawnee Tribe of Indians of Oklahoma (or Absentee Shawnee) is one of three federally recognized tribes of Shawnee people. Historically residing in the Eastern United States, the original Shawnee lived in the areas that are now Ohio, Indiana, Illinois, Kentucky, Tennessee, Pennsylvania, and other neighboring states. It is documented that they occupied and traveled through lands from Canada to Florida, from the Mississippi River to the eastern continental coast. In contemporary times, the Absentee Shawnee Tribe headquarters in Shawnee, Oklahoma; its tribal jurisdiction

---

[7] Federal Indian Law, Cohen; Pg. 147 Para. 1-2
[8] Curtis Act of 1898, Wikipedia

area includes land properties in Oklahoma in both Cleveland County and Pottawatomie County." [Today] "There are approximately 3,050 enrolled Absentee Shawnee tribal members, 2,315 of whom live in Oklahoma. Tribal membership follows blood quantum criteria, with applicants requiring a minimum of one eighth (1/8) documented Absentee-Shawnee blood to be placed on its membership rolls, as set forth by the tribal constitution. Though it is not a formal division, there is a social separation within its current tribal membership between the traditionalist Big Jim Band, which kept cultural traditions and ceremonies and has its primary populace in the Little Axe, Norman area, and the assimilationist White Turkey Band, which adopted European ways of the European majority, with many families based in the Shawnee area. Regardless of historical viewpoints, the bands cooperate for the future of the tribe."[9]

When this study was first pursued an old Xerox copy of a catalog that sat on the shelf for twenty five years was the first place searched for a viable source. It was titled, "Catalog of Microfilm Holdings in the Archives & Manuscripts Div. Oklahoma Historical Society 1976-1989". As mentioned in the description from this catalog's Introduction for the Sac and Fox Indian Agencies, it states, "In 1901 the Sac and Fox Agency was divided. The Sac and Fox Agency itself remained at the old site near Stroud with jurisdiction over the Sac and Fox and the Iowa. The Shawnee, Potawatomi and Kickapoo Agency (sometimes simply called the Shawnee Agency) was established about two miles south of Shawnee, Oklahoma. The agencies continued their separate existence until 1919 when they were merged becoming the Shawnee Agency.

Of course today in 2018, everything is digital and on the computer. You have to be thankful for having an old catalog and books on a shelf. There is nothing like the feel of holding a book in your hand. You can pick it up when you want and let your eyes travel to anywhere or any time in history. It has solid print that nobody can manipulate or change. It's just yours to wrap yourself up in without any glowing distractions as Native Americans call them, "Talking Leaves".

Jeff Bowen
Gallipolis, Ohio
NativeStudy.com

---

[9] Absentee-Shawnee Tribe of Indians Wikipedia

Sac & Fox – Shawnee Estates
1920-1924 Volume IX

Shawnee Indian Agency,
Shawnee, Oklahoma,
Sept. 27, 1922.

The Honorable Com.
of Indian Affairs,
Washington, D. C.

Dear Mr. Commissioner:

There is transmitted herewith the application for patent in fee by the heirs of Sarah Bear, Sac & Fox allottee No. 3, as declared in Law-Heirship 55822-21 SYT. and recommend that it be disapproved as recommended by Mr. A. B. Collins, United States Farmer.

Very respectfully,

9 od 27.
Incl. App. Pat.

J. L. Suffecool,
Supt. & Spl. Disb. Agt.

App. Patent
Thomas Jefferson
Buffalohorn
Sac & Fox No. 84.

Shawnee Indian Agency,
Shawnee, Oklahoma,
Sept. 26, 1922.

The Honorable Com.
of Indian Affairs,
Washington, D. C.

Dear Mr. Commissioner:

Transmitted herewith is the application for patent in fee by the heirs of Thomas Jefferson Buffalohorn, Sac & Fox allottee No. 84, covering the E/2 of SW/4 of Section 21, Twp. 11 N., Range 4 Est of the Indian Meridian in Pottawatomie County, Oklahoma.

These heirs when considered according to recent regulations probably would not measure up the standard of Competency required but in as much as this is inherited land it is considered best to recommend that a patent issue. All of them speak and write the English language, and there are no minors to consider.

1

Very respectfully,

9 od 29.   J. L. Suffecool,
Incl. App. Pat.   Supt. & Spl. Disb. Agt.

Land-Allots.
37176-13
55397-19
Mc P

The Honorable Com.
of Indian Affairs,
Washington, D. C.

Dear Mr. Commissioner:

This has reference to the allotment of Waw-paw-nab-ke-she-no-quah, deceased, Kickapoo No. 81, title to which was clouded by the action of the County Treasurer of Lincoln County, Oklahoma, in deeding the land to F. A. Rittenhouse for the delinquent taxes for the year of 1914.

There appeared in this office parties claiming to be the heir s[sic] of the above mentioned allottee and requested information with reference to the status of this allotment. In view of the fact that Manuel Mills is still in possession of the land it would appear that no action had ever been taken by this office to return to the Government and to the heirs when determined, the allotment in question.

For the information of the Office, it may be stated that an investigation was [illegible] and it was found that Manuel Mills is an old darky who is living on the land under the impression that he is the rightful owner by gift from the allottee in return for services he rendered during the last days of the allottee. He claims to have been defrauded by certain unscrupulous whites by getting away with his deed.

It is now desired by this office such instructions regarding possession of this allotment by Mills as willproperly[sic] dispose of this matter.

Very respectfully,

9 od 29.   J. L. Suffecool,
                                                   Supt. & Spl. Disb. Agt.

Probate
748121-22
WHG

Shawnee Indian Agency,
Shawnee, Oklahoma,
September 29, 1922.

The Honorable,
    The Commissioner
        of Indian Affairs,
            Washington, D. C.

My dear Mr. Commissioner:-

I have the honor to acknowledge the receipt of Office communication of above reference under date of September 26, 1922, in which was inclosed for immediate report and return of inclosure, the letter from Mr. James J. Mars, an attorney of Sapulpa, Oklahoma, with reference to certain mortgage held by the Tecumseh State Bank on the personal property of Polecat, deceased Shawnee Indian.

In reply, I have to advise that this matter has been partly investigated and it is found that the estate of Polecat, Shawnee Indian, has not been probated and the heirs are un-determined.

There is to his credit on the books of this office, the sum of $44.82. His wife, Mrs. Sapesa Polecat, has no funds at this unit, nor is she an allottee. It is not possible for this office to take any action with regard to the payment of this mortgage, which is one of many that has come to the attention of this office during the past few months. It appears that practically all of the Indians have mortgaged their personal property, some of them two or three times, and it is hardly ever a day passes but what some banker or money-lender comes to this office requesting settlement.

It is believed that if assistance is rendered in collecting indebtedness of this kind that it would be in violation of existing regulations governing such indebtedness; hence, about all this office does is to make a silent investigation of the status, and advise the banker or money lender that it is impossible for this office to take any action.

Mr. Mars' letter is returned herewith, as per request of the Office.

Very respectfully,

J. L. Suffecool
Superintendent.

JLS:EV.
INCL. 1.

3

Shawnee Indian Agency,
Shawnee, Oklahoma,
Sept. 29, 1922.

Mr. Charles Lybarger,
Sub-Station No. 2,
Kansas City, Mo.

Dear Mr. Lybarger:

Your letter to the Commissioner of Indian Affairs relative to the estates of Caroline Frayer and Helen Cook was refered[sic] to this office for the purpose of the issuance of a patent in fee to the Helen Cook allotment.

In connection with t he[sic] matter of a patent in fee for the Helen Cook allotment you are advised that an attempt was made to have the patent issue but it was discovered that Earl Frayer was then and is now a minor according to records in this office. He will not be 21 until next year. It appears that he was born in the year of 1908. However, if the mother of Earl Frayer can produce an affidavit by people who actually know the date of Earl's birth we can proceed to have the patent issued, provided, of course, the affidavit shows him to be of age.

You are probably aware of the fact that the patent in fee issued to the heirs of Caroline Frayer was delivered to Thomas Roy Lybarger of Ft. Scott, Kansas. Business in connection with this allotment is no longer under the supervision of the Government.

Very truly yours,

9 od 29.

J. L. Suffecool,
Superintendent.

Pet. Part.
Harry Hall
Allotment
Sac & Fox
No. 287.

Shawnee Indian Agency,
Shawnee, Oklahoma,
Oct. 10, 1922.

The Honorable Com.
of Indian Affairs,
Washington, D. C.

4

Dear Mr. Commissioner:

There are submitted herewith \[sic] petition for partition of the allotment of Harry Hall, with appraisements on from 5-110a, and the applications for patent in fee by Robert Charles Pate, and the Bigwalker heirs. Several attempts have been made to partition this allotment. The petition and report submitted herewith is about as equitable as it can be made, and it is therefore recommended for approval.

Very respectfully,

10 od 10   J. L. Suffecool,
Incl. Pet. Part.   Supt. & Spl. Disb. Agt.

Shawnee Indian Agency,

Shawnee, Oklahoma, Oct. 11, 1922.

Mr. Earl T. Miller,
   P. O. Box 538,
      Tulsa, Oklahoma.

Dear Sir:

This will refer to my letter of June 28, 1922, requesting that you send me addition bonus of $88.00 on the allotment of Jerome Wolf, deceased, to be paid to the Iowa heir Sa-ke no wa que, instead you send me a cashier's check for $188.00. You stated in your letter that you misplaced the letter written you.

It is requested that you send me a cashier's check for $88.00 as soon as possible. The check for $188.00 is herewith returned.

Very respectfully,

J. L. Suffecool,
Superintendent

TBA

Shawnee Indian Agency,
Shawnee, Oklahoma,
October 17, 1922.

Mr. O. K. Chandler,
Supt. Quapaw Agency,
Miami, Oklahoma.

Dear Sir:-

This will acknowledge receipt of your letter of September 27, 1922, in which you advise that Mrs. Nellie Kern, nee Jones, desires to know from what source the money represented in our official check No. 12520 was derived; and that she has not received any money from this estate in the last twenty years.

In reply to same, I have to advise that this money represents lease money paid to the estate of her grand-father, M-ta-ma-pa-ha-[??]-we, deceased. Her share in this estate equals to 65367/5556620. The reason that Mrs. Kern has not received any money from this estate in the last 20 years is because the heirs were not determined until 1918. Mrs. Kern's share of the lease rentals from this estate amounts to approximately $1.36 per year. The first year this lease rental was paid to this estate was in 1920. At that time Mrs. Kern received $.68 which amounted to one-half of her share of the lease rentals for that year. The other $0.68 was later placed to her credit, and has remained there to date in addition to the amounts of $1.36 placed to her credit last year from this lease; and $1.12 from the same lease, which represents her share for the year 1922. As you see this gives to the credit of Nellie Jones Kern, $3.84. This is the amount forwarded to her and is all that she has to her account at this office.

Trusting that this is the desired information, I am

Very respectfully,

J. L. Suffecool
Superintendent.

EV.

Shawnee Indian Agency,
Shawnee, Oklahoma,
Oct. 18, 1922.

Mrs. Victoria Nolen,
218 1/2 West 1st Street,
Tulsa, Oklahoma.

Dear Madam:

This replies to your letter of the 8th instant in regard to your interest in the John Taylor estate.

In connection with this matter you are advised that the heirs of said John Taylor have been determined. As determined they are the brother[s] and sister[s], and the children of the deceased brothers and sister ,[sic] of said John Taylor. If you claim heirship by being a decendent[sic] of the brother or sister you may have an interest in the estate. If otherwise it is believed you could not be considered.

As the case now stands there are about 26 heirs and the estate amounts to an allotment of 180 acres valued at about $1200.00. This you see would amount to but very little to each heir. You can decide for yourself whether it will pay you to go to the expense of proving your heirship. If you decide to do so it will be necessary for you to request for a rehearing, or a re-opening of the determination of the heirs of John Taylor by the Department, supported by affidavits of your relationship with Taylor.

This office will submit your application for re-hearing to the Indian Office for consideration whenever you make proper showing.

Very truly yours,

10 od 18.   J. L. Suffecool,
                                     Supt. & Spl. Disb. Agt.

PROBATE
77369-1915
60787-1922
  L A P
Heirship, Shawnee
Agency, Oklahoma.

Shawnee Indian Agency,
Shawnee, Oklahoma,
October 18, 1922.

The Commissioner
of Indian Affairs,
Washington, D. C.

S I R:-

Transmitted herewith are papers concerning the re-opening of the heirship case of Abbie Redrock, or E-fa-wi-si, deceased Sac & Fox allottee No. 478, Oklahoma. These papers have been prepared by Attorney, Willard E. Russell of Tama, Iowa, who represents the claimants. These papers were submitted to me through Mr. Jacob B. Breid, Superintendent of the Sac & Fox Sanatorium, Toledo, Iowa; and I am forwarding same to the Office for consideration, in as much as these people do not reside in this district.

The papers are forwarded un-accompanied by any recommendation of mine.

Very respectfully,

J. L. Suffecool
Superintendent.

JLR:EV.
ENCLS.

Shawnee Indian Agency,
Shawnee, Oklahoma,
Oct. 21, 1922.

Supt. George A. Hoyo,
Ponca Indian Agency,
Whiteagle, Oklahoma.

Dear Mr. Hoyo:

This refers to your recent inquiry concerning the estate of Kirwin Murray so far as Charles Watson is concerned.

Charles Watson has 1/4 interest in the estate, and has $9.00 to his credit in this office. The allotment consists of 80 acres situated a few miles east of Perkins, Oklahoma, described as the W/2 of SE/4, 11-17-3 E, No. 66. It is not covered by an oil lease. Robert Roubidoux had an agricultural lease on it last year. There appears to be no lease on it for this year. However, it may develop that Roubidoux is using it this year. This will be investigated and a report will be made to you of results.

The file numbers of Departmental Finding are as follows:- Law-Heirship 120580-12, 76610-16 SEB, final decision October 7, 1916.

Very cordially,

10 od 21

J. L. Suffecool,
Superintendent.

Shawnee Indian Agency,
Shawnee, Oklahoma,
Oct. 27, 1922.

Supt. A. R. Snyder,
Potawatomi Ind. Agency,
Mayetta, Kansas.

Dear Mr. Snyder:

This is in reply to your letter of the 16th instant relative to rentals that should be due to Nancy May and Anna Kaw-dott, heirs of Non-e-le-kat, from now occupied by Mary Rhodd, owner of 1/2 of the allotment. You are advised that the Rhodds have had two crop failures, last and this year. Hence, there will be no rentals coming to the Kaw-dott women.

A division by partition has been made by the Department which was recently approved setting aside 40 acres to the Kaw-dotts. An effort to lease their 40 will be made as soon as possible. It is doubtful that such can be done as the land is not very desirable. However, it is equally as good as the half that was given to the Rhodds.

Very cordially,

10 od 27.

J. L. Suffecool,
Supt. & Spl. Disb. Agent.

Shawnee Indian Agency,
Shawnee, Oklahoma
October 27, 1922.

Mr. J. A. Griffitts,
Ramona, Oklahoma.

Dear Mr. Griffitts:-

Referring to your letters of September 5th and October 6th, 1922, relative to the interest of Fannie Beaver, or McEwin, in the estate of Charley Beaver; I have to advise that this matter has been looked into, and it is ascertained that Fannie Beaver received her share of the proceeds derived from the sale of this allotment.

Photographic copies of the check drawn in her favor for $128.49 representing the proceeds have been obtained from the Treasury Department. Said check bears her endorsement made by her mark and witnessed by two people living in Tulsa.

Trusting that this is the information desired, and that same will clear up the situation, I am

Very respectfully,

J. L. Suffecool,
Superintendent.

JLR:EV.
ENCLS.

Shawnee Indian Agency,
Shawnee, Oklahoma,
October 27, 1922.

Mr. A. R. Snyder,
Supt. Mayetta, Kansas.

Dear Mr. Snyder:-

I am enclosing herewith a letter written to George Appletree, a Sac & Fox Indian under the jurisdiction of this office, by the Indian Office concerning the estate of Pah nah kah tho, a deceased Kickapoo allottee.

George Appletree left the letter here and requested that I forward same to you with the request that you notify him through this office as to the status of this matter. The interested heir Wah tho quah also requests if there is any money on deposit to her credit that same be transferred to this office for her use.

Very respectfully,

J. L. Suffecool,
Superintendent.

JLR:EV.

L-C
78051-23
11204-23
ERM

Shawnee Indian Agency,
Shawnee, Oklahoma,
Oct. 30, 1923[sic].

The Commissioner
of Indian Affairs,
Washington, D. C.

Dear Mr. Commissioner:-

Reference is made to Office letter dated October 10th, bearing above caption concerning complaints submitted by Zella Marie Graham of Emmett, Kansas in connection with the handling of the estate of Jospeh[sic] Welch, her grandfather--interest to which she but recently acquired by deed conveyed to her by her mother.

In this connection it may be stated that the estate of Joseph Welch is one of several that have been unearthed since my taking charge of the Shawnee Agency in 1921. There is no doubt of their[sic] being several other estates that will be discovered and reported to the Office as soon as congestion of office work will permit.

Shortly after Mrs. Graham acquired an interest in the said Joseph Welch estate, she was informed on February 24, 1923 that on account of a settlement of various matters which needed to be adjusted, such as claims against the estate by one of the heirs, that it would be quite a while before final settlement with the other heirs could be made, and that when finally settled, such settlement would be made for all time.

11

According to correspondence on file, it appears that Mrs. Graham was kept informed of the progress made in this settlement. On August 24, 1923 she was informed that a representative of this office called upon Mrs. Moutaw for the purpose of hastening the settlement of the claims of Mrs. Moutaw, and that it was then discovered that Mrs. Moutaw had recently died. Explanation was made to Mrs. Graham that this might be considered as the reason for the delay on the part of Mr. Moutaw to submit his claim against the estate of said Joseph Welch. However, on that date he agreed that he would submit his claim within the next few days. Ample time and opportunity was given Mr. Moutaw to submit his claims and finally on October 6, it was considered proper to modify Mr. Moutaw that he would be given until the 16th of October to submit his claims for final settlement. That date has now passed without Mr. Moutaw's having taken advantage of the time allotted for making his settlement.

There are, however, on record at Tecumseh, the County Seat of Pottawatomie County, probate proceedings in connection with the disposition of the estate of Joseph Welch; wherein, Wm. Moutaw was the administrator. There are certain claims, such as funeral expenses and care of the deceased shortly previous to his death that might be considered legitimate claims, included in Mr. Moutaw's report of the administration of the estate of Joseph Welch.

If the Office directs, certified copies of probate proceedings in connection with the estate of Joseph Welch, will be secured and submitted, or such other instructions that the Office sees proper to give will be followed.

Very truly yours,

J. L. Suffecool,
Superintendent.

CD:EV.
cc to Zella Marie Graham,
　　Emmett, Kan.

Land
Mary Spybuck,
dec., #64513
10-31-22   Shawnee Indian Agency,
JTW-REB   Shawnee, Oklahoma,
                             Nov. 4th, 1922.

Supt. Victor M. Locke, Jr.,
Union Indian Agency,
Muskogee, Oklahoma.

Dear Mr. Locke:

This is in reply to your letter dated Oct. 31, 1922, relative to the allotment of
Mary Spybuck, former deceased wife of George Spybuck, who died in 1904.

Will you please refer to our letter dated Sept. 22, 19022? You will notice that
the information requested for in said letter has no reference as to the interest of
George Spybuck. What is desired is the present status of the estate. If any part of the
land has been sold who sold it.[sic] What disposition was made of the proceeds? If the
heirs have been determines, who are they? In fact any thing of value concerning said
estate should be stated.

The parties making the inquiry claim to be the heirs and wish to establish that
fact if the estate is sufficiently valuable to make the expenditure in doing so.

Very cordially,

11 od 4   J. L. Suffecool,
                                      Supt. & Spl. Disb. Agt.

Land-Sales
58964-22
   N R   Shawnee Indian Agency,
                             Shawnee, Oklahoma,
                             Nov. 4th, 1923.

The Honorable Com.
 of Indian Affairs,
Washington, D. C.

Dear Mr. Commissioner:

There is submitted herewith deal from Eliza Colvin to Frank Smith covering her undivided one-twelvth[sic] inherited interest in and to the Martha Mullen allotment, Cit. Pottawatomie No. 303 accompanied by acceptance of sale by the heir, 5-110c, and affidavit of vendee, 3-110d.

The allotment herein considered is one of the three that was ruined by the Little River Drainage Ditch. In its present condition it is of but very little value, for this reason and for the reasons herein contemplated, viz. parttionment[sic], the appraisement on form 5-110a does not accompany the papers.

It will be remembered that the heirs herein are practically the same as those in the Josephine Bourassa estate considered in Land-Sales above reference under date of Sept. 12, 1922. It is the intention of these heirs to reduce the number of owners of their common estates. This deed eliminates Mrs. Colvin from any interest in the Martha Mullen allotment. It therefore respectfully recommended that the deed be approved. Consideration has been taken up, Spl. Deposits.

Very respectfully,

11 od 4.   J. L. Suffecool
Incl. deed   Supt. & Spl. Disb. Agt.

Shawnee Indian Agency,
Shawnee, Oklahoma,
December 5, 1922.

Mr. A. R. Snyder,
    Superintendent,
        Potawatomi Ind. Agency,
            Mayetta, Kansas.

Dear Mr. Snyder:-

There is inclosed herewith a statement made by various Indians and signed by them but not acknowledged, but is witnessed by John A. Snake, Chief of Police at this Agency. I personally saw the last two sign it.

As is explained in the statement, they claim to have an interest in the estate of Mak-kuk, deceased. I do not know whether their claim has any merit. I understand that the same was prepared by one Willie Whitewater, who I used to know in Kansas, and I presume that you know him better than I.

Please give this matter such consideration as the fact may warrant.

Very respectfully,

J. L. Suffecool
Superintendent.

JLS:EV.
Encl. 1.

****

[The above letter given again.]

L-Allot.
8635[?]-22
BDS

Shawnee Indian Agency,
Shawnee, Oklahoma,
November 9, 1922.

The Commissioner
of Indian Affairs,
Washington, D. C.

S I R:-

Replying to Office letter of November 6th, to which was attached a letter received from David Puck-pee of Mayetta, Kansas, concerning certain lands in Oklahoma; I have to advise that I am unable to connect his inquiry with any matter under this jurisdiction. It is impossible to determine his desires in the mater from the limited information given by him in his letter to the Land Office of September 25, 1922.

Returned herewith is Mr. Puck-pee's letter.

Very respectfully,

J. L. Suffecool
Superintendent.

JLR:EV.
ENCL: 1.

****

15

REFER IN REPLY TO THE FOLLOWING:

L-Allot.
86357-22
BDS

DEPARTMENT OF THE INTERIOR,

OFFICE OF INDIAN AFFAIRS,

WASHINGTON,

NOV -6 19224

ADDRESS ONLY THE
COMMISSIONER OF INDIAN AFFAIRS

Mr. J. L. Suffecool,

Supt., Shawnee School.

My dear Mr. Suffecool:

On October 12, 1922, the Office referred to the Superintendent of Potawatomi at Mayetta, Kansas, for report, a letter received from David Puck-kee of Mayetta, concerning certain lands in Oklahoma belonging to his uncle whose name was not given.

Superintendent Snyder advises that he is unable to connect the letter with any matter under his supervision. Mr. Puck-kee's letter is therefore being referred to you in the hope that you may be able to advise the Office of the matter inquired about. Please return the letter with your report.

Very truly yours,

CF Hauke
Chief Clerk.

11 CLR 3

Shawnee Indian Agency,

Shawnee, Okla.

Nov. 13, 1922.

The Commissioner of Indian Affairs,

Washington, D.C.

Sir:-

Transmitted herewith is my heirship report showing hearing fees collected during the First Quarter 1923. Also attached hereto is a list of all the outstanding fees at this unit. A notation has been made near each estate named, stating the status of the land. As regards those heirs that will receive lease money or land sale money trough[sic] this office, same will be required to pay their shares. Those heirs that have no funds to their credit on the books of this office will be called upon to remit amounts covering their proportionate shares of the fees. No knowing the financial status of all the heirs it is impossible to state whether [illegible] are in a position to make settlements at this time.

Incl.
JLR.   Very respectfully,

                                        _____

                                        J. L. Suffecool, Supt.

                                        Shawnee Indian Agency,
                                        Shawnee, Oklahoma,
                                        November 14, 1922.

Mr. Wiley W. Cook,
Supt. State Training School,
Winfield, Kansas.

Dear Sir:-

I am in receipt of your letter of the 13th concerning the estate of Priscilla Baylis, an Indian girl who has been a patient at the Osawatomie Hospital for about twenty-five years; and in which you request an appointment with me within the very near future, so that matters pertaining to this estate may be discussed.

I will be in my office Saturday, November 18th, and will be pleased to take up with you the matter referred to above.

                    Very respectfully,

                                        J. L. Suffecool
                                        Superintendent.

JLR:EV.

Shawnee Indian Agency.

Shawnee, Oklahoma,
November 22, 1923.

Mr. E. D. Reasor, Lawyer,
Shawnee, Oklahoma.

Dear Sir:

      I have your letter of the 20th, making inquiry for Miss Ada Smith concerning the estate of Jane Johnson, deceased mother of the young lady. You are advised that the estate of Jane Johnson is as yet not probated, there are no funds whatever to the credit of the deceased's account, and there are obligations to be met by any funds which may come into this office from the deceased's estate.

      Miss Smith should remember that when her mother was ill, that she was taken to the Shawnee Hospital where an obligation was incurred which has never been met, also that her mother's funeral expenses have never been entirely liquidated. These debts will be settled before any funds will be available for distribution to the heirs.

Very truly yours,

_____

J. L. Suffecool
Superintendent.

JLR:AMS

Shawnee Indian Agency,
Shawnee, Oklahoma,
November 23, 1922.

Dr. Jacob B. Breid,
  Supt. Sac & Fox San.,
    Toledo, Iowa.

Dear Sir:-

      This will reply to your letter of November 3, 1922 regarding inherited interest of Thomas Chuck in the estate of Gertrude Givens Pattequa.

Please inform the heir of Thomas Chuck that there is no sale contemplated in regard to the allotment of Gertrude Givens, and it is doubtful if any sale could be made at this time, for the reason that there is very little land being sold at this unit now. However, if in the near future anyone is interested in the purchase of this allotment, a movement to sell the same will at once be instituted.

Very respectfully,

J. L. Suffecool
Superintendent.

CD:EV.

Shawnee Indian Agency,
Shawnee, Oklahoma,
November 23, 1922.

Mr. George A. Hoyo,
Ponca Indian Agency,
Whiteagle, Oklahoma.

Dear Mr. Hoyo:-

This will reply to your letter of October 27, 1922 regarding the estate of Mary Grant as to the sale of Susie Deroin's interest to one William Atkins for a cash consideration of $1,500.00.

You will re-call that a few days previous to this letter, you wrote this office regarding the sale of the fore-going mentioned allotment requested for by some of the heirs. Now, it would appear necessary that one of these sales should be consummated before the other is started. Your advice as to which sale should be consummated first is respectfully requested.

However, I will say that the papers in the sale of said allotment have been turned over to the United States Farmer at Cushing, Oklahoma for investigation and report.

Very respectfully,

J. L. Suffecool
Superintendent.

CD:EV.

Shawnee Indian Agency,
Shawnee, Oklahoma,
November 24, 1922.

General Roy Hoffman,
906-912 State Nat'l Bank Bldg.,
Oklahoma City, Oklahoma.

Dear General:-

Permit me to acknowledge receipt of your letter of November 10, 1922.

I was in the city a few days ago, and I telephones your office but was advised by your Secretary that you were not in. I had intended to take this matter up with you at that time.

I might add that we have heard from the Indian Office this morning with reference to the partitioning of land belonging to Mrs. Bigwalker and others. While the partitioning of the land is not all that we desire; yet, it was opened up a way so that we can dispose of the matter in a manner that I presume will be satisfactory to all concerned.

Sincerely yours,

J. L. Suffecool
Superintendent.

JLS:EV.

Probate 101697-31
W H G

Shawnee Indian Agency,
Shawnee, Oklahoma,
November 28, 1922.

The Commissioner
of Indian Affairs,
Washington, D. C.

S I R:-

There is inclosed herewith a petition, or application, made by Tom Mitchell, an Indian under the Sac & Fox and Iowa jurisdiction; for the re-opening of the heirship case of Emily Johnson, or Ne ta wia, a Sac & Fox allottee of Oklahoma.

The Superintendent of the Sac & Fox Sanatorium, Toledo, Iowa informs me that the attorney who prepared the statement for Tom Mitchell advised him in discussing the matter with Tom Mitchell that he had indicated that his claim had very little merit, but that Tom Mitchell insisted that the statement be prepared for submittal.

In view of the above, and as I know nothing whatever of the case of Mitchell's, I am submitting his application to the Office for consideration without any recommendation whatever.

Very respectfully,

JLR:EV.   J. L. Suffecool
ENCLS. 2.   Superintendent.

Land-Sales
[??]119-22
SN R

Shawnee Indian Agency,
Shawnee, Oklahoma,
December 4, 1922.

The Honorable,
    The Commissioner
    of Indian Affairs,
    Washington, D. C.

My dear Mr. Commissioner:-

This will acknowledge the receipt of Office communication of above reference under date of October 16, 1922, in which was inclosed a letter from Roy Hoffman, an attorney of Oklahoma City, Oklahoma, with reference to certain notes in favor of Lelia Bigwalker, a non- competent Indian of the Sac & Fox Tribe.

In reply, I have to advise that I have encountered considerable trouble in making the necessary investigation, in order that I could report on this case--hence the delay in answering this letter. Recently I was in Oklahoma City and called on the United States Attorney; examined the file in this case and found that the notes referred to are not in the hands of the United States Attorney, nor do the files of this office disclose that they are here. While in Oklahoma City, I called upon Mr. H. S. Traylor, former United States Inspector of the Indian Bureau, who was detailed by your Office to make an investigation of this case. He informed me that he secured these notes, and that they were forwarded to your Office with his report.

With reference to the case against Amos Seaton, who procured signature of Lelia Bigwalker and other Indian heirs to deed to Trust Allotment of Harry Hall, deceased Sac & Fox allottee; I have to advise that the United States Attorney informs me that no action has been taken. In this connection I would respectfully call attention to Indian Office letter under date of December 7, 1921-- reference 88664-21--in which this Office saw fit to reprimand me in my report on this matter. In this connection, I would respectfully call the attention of the Office to my reply under date of December 17,1 1921; and to state that I feel now as I did then with reference to having this case prosecuted. True, Amos Seaton did quit claim this land back, but it was only, as I understand, upon the payment of certain notes, which General Hoffman refers to, by Lelia Bigwalker. It is to be remembered that the former Superintendent had recommended that she be given the unrestricted use of something like $4,000.00.

I am willing to give whatever assistance that I can to see that this matter is properly handled.

General Hoffman's letter is returned herewith as per request of Office.

Very respectfully,

J. L. Suffecool
Superintendent

JLS:EV.
ENCL. 1.

Shawnee Indian Agency,
Shawnee, Oklahoma, Dec. 5, 1922.

Mr. Edgar Creek,
Newalla, Okla. R# 2.

Dear Sir:

There is enclosed herewith check No. 4216, for $8.59, drawn on the Treasurer of the United States, representing your share of annuity payment in the estate of Black Wing, deceased.

Very respectfully,

J. L. Suffecool,
Superintendent

TBA

88845 OFFICE OF INDIAN AFFAIRS
5 deeds
and report

Washington, D. C., 1/23/22

The matter to which this slip is

attached is referred to the Superintendent of

.................................Shawnee............................
Record and delivery

for ⎰ ~~information and file~~

~~action and file~~

~~report~~

signature

completion of certificate

(lease blanks)

~~and return of papers~~

.......................W W Marschalk.....................

Chief, ...Land........Division

DO NOT REMOVE THIS SLIP

Number ....88845 – 22...............

Clerk ....MR..........................

Return date ....

****

Eliza Colvin	13/84 =	26/168
Zoa Denton	13/84 =	26/168
Nancy Fehligh[sic]	13/84 =	26/168
Nellie Wylie	19/84	38/168
Frank Smith	13/84	26/168
May Lewis	4/84	8/168
Rena Smith	13/168	13/168
Birdie Smith	13/168	13/168

174[sic]/168

****

Eliza Colvin	13/84 =	26/168
Zoa Denton	13/84 =	26/168
Nancy Fehligh	13/84 =	26/168
Nellie Wylie[sic]	19/84	38/168
Frank Smith	13/84	26/168
May Lewis	4/84	8/168
Rena Smith	9/168	9/168
Birdie Smith	9/168	9/168

This is correct

Dushane

N/2 of Sec 7, T. 8 N., R. 5 E.

Josepine[sic] Bourassa Estate

****

88845
5 deeds
and report

OFFICE OF INDIAN AFFAIRS

Washington, D. C., 1/23/22

The matter to which this slip is

attached is referred to the Superintendent of

................................Shawnee.............................
Record and delivery

for {
~~information and file~~

~~action and file~~

~~report~~

signature

completion of certificate

(lease blanks)

~~and return of papers~~
}

................W W Marschalk................

Chief, ...Land.......Division

DO NOT REMOVE THIS SLIP

Number ...88845 – 22.................

Clerk .....MR.........................

Return date ..._____....

****

Land-Sales
88845-22
88846-22
NR

DEC 12 1922

The Honorable

The Secretary of the Interior

(Through the Commissioner
of the General Land Office.)

Sir:

I have the honor to enclose five deeds conveying undivided interests in the allotments of Josephine Bourassa, #802, described as N 1/2, Sec. 7, T. 8 N., R. 5E, I. M., in Oklahoma, and Martha Mullens formerly Smith, #803, described as N 1/2, NW 1/4, Sec. 9, same township and range.

The heirs of Josephine Bourassa were determined by the Department on November 27, 1914, and the heirs of Martha Mullen[sic], a deceased heir of Josephine Bourassa, on March 22, 1918.

Certain of the heirs, eight in each case, have purchased the shares of others, and deeds approved conveying undivided interests, with restriction against alienation. If the enclosed deeds are approved, the interests of the heirs will be as follows:

Josephine Bourassa allotment:

Eliza Colvin, ...	24/168
Nancy Fehlig, ...	53/168
Nellie Wiley, ...	91/168

Martha Mullen (formerly Smith) allotment:

Eliza Colvin, ...	2/24
Zoa Denton, ...	2/24
Nancy Fehlig, ...	2/24
Frank Smith, ...	16/24
Rena Smith Richardson, ...	1/24
Birdie Smith, ...	1/24

The consideration paid in each case is the appraised value, except in deeds between Nellie Wiley and Frank Smith, where interests in the two allotments are exchanged. The Superintendent of Shawnee Agency recommends the approval of the following deeds and the Office concurs:

Sac & Fox – Shawnee Estates
1920-1924 Volume IX

Allotment of Josephine Bourassa:

Eliza Colvin, undivided 1/12 interest to Frank Smith;
Zoa Denton, undivided 1/7 interest to Nellie Wiley;
Frank Smith, undivided 1/7 interest to Nellie Wiley.

Allotment of Martha Mullen (Smith):

J. W. Mullen, undivided 1/2 interest to Nellie Wiley:
Nellie Wiley, undivided 1/2 interest (purchased from
Mullen) to Frank Smith.

Respectfully,

CF Hauke
Chief Clerk.

GENERAL LAND OFFICE,
WASHINGTON, D.C.   DEC 14 1922

There are no reasons appearing in the records of the General Land
Office why the deeds should not be approved as recommended.

Geo R Wickham

Assistant Commissioner.

DEPARTMENT OF THE INTERIOR,
OFFICE OF THE SECRETARY.
DEC 15 1922

Approved:
(Signed) F. M. Goodwin

Assistant Secretary.

And returned to Office of Indian Affairs.

12-MC-7

Shawnee Indian Agency,
Shawnee, Oklahoma,
December 15, 1922.

Supt. A. R. Snyder,
Potawatomi Ind. Agency,
Mayetta, Kansas.

Dear Mr. Snyder:-

There is returned herewith Petition for Sale of inherited land signed by the heirs of Pah-nah-kah-tho-no, allottee No. 223, which was referred to this office for the purpose of securing signatures thereto.

The heirs living in Oklaho ma[sic] have all signed the Petition and therefore it appears that your request has been complied with.

Very respectfully,

J. L. Suffecool
Superintendent.

CD:EV.
ENCLS.

Shawnee Indian Agency,
Shawnee, Oklahoma,
Dec. 16, 1922.

Mrs. Zelah Marie Graham,
P. O. Box, [sic]
Emmett, Kansas.

Dear Madam:

This is to acknowledge the receipt of an Indian Deed from Mary Deleye, nee Welch, your mother, to yourself covering an undivided one-fifth inherited interest in the allotment of Joseph Welch, Pottawatomie No. 945. This deed will at once be transmitted to the Department for appropriate action.

There are inclosed herewith correspondence relative to the estate of said Joseph Welch (carbon copies) for your information. You will be notified of further progress in this matter.

Sincerely yours,

1[?] od 16.   J. L. Suffecool,
Incls. Report &
    Letter to Moutaw

****

Land-Allot.
Joseph Welch
Cit. Pot. 945.   Shawnee Indian Agency,
    C D   Shawnee, Oklahoma,
                                      Dec. 9, 1922.

Supt. J. L. Suffecool,
Shawnee Indian Agency,
Shawnee, Oklahoma.

Dear Mr. Suffecool:

I have the honor to report the result of the investigation relative t o[sic] the rentals from the allotment of Joseph Welch, deceased Citizen Pottawatomie allottee No. 945, as follows:

1st. Mr. William Boler first leased this land from Joseph Welch just before his death in 1909 and moved upon the place in December of that year. Joseph Welch died, Sept. 20, 1909. Mr. Boler began paying rentals in 1910, continuing to stay upon the place by virtue of lease arrangements with William Moutaw, the husband of Amelia Moutaw, nee Welch, one of the heirs, and is still occupying the land as a lessee. Mr. William Moutaw was exercising this authority for the years of 1910 and 1911 as an administrator duely[sic] appointed by the Probate Court of Pottawatomie County, Oklahoma. However no cognizance is taken of Moutaw's authority to lease this land in as much as this is trust property and not subject to the jurisdiction of the local courts, preferring to place the burden of proof upon William Moutaw to show valid authority for exercising the same, namely, to lease and collect rentals.

2nd. Mr. Boler paid to William Moutaw as rentals for this place for the entire period that he occupied the land, viz., from 1910 to 1921, the date this office assumed control, the sum of $3958.00, as itemized particularly in his affidavit attached hereto. It is claimed by the heirs that he (William Moutaw) used the greater portion of said rentals collected for his personal use, and that only a very small amount of what he collected did he place upon the place as improvements. The place is now greatly in need of considerable repair. A farm producing as much revenue as

29

this farm does should never be allowed to deteriorate to the extent of being unfit for human habitation.

In view of the conditions existing upon the allotment of Joseph Welch as disclosed by this investigation the following recommendations are respectfully submitted:

1st. That Mr. William Moutaw of Lexington, Oklahoma, be required to show to this office for the benefit of the heirs all his transactions in the collection of rentals, and the disbursements of the proceeds supported by proper claims; that all proper claims against this estate, such as Doctor bills, funeral expenses, etc., be allowed, and that the remainder of all of his collections be brought to this office and placed to the credit of the heirs for equitable distribution. Upon failure of Mr. Moutaw to comply herewith it is recommended that the Indian Office, Washington, be asked for appropriate action to compel William Moutaw to reimburse the heirs for the money that he obtained from this farm, either by case payment or by the use of said allotment until such time as the heirs shall have been reimbursed.

2nd. That a regular governmental lease covering this land for the year of 1923 be made by this office t o[sic] Mr. William Boler for the sum of $400.00 and any and all claims he may have against the allotment on account of improvements he has placed thereon, or any other claim he may have against the estate of Joseph Welch. The sum of $400.00 for this year appears to be fair owing to the lateness of the season, and in view of the fact that $400.00 was collected by me as trespass fee for the year of 1922 and that it was also the consideration agreed to by Mr. Moutaw for the year of 1921, three hundred dollars ($300.00) of which was paid direct to Mr. Moutaw and $58.00 was put upon the place as improvements as follows:

    300 fence posts @ 6¢ , $18.00
    material, chick. house,   7.50
    repair of pump & well   10.50
    labor, hauling posts,   _ 12.00 _
           Total . . . $58.00

the remainder of $100.00 allowed for improvements for the year of 1921 which was not used amounting to $42.00 was collected by me and deposited in this office to the credit of the estate of Joseph Welch, with the trespass fee for 1922, all amounting to $442.00.

3rd. As stated before that this farm is badly in need of improvements, and the lateness of the season, that such improvements be considered by a lease for a term of at the least three years after the year of 1923. However, I will recommend that the well be repaired, or a new one dug, at an expense of not more than $75.00, and payment made from any funds available from the estate of Joseph Welch.

Sac & Fox – Shawnee Estates
1920-1924 Volume IX

Very respectfully,

12 od 9.   Charles Dushane
CC. Frank Welch &   Sac & Fox Lease Clerk
    Zelah Marie Graham.

****

Shawnee Indian Agency,
Shawnee, Oklahoma,
Dec. 16, 1922.

Hon. William Moutaw,
Lexington, Oklahoma.

My dear Mr. Moutaw:

You are hereby notified that this office has assumed administrative jurisdiction in accordance with Departmental Regulations over the estate of Joseph Welch, deceased Citizen Pottawatomie allottee No. 945.

After a thorough investigation by the field force of this office a report was made to me a copy of which is herewith inclosed. Therefore you will please render such claims, and report of transactions, relative to this estate in accordance with said report which will receive respect and proper courtesy.

Very truly yours,

12 od 16.   J. L. Suffecool,
Incl. Report.   Supt. & Spl. Disb. Agt.

CC   Frank Welck[sic] &
     Zelah Marie Graham.

Shawnee Indian Agency,

Shawnee, Oklahoma,

12/18/22

Mr. Charles W. Fear,
821 West 4th St.,
Joplin, Missouri.

31

Dear Mr. Fear:

This is to acknowledge receipt of notice informing me of the death of your wife, in St. Mary's Hospital of Jefferson City, Missouri, on December 5, 1922, and I am very sorry to hear of such.

Concerning the matter of the estate of your wife and heirs interested in the estate of her mother, Phoebe Keokuk, I have to advise that the Department of the Interior, probates the estates of deceased Indians who are wards of the Government. At certain times every year or so an Examiner of Inheritence[sic] is detailed to the agencies for the purpose of holding such hearings. At the time he arrives here, you will be notified as will all other interested persons in the estate of your deceased wife. You are advised that no portion of her allotment is held in trust by the Government as the patent and fee for same was issued in the years of 1906 and 1915.

Any funds derived from the estate of Phoebe Keokuk, in which she is interested will be returned by this office to the credit of her account until the determination of her heirs, and the same will be distributed to the rightful heirs.

There appears to be no record of any will having been made and filed with this office.

Very respectfully,

Enc.
MS

J. L. Suffecool
Superintendent

Shawnee Indian Agency,
Shawnee, Oklahoma,
January 2, 1923.

The Commissioner
    of Indian Affairs,
        Washington, D. C.

S I R:-

There are transmitted herewith petition for partition of the alltoment[sic] of Chief McKOsato[sic] allottee No. 101, described as the SE/4 of 17-11-5 in Oklahoma.

The necessary papers relative to patent in fee are herewith inclosed. The partition proceedings together with applications for patent in fee are respectfully recommended for approval, in as much as these heirs are considered sufficiently competent to take care of this allotment, and for the purpose of settlement of the estate.

Very respectfully,

J. L. Suffecool
Superintendent.

CD:EV.
ENCSS.

Shawnee Indian Agency,
Shawnee, Oklahoma,
January 2, 1923.

Supt. A. R. Snyder,
  Potawatomi Indian Agency,
    Mayetta, Kansas.

Dear Mr. Snyder:-

Information is desired by this office with reference to the heirs of one John B. Jackson, Citizen Pottawatomie Allottee of this Agency, deceased.

The heirs according to Department findings are as follows:

Minot Jackson
Jimmy Jackson
Charley Jackson, or Tip-ko-kuk
Mary Peamish

who appear to be residing under your jurisdiction.

Some of these heirs according to records in this office are dead and the heirs are still undetermined. All information relative to these heirs is desired for the purpose of completing a sale of the allotment of said John B. Jackson.

Very respectfully,

J. L. Suffecool
Superintendent;

CD:EV.

33

Shawnee Indian Agency,
Shawnee, Oklahoma,
January 2, 1923.

Mr. Ernest Pratt,
  R--Maud, Oklahoma.

Dear Friend:-

You will recall that in a recent discussion with you I explained the part on the Harriet Pratt land that came to your share to be fifty acres in an oblong form along the east end of this allotment.

Wont[sic] you please write me or this office by January 9, 1922[sic] as to why, giving all reasons in full, that you do not feel that this represents your part of this allotment. In other words why you do not want to sign for division of the allotment under those conditions.

On this date, January 9, we are to make some definite arrangement about it, and so I wish to impress upon you the importance of having your answer in by that time.

Very respectfully,

J. L. Suffecool
Superintendent.

C♦E:EV[sic].

Shawnee Indian Agency,
Shawnee, Oklahoma,
January 4, 1923.

The Commissioner
  of Indian Affairs
    Washington, D. C.

S I R:-

There is re-submitted herewith deed on form 5-183 covering the allotment of Robert Hunter allottee No. 509 of the Sac & Fox Tribe by the heirs of Robert Hunter to Henry Hunter, also an heir. A deed had been submitted heretofore covering this allotment but the form of acknowledgment required in such transactions did not conform to the law of the State of Oklahoma[sic] Therefore the deed was returned to this office in order that the proper form might be attached to a new deed.

This request of the Office has therefore been complied with and the deed is respectfully recommended for approval.

Very respectfully,

J. L. Suffecool
Superintendent.

CD:EV.
ENCLS.

Shawnee Indian Agency,
Shawnee, Oklahoma,
January 4, 1923.

The Commissioner
of Indian Affairs,
Washington, D. C.

S I R:-

There is transmitted herewith Indian Deed Inherited Lands (form 5-183) covering the allotment of Joseph Welch, deceased Citizen Pottawatomie allottee No. 945.

The heirs to the estate of said Joseph Welch were determined under L-H 107360-1914 97000-14 F W S and among these heirs is one Mary Deleye Welch. Mary Deleye Welch is now making her home with her daughter and son-in-law. Her daughter is Zella Marie Graham of Emmett, Kansas. Said Mary Deleye at present in in very poor health and it is her desire that her interest in the Joseph Welch allotment be transferred to her daughter, Zella Marie Graham.

For this purpose the deed herewith conveying the allotment to Zella Marie Graham was executed.

The deed appears to be regular being signed by thumb mark and the proper form of acknowledgment attached to the deed. It is therefore respectfully recommended that said deed be approved.

Very respectfully,

J. L. Suffecool
Superintendent.

CD:EV.
ENCLS.

Shawnee Indian Agency,
Shawnee, Oklahoma,
January 5, 1923.

Mr. S. Y. Tutwiler,
Examiner of Inheritance,
Kiowa Indian Agency,
Anadarko, Oklahoma.

Dear Mr. Tutwiler:-

Replying to your letter of the 3rd inst. requesting information regarding Franklin Wilmett; I have to advise that I was informed that Franklin Wilmett died January 31, 1922 at the age of 61 or 62 years. He has in trust under this jurisdiction 80 acres described as the E/2 of the NW/4 of Section 23, Twp. 7, North of Range 4 East. His allotment number is 1188.

As this man made his home in Kansas near Mayetta I am unable to advise you as to whether he has a widow or any children, or any other relatives. Information concerning this line may be obtained at Mayetta.

We have several cases at this Agency that need attention. When do you expect to make us a visit?

Very respectfully,

J. L. Suffecool
Superintendent.

JLR:EV.

Shawnee Indian Agency,
Shawnee, Oklahoma,
January 13, 1923.

Mr Grover Wakole,
Mercier, Kansas.

Dear Sir:-

This replies to your request under date of December 30, 1922 with reference to the allotment of Rufus Wakole. In previous correspondence you have been informed that the methods of removing restrictions from this land consists of about as follows:

Petition by partition; application for patent in fee; or a ale could be made by the heirs. As you are aware that you and your mother are the two heirs to this land, and that you have a two-thirds interest, for that reason partition could not be made, as divisions would be improper on account of the character of the land and the improvements thereon. Patent in fee could not be issued on account of the necessary competency required for the issuance of patent in fee. The sale of this land has been under consideration for sometime[sic] but in as much as lands are selling at such low figures, it has been considered best not to sell at the present time. However, if any party is discovered in the near future who is willing to give at least the appraisement, the sale of this land will be undertaken, and you will be so notified.

Trusting that this will be satisfactory, I am

Very respectfully,

J. L. Suffecool
Superintendent.

CD:EV.

Shawnee Indian Agency,
Shawnee, Oklahoma,
January 13, 1923.

The Commissioner of Indian Affairs,
Washington, D. C.

S I R:-

There is transmitted herewith the Application for Right of Way for a Pond Creek Drainage Ditch across certain restricted Indian lands by the County Commissioners of Pottawatomie County, Oklahoma in accordance with the Act of July 19, 1912; together with the necessary supporting papers.

The Office is respectfully advised that it may not be necessary that the Application be approved by the Department, in as much as there are two Indian allotments and in both instances the allottees are dead. The deceased allottees are Mary Schroepfer, Citizen Pottawatomie allottee No. 363, whose heirs are determined under Law-Heirship 127913-16, 15303-17 S E B; and John B. Jackson, whose heirs were determined Pur-Sup 6309-16, 69558-15 F W S. These heirs in both instances are living away from this Agency, most of them reside in Kansas. Correspondence with the view of locating these heirs has been directed to the Pottawatomie Agency, Mayetta, Kansas, for the purpose of effecting the sale of both allotments.

In view of the fact that an early action is desired by the Commissioners of Pottawatomie County, an immediate sale of these two tracts of land should be made. The Office is respectfully requested for authority to consummate an immediate sake with as short period of advertising as may be consistent. Further, if the Office can consistently approve the sale of these two allotments without the acceptance of sale on the part of the heirs of the two deceased allottees the completion of the application for right of way can at once be consummated.

An investigation has been made as to the value of these two allotments and appraisements have been made showing that the lands under present conditions are valued in the case of John B. Jackson at $20 per acre, and in the case of Mary Schroepfer at $30 per acre. The purchaser of these two tracts of land will necessarily have to pay not only the $20 and $30 respectively. but there must be added thereto the assessment which amounts to practically $15 per acre--making the total cost at $35 and $45 per acre.

If no sale is made of these two tracts of land, the application of County Commissioners for right of way across these two allotments is respectfully recommended for approval. This matter was called to the attention of this office with the request for an immediate report under Office letter, caption as above.

Very respectfully,

J. L. Suffecool
CD:EV.   Superintendent.

Shawnee Indian Agency,
Shawnee, Oklahoma,
January 15, 1923.

Mrs. Dora Harry,
  Edna, Oklahoma.

Dear Madam:-

Your inquiry relative to the sale of the Nancy Joe Billy land was received.

In connection with this, you are informed that partition proceedings are being made, and that one-half of the said allotment is being given to Billy

Williams, and the remaining one-half of the same will be given to all of the other heirs in accordance with Departmental findings of heirs. After the partition proceedings are approved, the sale of one-half of the allotment belonging to the several heirs will be made. The appraisement of the allotment has recently been made. As soon as papers are completed in this matter, you will be notified accordingly.

Very respectfully,

J. L. Suffecool
Superintendent.

CD:EV.

Shawnee Indian Agency,
Shawnee, Oklahoma,
January 15, 1923.

Supt. Victor M. Locke, Jr.,
  Muskogee Indian Agency,
  Muskogee, Oklahoma.

Dear Sir:-

This has reference to the heirship matter pertaining to the estate of Wantay Davy, Creek allottee No. 8513.

You will re-call that Wantay Davy was allotted the Shawnee allotment No. 467 which has recently been cancelled. Carbon copy of Office letter was mailed to you from the Indian Office.

Will you please furnish this office with probate records of this allottee in order that it may be shown that Jim Gibson is or is not one of the heirs of said allottee[so that proper disposition can be made of funds held in this office pending determination of said heirship.

If you have any advice or wishes in this matter please feel free to suggest such in order that this transaction shall be definitely closed.

Very respectfully,

J. L. Suffecool
Superintendent.

CD:EV.

Shawnee Indian Agency

Shawnee, Okla.

Jan. 18, 1923.

Mr. S. Y. Tutwiler,

Anadarko, Okla.,

Dear Mr. Tutwiler:-

Complying with your request in your letter of the 13th inst., I am enclosing herewith certificate of appraisement on Franklin Wilmette's allotment. At this time he has no funds to his credit. He holds no inherited interests under this jurisdiction.

In my former letter I stated that he died at the age of about 62 years, but I have later found a death certificate which states that he dies at the age of 60 years-it also shows his date of birth as 1854. Mr. Snyder will be able to acquaint you with other matters pertaining to the old man prior to his death etc.

Very respectfully,

J. L. Suffecool,
Superintendent.

Land-Sales
60885-13
91151-22
 FIP

Shawnee Indian Agency,
Shawnee, Oklahoma,
January 22, 1923.

The Commissioner
 of Indian Affairs,
   Washington, D. C.

S I R:-

This has reference to Office letter under date of January 5, 1923 of the above reference relative to the allotment of Wm. Shawnee, Sr.

Mr. G. M. Griffin purchaser of the N/2 of the NW/4 of the NE/4 of 35-10-3 of said allotment of Wm. Shawnee, Sr. has made payment in full as the Office was informed by wire of recent date.

Mr. Charles E. Wells a grantee of F. B. Reed has executed a Quitclaim deed according to instructions contained in Office letter mentioned before. The Office is advised that the 6/39ths if the Wm. Shawnee allotment claimed by Reed as belonging to him under foreclosure proceedings covers more than 24 acres; whereas the Quitclaim deed rendered by Mr. Charles E. Wells covers only 20 acres. In conference with Mr. Wells he stated that he was willing at any time to execute any deed covering the entire 6/39ths claimed by him through the interest of Mr. Reed.

It would appear to this office that such a deed might be necessary in order that Well's[sic] and Reed's interest may be entirely conveyed to the Wm. Shawnee heirs.

The mortgage in favor of the Farmers National Bank at Tecumseh, Oklahoma which was called for in said Office letter is herewith inclosed. It is the understanding of this office that it is the intention that the twenty acres sold to G. M. Griffin should be the entire amount of land unrestricted of the Wm. Shawnee allotment. While this is not actually the case and encumberances[sic] similar to the Farmers National Bank's mortgage will continue to be a source of annoyance for the reason that there will remain something more than four acres of the Wm. Shawnee allotment without Governmental restrictions.

According to Office instructions it appears that all of the heirs of Wm. Shawnee who have not disposed of their interest will participate in the proceeds of the sale to G. M. Griffin. As before stated the 6/39ths interest unrestricted owned by Julia Shawnee amounts to more than the twenty acres sold to G. M. Griffin. It does not appear from this fact that the other heirs other than Julia Shawnee would be entitled to participate. However, this office intends to follow the instructions as given.

The attention of the Office is called to this fact merely that if it is an over-thought that such may be corrected. If no further instructions with reference to the disposition of the proceeds of the Griffin sale are received, immediately after the issuance of patent in fee the said proceeds will be disbursed accordingly.

Very respectfully,

J. L. Suffecool,
Superintendent.

CD:EV.
1 incl.

Shawnee Indian Agency,
Shawnee, Oklahoma,
January 22, 1923.

Commissioner of Indian Affairs,
Washington, D. C.

S I R:-

There are transmitted herewith two deeds; one from Andrew Conger to George Oliver Morton covering the allotment of Jasper Conger, Sac & Fox allottee No. 383. The heirship in this matter was declared under Law-Heirship 60650-14 under date of August 18, 1914. The other from George Oliver Morton to Andrew Conger covering the allotment of Hattie Conger, allottee No. 386, Law-Heirship in this case was declared under Law-Heirship 60663-14, dated August 18, 1914.

These two deeds are partition proceedings in order that Andrew Conger and George Oliver Morton's shares may be placed in the allotments of Grace Mason and Hattie Conger.

The appraisement on Form 5-110a is herewith included. The deeds are respectfully recommended for approval.

Very respectfully,

J. L. Suffecool
Superintendent.

CD:EV.
ENCLS.

Shawnee Indian Agency,
Shawnee, Oklahoma,
January 22, 1923.

The Commissioner
of Indian Affairs,
Washington, D. C.

S I R:-

There are transmitted herewith two Indian deeds inherited lands; one from Ellen Mason to Hattie Mason covering her share of the Samuel L. Moore allotment, Sac & Fox no. 499, which was partitioned to her under Land-Sales 110055-14 and

52120-22 J T M; the other deed from Hattie Mason to Ellen Mason covering the Grace Mason allotment of that portion belonging to her under Law-Heirship No. 119811-13 F E, date of decision being February 5, 1914.

The Office is respectfully advised that this is merely partition proceedings in order that the property of these two girls may be separated and each heir's share will be so that Hattie Mason will be sole owner of the Grace Mason allotment, and Ellen Mason will be the sole owner of the Samuel L. Moore allotment.

These two deeds are respectfully recommended for approval as they are practically of equal value and are satisfactory to the two girls.

Very respectfully,

J. L. Suffecool
Superintendent.

CD:EV.
ENCLS.

L-c
1745-23
E R M

Shawnee Indian Agency,

Shawnee, Oklahoma, Jan. 22, 1923.

The Commissioner of Indian Affairs,

Washington, D. C.

Sir:

Reference is made to Office letter dated Jan. 17, 1923, above caption, relative to the proposed lease signed by the heirs on the allotment of Big Jim, deceased.

In connection with my letter of January 3, 1923, I have the honor to request that the leases and correspondence in this case be returned, if not needed any longer by the Department.

Very respectfully,

J. L. Suffecool,
Superintendent

TBA

[The following page was badly destroyed. Information obtained where legible.]

[Illegible...] Jan. 14, 1900, leaving as her heirs Ti-an-koo-hah, her [illegible] 1/3; John Grant, brother, sharing 1/3; Charles Murray, [illegible...].

[Illegible...] died July 3, 1900, leaving his 1/3 interest to his wife and [illegible...] [fo]llows:

[Illegible], wife 1/3 of his 1/3 or 1/9 interest.

[Illegible...] 1/4 of remaining 2/3 of 1/3 or 1/18.

[Illegible...] Grant, dau., 1/4 of remaining 2/3 of 1/3 or 1/18.

[Illegible...] Grant, son, 1/4 of remaining 2/3 of 1/3 or 1/18.

[Illegible...] Grant, "   "   "   "   "   1/18.

[Illegible...] 25, 1905, leaving her 1/18 interest to her mother, [illegible...], as follows:

[Illegible...] shares 1/4 of her 1/18 int or 1/72; Annie Nellie [Illegible...] 1/4 of her 1/18 int or 1/72; Vestina Grant, niece, [illegible...] Grant, deceased, who was a brother of Jane Ely) [illegible...] or 1/72 by right of representation; Frank, Anna, [illegible...] Morris [or Norris], Ralph Green and Jefferson Green, nieces [illegible...] children of William Green Grant, deceased, who was a brother [illegible...] other 1/4 of her 1/18 or 1/72 int. There being six [illegible...] shares 1/6 of 1/72 or 1/432 int. each by right of represent[tation].

[Illegible] Nellie Grant (Atkins) died Oct. 8, 1906, leaving her 1/18 int from [illegible...] Grant, her father, and her 1/72 int. through her sister, Jane Ely or a total of 1/72 int. in the original estate of May Murray) to her husband and children as follows:

William Atkins, husband, shares 1/3 of her 5/72 or 5/216; Zolo Grant, shares 1/[?] of remaining 2/3 of her 5/72 or 5/432; William Atkins, Jr., shares 1/4 of remaining 2/3 of her 5/72 or 5/432; Harvey Atkins shares [illegible] of remaining 2/3 of her 5/72 or 5/432; Hiawatha Atkins, 1/4 of 2/3 of 5/72 [or 5/432].

[Illegible] Stanley Grant died Dec. 11, 1900, leaving his 1/18 int. to his [illegible] children as follows:

[Illegible...], wife, shares 1/2 of his 1/1[?] int. or 1/36 int.

[Illegible] Grant, dau. "   "   "   1/36 "

William Green Grant died Jan. [Illegible..] leaving his 1/18 int. to his [illegible] children as follows:

[Illegible] Green Grant inherits 1/[?] of his 1/19 or 1/34; Frank [Illegible...]

[Remainder of page completely illegible]

* * * * * * * * * *

[Complete left side of the following page missing]

[Illegible...], a surviving child of Annie Nellie Grant, Atkins, [illegible...] not having been married, on or about the 13th [illegible...] at the age of 5 mo. and 5 days, leaving his [illegible...] in equal shares to the other children of the said [illegible...] namely:

Zolo Grant, William Atkins, Jr., and [illegible...] to each 1/3 of 5/432 or a 5/1296 interest in the [illegible]

[Illegible] Jefferson Green died on the 2nd of May, 1907, leaving his [illegible] in this estate in equal shares to Frank Grant, Thelma Grant, [Illegible] Grant, Ralph Green, and Eva B. Morris, children of his father, William Green Grant, deceased, each receiving 1/5 of 11/1896 or [illegible] int in estate.

Recapitulation:

Ti-an-koo-hah,	1/3.
Mary Grant, sister-in-law,	1/8.
Mary Harragara, brother's dau.-in-law,	1/36
Vestina Grant, niece,	1/24.
William Atkins, brother's son-in-law,	5/216.
Zolo Grant, niece,	5/324
William Atkins, Jr., nephew,	5/324
Harvey Atkins, "	5/324
Anna Grant, niece,	11/1020
Frank Grant, nephew,	"
Thelma Grant, niece,	"
Eva B. Morris, "	"
Ralph Green, nephew,	"
Mary Green Grant, brother's sister-in-law,	1/54.
Emily Roubideaux, nephew's wife,	1/9
Kirwin Murray, Grand nephew,	1/27
Franklin Murray, " "	"
Pearl Murray, " niece,	"
Vestina Murray, " "	"
Kate Murray, " "	"
Velinda Murray, " "	"

Shawnee Indian Agency,
Shawnee, Oklahoma,
January 27, 1923.

Mr. Robert Roubidoux,
 Perkins, Oklahoma.

Dear Sir:-

Referring to my conversation with you on the 19th with reference to the partitioning of the Kirwin Murray allotment, you are advised that I have referred this matter to Mr. Dushane, and he has taken the matter under consideration and just as soon as time can be secured to look into the matter, you will be further communicated with.

Please do not forget the meeting of the Sac & Fox, and Iowa people on the 31st of this month. We anticipate a large crowd and will have many things of interest for the Indian people. If there is any possible way by which you can be present, please do so.

Expecting to have you present on that date, I am

Very respectfully,

J. L. Suffecool
Superintendent.

JLS:EV.

Shawnee Indian Agency,
Shawnee, Oklahoma,
January 31, 1923.

Mr. J. B. Vanmeter,
Maud, Oklahoma, R#3.

Dear Sir:-

Your inquiry with reference to N/2 of the NW/4 of 9-8-5 E. of the I.M. was received; and you are advised that said land belongs to the heirs of Martha Smith.

Frank Smith has the greatest interest in this allotment, and the same is still held in trust by the Government.

In your letter you also requested as to what provisions were made in the McKowan-Snyder Bill with reference to rights of way across restricted Indian lands for drainage or ditch purposes.

In connection with this bill you are advised that we are not informed and do not have a copy of said bill. The Indian Office, Washington will be asked to furnish this office with copy of the bill, and later if you still desire this information, the same will be given you.

Very respectfully,

J. L. Suffecool
Superintendent.

CD:EV.

Shawnee Indian Agency,
Shawnee, Oklahoma,
February 1, 1923.

The Honorable,
   The Commissioner
   of Indian Affairs,
      Washington, D. C.

My dear Mr. Commissioner:-

   I have the honor to bring to your attention conditions surrounding Ruth
Pennock, wife of David Pennock, now deceased; and her two minor
children--David Pennock, age three years, and William Pennock, age six
months.

   On the 18th day of January, David Pennock was killed.   This
circumstance was reported to the Office by wire, and a full report of the
same is now being compiled and will be forwarded to the Office within a
few days.

   David Pennock, deceased has at this office $2, 571.35 in cash, and
$3,500 in Liberty Bonds. This of course will be distributed after his estate
has been properly probated to his heirs, which presumable will be the wife
and two small children.   But in te meantime some assistance must be
granted this young woman. She has the sole care and custody of the two
small children; has no home other than that of her father and mother; and I
would respectfully request that authority be granted this office to disburse
from the account of David Pennock, her husband, payments not exceeding
$50.00 a month for the support of the wife, Ruth Pennock, and her two
minor children. The circumstances under which this woman is left are
pitiful and some steps must be taken to relieve her wants immediately.

                                Very respectfully,

                                J. L. Suffecool
JLS:EV.   Superintendent.

47

Shawnee Indian Agency,
Shawnee, Oklahoma,
February 3, 1923.

Mr. J. W. Mullen,
Maud, Oklahoma, R#3.

Dear Sir:-

There is inclosed herewith my official check No. 14172, drawn from the account of payee, and payable to your order in the sum of $792.50. This check represents proceeds of land-sale of Martha Mullen estate.

Very respectfully,

J. L. Suffecool
Superintendent.

EV.
ENCLS. ck.

Shawnee Indian Agency,
Shawnee, Oklahoma,
February 8, 1923.

Mr. O. K. Chandler,
Supt. Quapaw Ind. Agency,
Miami, Oklahoma.

Dear Sir:-

This will reply to your letter of January 30th relative to the share of Mrs. Margaret Phelps Holmes in her father's allotment.

You are advised that a careful search has been made of the files in this office, but we have failed to establish any connection with Mrs. Holmes[sic] share in the William Phelps allotment. There has been several changes in the location of the Shawnee Indian Agency, it having been at one time located near Stroud, Oklahoma, and other changes following have caused some confusion relative to records in connection with estates; especially with reference to the Potawatomi. It is very probably that there are some records but such have not yet been located.

A further examination of the records will be made and when found, Mrs. Holmes will be duly notified through your office.

Very respectfully,

J. L. Suffecool
Superintendent.

CD:EV.

Shawnee Indian Agency,
Shawnee, Oklahoma,
February 8, 1923.

Dr. Jacob Breid,
  Sac & Fox Sanatorium,
    Toledo, Iowa.

Dear Sir:-

This replies to your letter under date of January 22, 1923, and also of January 27, relative to the inherited interest in the estate of Andrew Barker, which the heirs up there wish to sell and retain mineral rights therein.

You are advised that sale made in that form would have little consideration for the reason that purchasers of this allotment would make purchase for the purpose of obtaining full right and title in this allotment. Therefore, you will please inform these parties that a sale cannot be made.

Very respectfully,

J. L. Suffecool
Superintendent.

CD:EV.

Shawnee Indian Agency,
Shawnee, Oklahoma,
February 8, 1923.

The Commissioner
  of Indian Affairs,
    Washington, D. C.

S I R:-

49

This has reference to the estate of Philola Green nee Le Point, deceased Citizen Pottawatomie No. 1083, whose heirs were determined under Law-Heirship 75250-15 E G T.

The Office is respectfully advised that in response to Office letter dated Jan. 24, 1918 captioned "Land-Sales ESS" the matter of issuance of patent in fee was submitted to the Office under Declaration of Policy then in force, but for some reason said patent was not issued. It will be noted that all of the heirs in this case are white people whose ages all appear to be above twenty-two years. It appears that these people should have a patent in fee issued.

The reason for a patent in fee not having been issued was probably due to the fact that the hearing fee of $15.00 had not been paid. 5 The estate is now under the control of only one of the heirs; namely, F. Green who is holding said allotment under an agreement existing between himself and all of the other heirs who live outside of this State. As the revenue from this allotment never came through this office, therefore said probate fee remains unpaid.

If the Department will issue patent in fee covering this allotment upon payment of said probate fee, information will be submitted to the heirs with the request that they pay the probate fee at once in order that patent in fee may be issued.

Very respectfully,

CD:EV.

J. L. Suffecool
Superintendent.

Ed-Ind.
4102-23
ESS

Shawnee Indian Agency,

Shawnee, Okla.

Feb. 9, 1923.

The Commissioner of Indian Affairs,

Washington, D.C.

Sir:-

Replying to carbon copy of Office letter dated Feb. 1, 1923 and bearing file number as stated above requesting information concerning distribution of funds carried to the credit of Maggie Sullivan (Harris) and which matter one, Louis Sullivan, has made inquiry, I have to inform the Office that the allottee died July 22, 1922 and up to the present time no hearing has been held to determine her heirs.

Upon the examiner of inheritance's next detail here this estate will be probated.

Returned herewith is Mr. Louis Sullivan's letter to the Office.

Incls.   Very respectfully,
JLR.

_____

J. L. Suffecool,
Superintendent.

Shawnee Indian Agency,
Shawnee, Oklahoma,
February 9, 1923.

The Commissioner
  of Indian Affairs,
    Washington, D. C.

S I R:-

There is transmitted herewith Indian deed on inherited lands on Form 5-183 covering the allotment of Louis Ogee, deceased Pottawatomie allottee No. 1112, whose heirs were determined under Law-Heirship 73143-14 FWS, made by Mary Ogee, Shawnee, Oklahoma; Clarence Ogee, Pocatello, Idaho; Thurman A. Ogee, Lima, Montana; and Carl S. Ogee of Pocatello, Idaho in favor of Marvin R. Ogee, also an heir.

According to records in this office the grantors in this deed are all adults and most of them live outside of this State and their financial conditions are unknown to this office. Marvin R. Ogee, the grantee is a minor under the care of his mother, Mary Ogee.

It appears to be the intention of these people that the said Marvin R. Ogee be the sole owner of the allotment of Louis Ogee.

I respectfully recommend approval of the deed.

Very respectfully,

J. L. Suffecool
CD:EV.   Superintendent.
ENCLS.

Shawnee Indian Agency,
Shawnee, Oklahoma,
February 10, 1923.

The Commissioner
of Indian Affairs,
Washington, D. C.

S I R:-

There is transmitted herewith Indian Deed Inherited Land form 5-183 covering the undivided interest of Thomas Hartico in the allotment of Hog-gra-ah-chey, deceased Iowa allottee No. 28, in favor of Anna Bassett, daughter of Mary Ford Bassett, one of the heirs of the deceased allottee.

The matter of the sale of the undivided interest of Hartico was submitted to this office for consideration by letter from Supt. George A. Hoyo of Ponca Agency, Whiteagle, Oklahoma; his letter is herewith inclosed. The consideration in this sale is in the form at present of a bond of $500--$400 of which is the consideration in the deed. If said deed herewith is approved by the Department, the bond of $500 herewith inclosed should be converted into a negotiable bond, so that $400 of said bond may be applied to this sale and the remainder placed to the credit if the grantee.

There is also inclosed a copy of letter from Supt. George A. Hoyo, Ponca Agency, transmitting the $500 bond to this office.

Tom Hartico is an adult Indian and under advises[sic] from Supt. Geo. A. Hoyo, it appears that he has recently been divorced from his wife, which is set out in Supt. Geo. A. Hoyo's letter. Hartico, it will be observed, lives under the jurisdiction of Supt. Hoyo. Anna Bassett is a minor also under the jurisdiction of Supt. Hoyo, therefore the financial condition of Hartico and Anna Bassett is not very well known to this office. However, it appears that this is a legitimate transaction and should be approved, and therefore I recommend its approval.

Very respectfully,

J. L. Suffecool
Superintendent.

CD:EV.
ENCLS.
cc to George A. Hoyo
Ponca Agency,
    Whiteagle, Okla.

Shawnee Indian Agency,

Shawnee, Oklahoma,

2/10/23

The Commissioner of

    Indian Affairs

        Washington, D. C.

Sir:

Transmitted herewith is my Heirship Report for the second quarter 1923, attached thereto is the list showing estates on which amounts are still delinquent. Efforts are being made to collect all outstanding fees.

Very respectfully,

Encl.
JLR/MS

J. L. Suffecool,
Superintendent.

Shawnee Indian Agency,
Shawnee, Oklahoma,
Jan. 31, 1923.

Mrs. Zoa Allen,
Tonkawa, Okla.

Dear Madam:

This acknowledges the receipt of your letter of the 20th instant regarding the estate of your mother Madeline Bourbonnais in connection with the road matter.

You are informed that the Indian Office authorized the opening of the highway you mentioned by recommendation of Mr. Deaver, the Superintendent at that time. The damages assessed were $40.00 and your share amounts to $13.34. You will find inclosed herewith my official check No. 10051 i the Shawnee National Bank for $13.34 which is all you have to your credit in this office.

Very truly yours,

1 od 31.   J. L. Suffecool,
Incl.   Superintendent.

Shawnee Indian Agency,

Shawnee, Okla.

Feb. 19, 1923.

Mr. A. R. Snyder:- Supt.,

Mayetta, Kansas.

Dear Mr. Snyder:

Your letter of the 15th inquiring as to the the[sic] relationship of Mrs. Whitewater or Wah-pe-pah-ke-ah, to Ka-ah-tah-be-ah received and in reply I have to state that Mrs. Whitewater is not the wife of Ke-ah-tah-be-ah and that Mrs. Whitewater or Wah-pe-pah-ke-ah and Wah-pah-nah-pe-quah are two separate and distinct persons.

You may forward the $43.93 to this agency to be taken up to the credit of Wah-pah-nah-pe-quah, the wife and sole heir of Ke-ah-tah-be-ah. Please give us the file number of the approved hearing at the time you transmit the check.

JLR.

Very respectfully,

_____

J. L. Suffecool,
Superintendent.

Shawnee Indian Agency,

Shawnee, Oklahoma,

Feb. 19, 1923.

United States Land Office,

Las Cruces, N.M.

Sir:-

The enclosed reisgtered[sic] letter addressed to the heirs of Aaron M. Bourbonnaise, Quemado, N.M. and forwarded to Shawnee, Okla., care of me as Indian Agent and which was receipted for [illegible] Agent, is returned with the information that none of the heors[sic] are present at this time-one who resides near Shawnee is away at a hospital for treatment, one lives in Oklahoma City and others live in New Mexico. Some of the addresses are as follows and are all that this office knows:

Anthony Bourbonaise[sic], Oklahoma City, Okl.
C/o Masonic Temple.

Mrs Rosetta Jenks, Artesia, New Mexico.

John Burbonaies[sic], Shawnee, Okla..

The one to whom I would suggest writing is Mrs. Jenks at Artesia, New Mexico. She appears to be the business head of the estate and is in a position to give you information as to the where-abouts of the others.

JLR.   Respectfully,   Supt.

Shawnee Indian Agency,
Shawnee, Oklahoma,
Feb. 21, 1923.

The Honorable Com.
of Indian Affairs,
Washington, D. C.

Dear Mr. Commissioner:

There are transmitted herewith the papers in the sale of the allotment of Samuel L. Brown, dec. Sac & Fox allottee No. 60, described as the Lots 3 & 4 and S/2 of NE/4 all in Sec. 4, Twp. 16 N., R. 6 E. I. M. in Oklahoma.

This is not agricultural land. Fryor Brown who is the sole heir in this estate can get material assistance from the sale of this land in as much as it will provide him with funds for necessary supplies, home improvements, etc. The land in its present condition affords him with very little revenue and that the price offered is very good. I unhesitatingly approve that this sale be approved.

Very respectfully,

2 OD 21.   J. L. Suffecool,
Incl. sale-papers.   Supt. & Spl. Disb. Agt.

Shawnee Indian Agency,
Shawnee, Oklahoma,
February 24, 1923.

Mrs. Zella Marie Graham,
    Emmett, Kansas.

Dear Madam:-

There is inclosed herewith receipts for deed covering your mother's undivided one-fifth interest in the allotment of Joseph Welch, your grandfather. Please sign this receipt and return at your convenience.

The deed covering this interest has been approved by the Department and is now held in this office and will be held here until it has been recorded in Tecumseh, Oklahoma. You should remit $1.00 for the necessary recording fee. After the deed has been recorded it will be mailed to your address.

Your letter to Senator Charles Curtis of Kansas was referred to the Indian Office and by that Office referred to this office for report.

A complete report of the estate of Joseph Welch is being prepared for consideration of the Indian Office and will take sometime[sic] for the final settlement of this estate, for the reason that there are several matters to be adjusted before final settlement can be made. However, as rapid progress as possible under the circumstances will be made so that this estate when finally settled will be settled for all time. If you should desire further information, sometime in the future when you think the progress is not sufficiently advanced, please address this office for such information and the same will be freely given you.

Very respectfully,

J. L. Suffecool
Superintendent.

CD:EV.
ENCLS.
cc to Indian Office

Shawnee Indian Agency,
Shawnee, Oklahoma,
Feb. 27, 1923.

The Honorable Com.
of Indian Affairs,
Washington, D. C.

Dear Mr. Commissioner:

There are transmitted herewith the papers in the sale of the allotment of Mary Hodge, deceased Sac & Fox allottee No. 538, whose heirs were determines under L-H, as modified, 113285-13, 26061-14 FWS, April 13, 1914, covering the 1/3 inherited interest of Andrew Conger to Florence Grass.

Partition in this case is not as practical as a sale for the reason that Andrew Conger is in need of funds and that Florence Grass has sufficient funds. In order that a settlement of the estate be made equitable, and satisfactory to these two heirs this sale is respectfully recommended.

Very respectfully,

2 od 27.   J. L. Suffecool,
Incls. pet. for sale, Etc.   Supt. & S. D. A.

Shawnee Indian Agency,
Shawnee, Oklahoma,
February 28, 1923.

Mrs. Eva S. Lowe,
  Langston University,
  Langston, Oklahoma.

Dear Madam:-

Under date of January 31, 1923, you were informed that a portion of the Wm. Shawnee land was sold, and that you might participate in the proceeds of the sale, but that in as much as your mother, Julia Shawnee was selling said twenty acres of land deeded to her by three of the boys, the Department at Washington issued instructions that all of this money from this sale should be made to Julia Shawnee.

You are therefore again informed that your interest in this allotment will continue to be held in trust in the same proportion and manner as before the sale. Owing to the fact that Julia Shawnee holds this allotment under homestead rights, it will be impossible for you to dispose of your interest excepting to Julia Shawnee, herself, or to some of the other heirs subject to the homestead right of Julia Shawnee.

Very respectfully,

J. L. Suffecool
Superintendent.

CD:EV.

Land-Sale
119811-13
100055-14
7588-23
   J T H

Shawnee Indian Agency,
Shawnee, Oklahoma,
February 28, 1923.

The Commissioner
   of Indian Affairs,
      Washington, D. C.

S I R:-

This will comply with instructions given under date of February 16, 1923 bearing above reference relative to partition proceedings in favor of Ellen and Hattie Mason, inclosing official appraisement on form 5-110a.

Very respectfully,

J. L. Suffecool
Superintendent.

CD:EV.
ENCLS.

Land-Contract
18033-19
78116-22
C H I

Shawnee Indian Agency,
Shawnee, Oklahoma,
March 1, 1923.

The Commissioner
   of Indian Affairs,

Dear Mr. Commissioner:-

Reference is made to Office letter under date of October 13, 1922 bearing reference above relative to the application of the Township Board of the Eason Township, Pottawatomie County, Oklahoma for permission to open the public highway across the allotment of Joseph Melott, Pottawatomie allottee No. 92.

There are inclosed herewith linen tracings called for; and the Office is advised that statements of only four of the heirs have been procured and are also herewith inclosed. The heirs submitting these statements all belong to the same family with Marie Alice Upton Wynn. The other heirs have been appealed to and refuse to take any action and have never given reasons for their attitude in this matter. However, it might be presumed that in as much as they have in time past signed papers for application for patent in fee in favor of Marie Alice Upton Wynn; and for that reason they may presume that they have no interest in this land any more.

The Office has requested that a report in this matter be made; that a card was written in reply to the request and the Office was informed that said report would be forwarded at an early date, but that owing to the hope that some explanation might be procured from the other heirs, the report therein was this long delayed.

Very respectfully,

J. L. Suffecool
Superintendent.

CD:EV.
ENCLS.

Shawnee Indian Agency,
Shawnee, Oklahoma,
March 1, 1923.

The Commissioner
of Indian Affairs,
Washington, D. C.

S I R:-

There is transmitted herewith the application for patent in fee by the heirs of Sarah Bear, Sac & Fox allottee No. 3-- heirs being determined under law-heirship 55623-21 SYT--which is recommended for approval for the reason the George O. Morton, one of the applicants has considerable inherited landed[sic] interests; and for the further reason that he has executed a deed covering some of his inherited land in favor of his two children to be submitted to the Office at a later date. Also, he is sufficiently competent to take care of his allotment without Government control.

Sac & Fox – Shawnee Estates
1920-1924 Volume IX

The other heirs, Mamie Jennings Blackburn still holds her own allotment and she has inherited interests in other land. She is married to a white man who bears a good reputation and is capable of supporting a family.

Very respectfully,

J. L. Suffecool,
Superintendent.

CD:EV.
ENCLS.

Shawnee Indian Agency,
Shawnee, Oklahoma,
March 1, 1923.

Supt. A. R. Snyder,
    Potawatomi Indian Agency,
    Mayetta, Kansas.

Dear Mr. Snyder:-

An Indian by the name of Daniel O'Brien recently came into this office and requested that we write you with reference to the disposition of the estate of Edward O'Brien, allottee No. 100, whose allotment was described as the NE/4 of the NW/4 of 5-9-11 and the SE/4 of the SW/4 of the NW/4 of 5-9-11 and the SE/4 of the SW/4 of 32-8-11. Also, the allotment of Julia E. O'Brien, allottee No. 1432, described as the W/2 of the NW/44 of 32-8-11, containing eighty acres.

This man is under the impression that the sale of land in these two estates was irregular and desires information as to what interests or rights, if he has any, remaining in these two estates.

If after you have sufficient information covering these two allotments you will forward the same to this office and an explanation of his rights and interests will be made to him by us.

Very respectfully,

J. L. Suffecool
Superintendent.

CD:EV.

Shawnee Indian Agency,
Shawnee, Oklahoma,
March 1, 1923.

Mr. Farron Roubidoux,
Perkins, Oklahoma.

Dear Sir:-

Under date of February 13, 1923, you requested information with reference to a certain deed covering the allotment of Lee Patrick Tohee executed by your mother, Annie Perry Tohee.

You are informed that owing to the fact that Annie Perry Tohee has a grand-child who would share alike with you in case of the death of Annie Perry Tohee, the deed you mention could not be approved. For that reason said deed was never submitted to the Indian Office for action.

Very respectfully,

J. L. Suffecool
Superintendent.

CD:EV.

Shawnee Indian Agency,

Shawnee, Oklahoma,

Mar. 2, 1923.

Mr. Geo. A. Hoyo, Supt.,

Whiteagle, Okla.

Dear Mr. Hoyo:-

In compliance with your request of the 1st, inst., I am enclosing herewith the approved Departmental findings in the case of Sophia Embler Lincoln, deceased Iowa Allottee No. 15, with some testimony which might be interesting to you.

When you have finished with same please return to me.

Very truly yours,

Incls.

JLR.

_____

J. L. Suffecool,
Superintendent.

Shawnee Indian Agency,

Shawnee, Oklahoma, March 5, 1923.

Mr. Chas. L. Austin,
Norman, Oklahoma, R# 6.
Dear Sir:

This is to advise you that your lease is signed by Go do pea se, described as the S/2 of section 9, township 0 north, range 1 east.

Please call at this Office and complete same as soon as possible.

Very respectfully,

J. L. Suffecool,
Superintendent

TBA

Shawnee Indian Agency,

Shawnee, Oklahoma, March 5, 1923.

Mr. C. Files,
Norman, Oklahoma.

Dear Sir:

Reference is made to your letter of the 2nd instant, I have to advise you that the heirs reuse to consider $15.00 for the N/2 of the NE 1/4 of section 17, township 9 north, range 1 east.

They claim that the consideration is inadequate.

Very respectfully,

J. L. Suffecool,
Superintendent

TBA

Shawnee Indian Agency,

Shawnee, Okla.

March 10, 1923.

Mr. Claude Hendon, Co., Att'y.,

Tecumseh, Okla.

Dear Mr. Hendon:-

Replying to your letter of the 9th, inst., concerning the rights of Mrs. Bertha E. Myers, nee Edna Kennedy, the daughter of Geo. A. Kennedy, I have to advise that the records of this office disclose that Geo. A. Kennedy received a patent-in-fee for the SW/4 of SW/4 of sec. 25, Twp. 11 Range 4 and Lot 3 of SW/4 of Sec. 25, Twp. 11 Range 4 and Lot 3 of SW/4 of Sec. 31, Twp. 11 Range 2 E, in June 1907. This represented all his land and holdings under this jurisdiction, as far as we are able to ascertain. Therefore his daughter holds no interest therein;

His first wife, who was the mother of Edna Kenneday[sic], was a white woman and had no interests here. As far as we are able to ascertain she has no tribal rights at this time, however the members of the Pottawatomie tribe of Indians have held a meeting or two at which tribal matters were discussed regarding claims they allege to have against the Government. It may be she is referring to these matters.

JLR.

Very truly yours,

_____

J. L. Suffecool,
Superintendent.

Shawnee Indian Agency,
Shawnee, Oklahoma,
April 4, 1923.

Mrs. Leonard Thompson,
Waubum[sic], Minnesota.

Dear Madam:-

There is acknowledged herewith the receipt of your letter to this office under date of March 30, 1923, in which you request information to your grandmother's land, and who is living on it.

In reply I have to advise that if you will give us more information, such as the name of your grandmother or the location of the land e may be able to give you the desired information; but at present we cannot give any information as we do not have the name of your grandmother.

Very respectfully,

J. L. Suffecool,
Superintendent.

EV.

Shawnee Indian Agency,
Shawnee, Oklahoma,
April 9, 1923.

Mr. A. R. Snyder,
Supt. Pott. Indian Agency,
Mayetta, Kansas.

Dear Mr. Snyder:-

There are returned the papers in the sale of the allotment of O-ketch-e-show-o-now allottee No. 527 belonging to your Agency un-signed for the reason that the heirs consider this allotment to have greater value than as appraised. The heirs of course took it for granted that the appraisement would be as shown in the petition, however if the appraisement is greater than shown in said petition then you will return these papers and the matter will again be submitted to them for their consideration.

Very respectfully,

J. L. Suffecool,
Superintendent.

CD:EV.
ENCLS.

Shawnee Indian Agency,
Shawnee, Oklahoma,
April 9, 1923.

Mrs. Vestina Burgess.
Marland, Oklahoma.

Dear Madam:-

I have your letter of the 2nd inst. regarding the sale of the Mary Grant allotment; and in connection therewith you are advised that a sale of this allotment will be made sometime this Spring. An appraisement by Mr. Collins has not yet been made and for the reason that other allotments are being considered for sale at the same time, delay will be necessary for a short while.

It is the intention of this office and of the Indian Office at Washington that settlements be made in inherited estates where convenient either by partition or by sale.

The reasons for sale are considered reasonable and if land can be sold this office will gladly assist in fulfilling your request.

Very respectfully,

J. L. Suffecool,
Superintendent.

CD:EV.

Shawnee Indian Agency,
Shawnee, Oklahoma,
April 9, 1923.

Mr. Wm. Moutaw,
Lexington, Oklahoma.

Dear Mr. Moutaw:-

Further reference is made to the estate of Joseph Welch to which your attention was called sometime[sic] ago when this office took charge of said allotment.

In connection with this matter you are informed that the papers consisting of your letter of transmittal of certain affidavit together with the affidavit that sets out the whole controversy between your wife and the heirs in connection with said estate were submitted to the Department for consideration, and in reply we received Office letter under date of March 19, 1923, a copy of which is inclosed.

You will please submit all claims that you have against said estate supported by reports or affidavits that may be considered in the settlement so that proper credits may be placed to the credit of all the heirs.

Very respectfully,

J. L. Suffecool,
Superintendent.

CD:EV.
ENCL. 1.

Shawnee Indian Agency,
Shawnee, Oklahoma,
April 9, 1923.

Supt. A. R. Snyder,
Mayetta, Kansas.

Dear Mr. Snyder:-

On Marth 17th, there was transmitted to you sale papers in the sale of John B. Jackson allotment to be signed by the heirs who reside near your Agency. What is further desired now since the papers mentioned before have been received and sale having been accomplished wherein the bid was $3,250, is that the heirs give their consent to the sale on deferred payments.

Please obtain their written consent to this manner of sale so that the papers may be submitted in that form for consideration of the Department.

Very respectfully,

J. L. Suffecool,
Superintendent.

CD:EV.

Land-Sales,
6993-23

Shawnee Indian Agency,
Shawnee, Oklahoma,
April 9, 1923.

The Commissioner
of Indian Affairs,
Washington, D. C.

S I R:-

Further reference is made to Office letter captioned as above dated February 27, 1923 relating to the allotments of Priscilla and Elmira Bayliss.

Former reports show that there has not been any considerable amount of walnut logs out from this allotment; and that the logs that remain on said allotment, numbering about twenty-eight, were out partly from other allotments. Therefore, it is suggested that with reference to timber depredations on this allotment that that phase be considered settled.

With reference to the notice of sale not showing specific assessments. On account of drainage ditch and in as much as the land did not sell at the date mentioned before the land was again re-advertised and regulations as to the form of advertising in connection with assessments were made. The date of the last sale has passed and no bids were received upon upon[sic] this land. There is inclosed herewith for the information of the Office advertising of the land in question.

Referring to the estate of William C. Bayliss, the matter pertaining to his death was over-looked in the last report. It appears that William C. Bayliss spent his last days in Kansas and re-married-- raising one child. Sometime before his death, he and his last wife separated and lived away from his family. It also appears that he was given some information that it would probably be that there would a suit instituted against him for the maintenance of Priscilla Bayliss, who was then and is now in the State Hospital for the Insane at Osawatomie, Kansas. That in order that he would be without property, he deeded some valuable property in Kansas to his daughter from his last wife, but never the less it might appear that these heirs in Kansas may be able to show that they are entitled to any inherited interest William C. Bayliss may have in Oklahoma.

In the last report from this office, information was requested concerning records of the remaining portion of the Elmira Bayliss allotment with reference to its description, as it was suggested in said report that records in the county office and this office do not coincide. Instructions with reference to the disposition of this estate are respectfully desired.

Very respectfully

J. L. Suffecool,
CD:EV.   Superintendent.
ENCL. 1.

Shawnee Indian Agency,
Shawnee, Oklahoma,
April 9, 1923.

The Commissioner of
  Indian Affairs,
    Washington, D. C.

S I R:-

The accompanying sale papers of the allotment of Jim Bullfrog together with a letter by the parties at interest requesting that patent in fee be issued, although not just as directed by the Office in connection with the sale of this tract of land by wire dated January 23, 1923 and Office letter 101173 dated January 23, 1922. However, these parties have submitted quit claim deed, and in view of all circumstances in connection with this sale it may be possible for the Department to issue a patent in fee covering this land.

The Superintendent's report shows that none of the heirs have any assignable portion of the proceeds to be derived from this sale for the reason that it is unknown what proportions will fall to their share on account of Charley Tyner having sold his inherited interest to E. T. Carson, and in fact sole greater than said inherited interest; and in view of this fact and he recognized by the Office Charley Tyner may not participate in the proceeds of this sale. However, such instructions with reference to the proceeds of the sale, if approved, are desired by this office.

If the Office desires, a deed will be procured from the heirs and submitted for consideration in connection with the sale.

Very respectfully,

J. L. Suffecool,
Superintendent.

CD:EV.

Shawnee Indian Agency,

Shawnee, Okla.

April 12, 1923.

Mr. Charles W. Fear,

Joplin, Mo.

Dear Mr. Fear:-

I have your letter of the 5th inst., relative to the estate of your deceased wife and in reply I have to state that at the present time there is no examiner of inheritance at this agency, but it is expected that one will be here sometime time spring or summer. When he does arrive and take up the heirship work you and your daughter will be notified.

As to the feasibility of you and your daughter giving testimony elsewhere in this matter, I am not in position to state, as this will be left with the examiner. You might take the matter up with him and get his advice. His address is: S. Y. Tutwiler, Indian Agency, Anadarko, Okla.

An agricultiral[sic] issue has been made on the estate for the year 1923, for $300.00 and has been paid in full. The payment on the oil and gas lease is due July 31, 1923 and if $320.00.

The share of Mrs. Fear will be retained to the credit of her account until her heirs have been determined by the Department. Under the law no disbursements may be made until the heirs are determined.

The address of John Keokuk is Shamrock, Okla.

JLR.
Carbon copy   Very truly yours,
to Mrs. Ruby Carter
936 Putnam St.
Detroit, Mich.

_____

J. L. Suffecool, Supt.

---

303 Wichita

Joseph Edmonds.

Shawnee Indian Agency,

Shawnee, Okla.

April 12, 1923.

Mr. John A. Buntin, Supt.,

Anadarko, Okla.

Dear Sir:-

Replying to your letter of the 3rd, relative to the interest Joseph Edmonds and his children have in the Little Fish estate under this jurisdiction I have to state that at the present time no lease is on this land and that no funds are to the credit of their accounts derived from rentals. There is a small balance to credit of the Edmonds heirs, something like 80¢ which was transferred from some old account and this will be sent them in the course of business.

Their inherited interests are as follows:

Joseph Edmonds- - -60/1440
Scipio Edmonds- - - 40/1440
Houston Edmonds- -40/1440
Taylor Edmonds- - - 40/1440

L-H- 134177-15 F.E.

71

JLR.   Very respectfully,

_____

J. L. Suffecool,
Superintendent.

Shawnee Indian Agency,
Shawnee, Oklahoma,
April 13, 1923.

General Roy Hoffman,
  906-912 State National Bank Bldg.,
    Oklahoma [sic], Oklahoma.

Dear General Hoffman:-

I thought perhaps that you would be interested in knowing the status of the Bigwalker-Hall land-sale. I am pleased to state that we have been very fortunate in this matter and have secured all of the signatures necessary in this matter and the heirs are very willing to complete the necessary arrangements. The papers are signed and will be forwarded in a few days to Washington for approval. Upon receipt of notice of approval, I will be pleased to advise you and a meeting will be held where it is possible that a settlement can be effected that will not only be fair to your client but to the other heirs as well.

Very truly yours,

J. L. Suffecool,
Superintendent.

JLS:EV.

Shawnee Indian Agency,

Shawnee, Okla.

April 15, 1923.

Mrs. H. E. Carter,

    838 Putnam Street,
    Detroit, Mich.,

Dear Mrs. Carter:-

    My letter of recent addressed to Mr. Charles Fear of Joplin, Mo., a carbon of which was forwarded to you, will explain, I believe, the status of your mother's estate.

    Any funds derived from the estate your mother was interested in will be held intact on the books of this office until the heirs are determined. No distribution of the funds can be made until that time.

    Under the laws of decent in Oklahoma it is believed that both you and your step-father will inherit in the estate of your deceased mother.

JLR.   Very respectfully,

                                  J. L. Suffecool,
                                  Superintendent.

                                  Shawnee Indian Agency,
                                  Shawnee, Oklahoma,
.   April 18, 1923.

Mr. Levi Jones,
    Office of Court Clerk,
        Sapulpa, Oklahoma.

Dear Mr. Jones:-

    Under date of February 23, 1923 you were requested by Mr. Dushane of this office to procure certain deed covering the allotment of Wantay Davy, Creek allotment No. 8512.

    This deed does not connect up with other papers in connection with the tract of land and there appears to be another deed wherein James Gibson is one of the grantors. If you will be able to locate this deed which covers the S/2 of the NE/4, and the NW/4 of the SE/4 3-14-8, please have certified copy made and have it sent to this office submitting at the same time charges in connection therewith, we will be greatly obliged to you. For your information notations on correspondence shows there are two deeds--one deed dated August 10, 1914--another deed dated January 17, 1913. However if neither of these show that James Gibson is one of the grantors this office will not be able to make use of it. The only deed that can be used will be that, as stated, which shows James Gibson as one of the grantors.

Very respectfully,

J. L. Suffecool,
Superintendent.

CD:EV.

Shawnee Indian Agency,
Shawnee, Oklahoma,
April 18, 1923.

Mrs. Zella Marie Graham,
 Emmett, Kansas.

Dear Madam:-

This replies to your letter of the 9th inst. regarding your deed covering your mother's inherited interest in the Joseph Welch allotment.

On the same date that your letter was received the deed mentioned was returned from Tecumseh, Oklahoma where it was sent for the purpose of recording. The deed is herewith inclosed. Please sign the receipt accompanying the same and return at your convenience.

There was received a letter of instruction from the Department to the effect that the heirs in the estate of Joseph Welch have not been changed on account of affidavits furnished or submitted by Mr. Wm. Moutaw, and that the shares would continue to be as the Department found, which appears to be one-fifth to your mother in the estate; and that the deed by your mother appears to cover her share of the allotment of Joseph Welch.

When settlement is finally made with Mr. & Mrs. Moutaw, there will be some money due your mother on account of rentals from this land. As soon as arrangements are completed you will be further notified.

Very truly yours,

J. L. Suffecool,
Superintendent.

CD:EV.

Shawnee Indian Agency,
Shawnee, Oklahoma,
April 18, 1923.

Mr. W. N. Dannenburg,
United States Probate Attorney,
Muskogee, Oklahoma.

Dear Sir:-

Information is desired in this office regarding the heirs of Wantey Davey, Creek allottee No. 3512, a portion of whose allotment was sole, same being described as S/2 of NE/4, and NW of the SE/4; according to records at Sapulpa, Oklahoma.

It is particularly desired by the Department to be informed as to whether James Gibson is an heir or not an heir of Wantey Davy, mentioned before.

If this information desired can be furnished by you at a very early date, it will be greatly appreciated.

Very respectfully,

J. L. Suffecool,
Superintendent.

CD:EV.

Sac & Fox – Shawnee Estates
1920-1924 Volume IX

Shawnee Indian Agency,
Shawnee, Oklahoma,
April 25, 1923.

Mr. S. Y. Tutwiler,
  Kiowa Indian Agency,
    Anadarko, Oklahoma.

Dear Mr. Tutwiler:-

Replying to your letter of the 23rd inst., calling for information concerning the estates of Ketumwah and Joseph M-zam-quah, Citizen Pottawatomie allottees Nos. 1070 and 55 respectively; I have to advise that both of the above received allotment on the Pottawatomie reservation under this Agency.

The heirs of Ketumwah appear to have been Peter Soldier, or Nash-ne-ce Piano, who is now dead and whose heirs were determined April 18, 1919 and are Irene Marshall, or Mac-goo-see, wife--one-half; and Mahb-en-wah, daughter--one-half. The heirs to Ketumwah estate were determined June 30, 1920 (Probate 46211-14; 121741-15; 25327-22 LAP).

The heirs of M-zam-quah were determined by the Business Committee of the Citizen Pottawatomie Indians and approved by the Department August 25, 1905. The land of this allottee was sold May 21, 1904. I do not have on file a copy lf said determination but it appears from records that Mr. Upton held a hearing in 1914 at which he determined the heirs, as follows:

Mah me ah--wife......................................297/810
Louis Zahn-quah, son...............................171/810
John Zahn-quah, son................................171/810
Peter McCoonse, husband of subsequently deceased
daughter... 57/810
Joseph McCoonse, Grand-son..................... 38/810
James McCoonse, Grand-son.......................38/810
Francis McCoonse, Grand-son.....................38/810

I do not know whether the findings as presented by him were ever approved or not, however, the Indian Office under date of October 26, 1921 (probate 12742-15 LAP) advises that the final disposition of this matter has been made, and: "That at this late date, nearly 16 years after the land was sold and the proceeds finally distributed, that a re-opening of the heirship is not warranted in view of the conflicting evidence in the records".

Sac & Fox – Shawnee Estates
1920-1924 Volume IX

It appears that the heirs, or rather the alleged heirs have had considerable correspondence with the Indian Office, Mayetta, and this office relative to these two estates. The letters are many and for one to thoroughly understand the case the files would have to be looked over.

I fail to find the copy of the letter which you supposed was written to Mr. Patrick Matchie of Mayetta, Kansas.

Very truly yours,

J. L. Suffecool,
Superintendent.

JLR:EV.

Shawnee Indian Agency,
Shawnee, Oklahoma,
April 26, 1923.

Mr. S. Y. Tutwiler,
  Kiowa Indian Agency,
  Anadarko, Oklahoma.

Dear Mr. Tutwiler:-

There is inclosed herewith at your request a copy of the findings in the case of Phoebe Keokuk, deceased.

Mrs. Charles W. Fear was allotted as Mrs. Marie Whistler (Fear). Allotment described as follows: W/2 of NW/4 of Lat. 1--Sec. 3--11--5--109.40 Acres; and E/2 of NW/4 of Lat. No. 2--Sec. 20--11--5, #144 allot. This land has been released from trust.

Mrs. Phoebe Keokuk's allotment is described as Sac & Fox allottee No. 261--Lots 3 & 4 of the E/2 of SW/4 of Sec. 31-17-6; same being still held in trust.

Very truly yours,

J. L. Suffecool,
Superintendent.

EV.
ENCL. 1.

Shawnee Indian Agency,
Shawnee, Oklahoma,
April 26, 1923.

Mr. A. R. Snyder,
Supt. Potawatomi Indian Agency,
Mayetta, Kansas.

Dear Mr. Snyder:-

      Lily Gokey and Isadore Neal, who inherited one-fourth
interest in the Sac & Fox allotment, number which I am unable to state,
but the allottees[sic] name is Wah-see-se-quah in the office a few days ago
and asked that you prepare a petition for the sale of this land and sent the
same to this office for their signatures. The other heir is John Wapp, who
I understand has the other one-half interest.

      I do not know that it is desirable to sell this land at this
time but I am complying with the request of the parties named above.

      I will be pleased to hear from you at an early date
concerning this matter.

Very respectfully,

J. L. Suffecool,
JLS:EV.   Superintendent.

Probate
46211-14
121741-15
25327-22
  LAP

Heirship, Potawatomi
Agency, Okla.

Shawnee Indian Agency,
Shawnee, Oklahoma,
April 26, 1923.

The Commissioner of
Indian Affairs,
Washington, D. C.

S I R:-

Will you please furnish this office with a copy of the finding in the case of Ke-tum-wa, or Piano, deceased Citizen Potawatomi allottee No, 1070, the heirs to which estate were said to be determined June 30, 1920.

This office's copy of said finding seems to have been lost or mis-placed and we would respectfully request that a copy of same be sent us.

Very respectfully,

J. L. Suffecool,
Superintendent.

EV.

Shawnee Indian Agency,

Shawnee, Okla.

Apr. 30, 1923.

Dr. Jacob Breid, Supt.

Toledo, Iowa.

Dear Sir:-

Replying to your letter of the 27th inst., concerning the heirs of James, Jane and John Wolf, I have to advise that Thomas E. Oliver, of Mayetta, Kansas was determined the sole heir of all three estates June 16, 1922 (46785-22 S YT)

The heirs of Cora Shaquequot were determined January 24, 1913 and were found to be:

Pa-phia-na----------------------------3/10
Ne-paw-sa-qua----------------------- 3/10
Ma-ke-so-pe-at---------------------- 3/10
Pone-wya-tah------------------------1/10

(Law 30955-13 WDG)

JLR.   Very truly yours,

_____

J. L. Suffecool,
Superintendent.

DR. JACOB BREID
SUPERINTENDENT AND
PHYSICIAN

DEPARTMENT OF THE INTERIOR

UNITED STATES INDIAN SERVICE

SAC & FOX SANATORIUM
TOLEDO, IOWA

RECEIVED
APR 30 1923
SHAWNEE INDIAN
AGENCY

April 27, 1923

Mr. J. L. Suffecool,
    Supt., Indian Agency,
      Shawnee, Okla.

<u>46785- 22 S Y T.</u>

My dear Mr. Suffecool:

    Pone-Way-tah came to the office this morning and requested information regarding the heirs of John, Jane and James Wolf in whose estates she claimed an inheritance as per affidavit submitted by us under date of March 10, 1921. Hearing was set for October 5, 1921, in these cases and I assume that a decision has been rendered. 6-16-22.

    Wa-ko-si-ke-ta or John Wayne wishes to know if the heirs of Cora Shaw-que-quot have been determined, and, if so, please forward me a copy of the decision.

Very respectfully,

Jacob Breid

JB:S.

Shawnee Indian Agency,

Shawnee, Okla.

Apr. 30, 1923.

Dr. Jacob Breid, Supt.

    Toledo, Iowa.

Dear Sir:-

    Replying to your letter of the 27th inst., concerning the heirs of James, Jane and John Wolf, I have to advise that Thomas E. Oliver, of Mayetta, Kansas was determined the sole heir of all three estates June 16, 1922 (46785-22 S YT)

The heirs of Cora Shaquequot were determined January 24, 1913 and were found to be:

Pa-phia-na----------------------------3/10
Ne-paw-sa-qua---------------------- 3/10
Ma-ke-so-pe-at---------------------- 3/10
Pone-wya-tah------------------------1/10

(Law 30955-13 WDG)

JLR.   Very truly yours,

J. L. Suffecool,
Superintendent.

Shawnee Indian Agency,
Shawnee, Oklahoma,
April 30, 1923.

Mrs. Etta Richards, nee Davenport,
Pawnee, Oklahoma,
c/o Indian School.

Dear Madam:-

According to my promise to you recently, there is herewith the information you desire. The description of the allotment of Addison Doc Davenport is, as follows: S/2 of NE/4 of Section 19; Township 9, North; Range 3 east. The allotment is leased to Richard Curry of Tecumseh, Oklahoma for the sum of $60 per annum.

There are as[sic] heirs in this estate:

Benjamin Davenport
James Davenport   Inclosed check No 15133
Ira Davenport
Isaac Pappan   in your favor, $13^{33} all
Steven Pappan
Etta Davenport   you have to your credit
Irene Davenport
                         in this office.

Sophia Pappan
Ruby Pappan

each receiving one-ninth interest.

The revenue from the allotment of Addison Doc Davenport in the form of rentals has been credited to the different heirs and checks covering their respective shares will be forwarded to them at an early date. Please furnish this office with the addresses of all the heirs mentioned above.

Very truly yours,

J. L. Suffecool,
CD:EV.   Superintendent.

Land-Sales
28053-23
4602-23
16676-23
   JTH

Shawnee Indian Agency,
Shawnee, Oklahoma,
April 30, 1923.

The Commissioner of Indian Affairs,
Washington, D. C.

S I R:-

Reference is made to land-sales as above dated April 18, 1923 relative to the sale of the allotment of Mary Schroepfer within the Pond Creek Drainage District No. 3. said letter being addressed to W. C. Schroepfer, 342 Myrtle Avenue, Kansas City, Missouri, wherein this office was requested to give an early report.

There are nine heirs in this estate and the allotment affords a revenue of something like $100 annually. Disbursements of Indian Moneys since 1921 show that Mr. W. C. Schroepfer has been paid $55.17. This appears to represent his share of the revenue of this allotment to date. There is now nothing to his credit in this office, therefore the statement Mr. Schroepfer makes in regard to non-payment of rentals appears to be unfounded.

The matter of the sale of this allotment has been again submitted to Mr. W. C. Schroepfer for his further decision in the matter of the sale. Some of the other heirs have also been addressed in this respect and their replies have not been received as yet.

The bids in this sale will be opened on Saturday, May 5th. The Office will be notified further with reference to the sale of this allotment.

Very respectfully,

J. L. Suffecool,
Superintendent.

CD:EV.

Shawnee Indian Agency,

Shawnee, Oklahoma, May 1, 1923.

Messrs. Lydick & Arrington,
Attorneys at Law,
Shawnee, Oklahoma.

Gentleman[sic]:

Reference is made to your letter of the 27th ultimo, relative to the present addresses of the heirs of Elizabeth Pappan, deceased, a Citizen Pottawatomie Indian who dies about 1904.

The present addresses of the heirs are unknown to this Office, but your[sic] might write to Supt. George O. Hoyo, Supt., of the Ponca Indian Agency, Whiteagle, Oklahoma, he may be aboe[sic] to give you the information desired.

Very respectfully,

J. L. Suffecool,
Superintendent

TBA

Shawnee Indian Agency,
Shawnee, Oklahoma,
May 3, 1923

Mrs. Katie English,
 Red Rock, Oklahoma.

Dear Madam:-

Replying to your letter of April 27th concerning rentals due you from the John Moses estate, you are advised that check covering same was mailed you April 28, 1923.

In reference to the sale of the John Moses estate by Tom Lincoln to Dr. Holbrook of Perkins, you are advised that I have no knowledge of such a transaction. This land cannot be sold except through this office.

Several months ago this allotment was advertised for sale and a bid was made by Dr. Holbrook but as the heirs failed to accept Dr. Holbrook's bid the sale was never completed.

Very truly yours,

J. L. Suffecool,
Superintendent.

JLR:EV.

Shawnee Indian Agency,
Shawnee, Oklahoma,
May 7, 1923.

Mr. Albert Moore,
 c/o Sheriff,
  Stillwater, Oklahoma.

Dear Sir:-

This will acknowledge the receipt of your letter of April 3rd, and in reply I have to advise that the office is not in a position to send your check just at this time but just as soon as the money can become available it will be forwarded. We are extremely busy with our work here at the present time.

With reference to the division of the 160 acres east of Cushing, known as the estate of Watt Grayson, I doubt very much if it is possible to make a partitionment that will be agreeable to all concerned. I expect that the proper way, if you wish to dispose of your share, would be by addressing the Office and securing authority for the sale of an undivided interest that you claim. I, personally, would approve of this proposition but cannot assure you that it will be agreeable to the Office in Washington.

It is to be regretted, Albert, that you will insist in using intoxicating liquors. I feel that probably this is one of your weak points. You have certainly lived in this world long enough to know that the use of liquor will not do anyone good and will always get them into trouble. It would be very pleasing to me and your many people who are interested, if you would be careful and not use that which has and will always get you into trouble. These are just a few words from one who has seen the use of liquor among Indian people and feels that he knows what the ultimate result will be.

Very truly yours,

J. L. Suffecool,
Superintendent.

JL:EV.

Shawnee Indian Agency,
Shawnee, Oklahoma,
May 7, 1923.

The Commissioner
of Indian Affairs,
Washington, D. C.

S I R:-

This will comply with Office letter bearing above reference dated April, 1923 requesting certificate of appraisement for the allotment of Irene Clark, deceased Shawnee allottee No. 548, described as the N/2 of the SE/4 of Sec. 26, T. 10 N. R. 2 E. of the Indian Meridian. Appraisement on form 5-110a is herewith inclosed.

Very respectfully,

J. L. Suffecool,
Superintendent.

CD
EV
encls.

Shawnee Indian Agency,

Shawnee, Okla.

May 12, 1923.

Mr. George Appletree,

  C/o Richard Duncan
  Meeker, Okla.

Dear George:-

  I am enclosing the papers you asked to have signed. I beleive[sic] they are now in proper shape. You may forward them to Mr. Snyder now at the same time telling him what you desire in the matter. Mr. Snyder, I believe has the other papers in the case and in-as-much as the original estate is under his jurisdiction it is proper for him to take the matter up with the Office at Washington.

Incls.   Very truly yours,

                J. L. Suffecool,

Shawnee Indian Agency,
Shawnee, Oklahoma,
May 16, 1923.

The Commissioner
 of Indian Affairs,
  Washington, D. C.

S I R:-

  In accordance with Office instructions under date of May 11th, 1923, reference is above, there are transmitted the several deeds covering inherited interests to the allotment of Josephine Bourassa, Pottawatomie allottee No. 802; as follows:

May Coleman, now Lewis	to	Nancy Smith Fehlig
J. E. Mullin	to	Josephine Bourassa
Eliza. Smith, now Colvin	to	Nancy Smith
Birdie Smith	to	Nellie Wylie

Birdie Smith	to	Nancy Smith Fehlig
Zoa Denton	to	Nellie Wiley
Zoa Denton	to	Nellie Wiley
Frank Smith	to	Nellie Wiley
Frank Smith	to	Nellie Wiley
Rena Richardson	to	Nancy Smith
Rena Richardson	to	Nancy Smith

which are to be made the basis of issuance of a patent in fee to certain heirs and purchasers, or present owners of the Josephine Bourassa allotment.

Very respectfully,

J. L. Suffecool,
Superintendent.

CD:EV.

7587-23

Shawnee Indian Agency,
Shawnee, Oklahoma,
May 16, 1923.

The Commissioner
of Indian Affairs,
Washington, D. C.

Sir:-

Under date of May 7, 1923 instructions were given concerning new deeds to be signed by Andrew Conger and George Oliver Morton in a partition proceeding where it appears that these two heirs signed the wrong deeds in this transaction.

The deeds are therefore herewith inclosed.

Very respectfully,

J. L. Suffecool,
Superintendent.

CD:EV.
encls.

Shawnee Indian Agency,

Shawnee, Oklahoma, May 18, 1923.

Messrs Anglin & Stevens,
   Attorneys at Law,
      Holdenville, Oklahoma.

Gentleman[sic]:

Reference is made to your letter of the 14th instant, relative to Garfield Ellis, deceased, Abs. Shawnee allottee No. 107, who was allotted the NW1/4 of NW1/4 of section 22, township 10 north, range 3 east an containing forty acres.

The record of the correspondence of this Office shows that Garfield Ellis died at Leavenworth, Kansas, November 4, 1901. It appears that he was living with Nancy Marhardy at the time he went to the Pennitentiary[sic] and also, have a son Daniel Ellis or Daniel Chisholm from his former wife Alice Chisholm from who[sic] he was divorced according to Indian Custom.

It appears from Office letter land 20302-1901; 22080-1901, which was addressed to Lee Patrick, United States Indian Agent, Sac & Fox Agency, Oklahoma, under date of April 28, 1901, that the allotment of Garfield Ellis, was conveyed to George M. Morgan for the sum of $725.00, said deed being approved April 23, 1901.

It also appears that Garfield Ellis has some money on deposit at the Fort Leavenworth Pennitentiary at the time of his death, it is presumed it is derived from the sale of his allotment. The Warden R. W. McClaughry, writes to Nancy Wilson, mother of Garfield as follows:

> "You[sic] son left some money on deposit in this office, which can be paid only to the administrator of his estate, when one is appointed. I would suggest that you go before the county clerk and have such administrator appointed, and ask him to communicate with me."

This Office is unable to learn who this money was paid to.

Nancy Wilson died in 1915, mother of Garfield Ellis, leaving an inheirted[sic] estate in the allotments of Jerry Wilson and Laura Wilson, and thru the grandmother Nancy Wilson, Daniel Chisholm or Daniel Ellis heirs in the above estates. The two allotments consist of 120 acres.

Daniel Ellis or Daniel Chisholm died June 30, 1918, leaving a wife May Chisholm and a son named Bennie Chisholm.

This Office can furnish[sic] you a certified copies[sic] of the Approved hearing in the estate of Nancy Wilson, mother of Garfield Ellis, deceased, or other testimony that you may desire in the above estates. There is no approved hearing in the estate of Garfield Ellis.

Very respectfully,

J. L. Suffecool,
Superintendent

TBA

Ed-Ind
36558-23
ESS

Shawnee Indian Agency,
Shawnee, Oklahoma,
May 21, 1923.

The Commissioner
of Indian Affairs,
Washington, D. C.

My dear Mr. Commissioner:-

Receipt is acknowledged of carbon copy of a letter addressed to Mr. Walter Washington, Shawnee, Oklahoma and his letter addressed to you, making inquiry concerning the status of the Lizzie Washington estate; and in reply to the same I have to advise that a hearing wa held in 1914 determining the heirs of this deceased Indian (L-H 91746-12, 10027-13, 31591-13 EGT.)

The Washington children are dis-satisfied with the result and assert that Claude and Charley Tyner should not be determined as heirs to this estate and as a result they have petitioned the Office for a re-hearing. Up to date no action has been taken in the matter towards re-opening this hearing.

Upon the next visit of the Examiner of Inheritance, this matter will be looked into further and if it is thought justifiable, papers will be prepared and forwarded to the Office for its action.

There are funds to the credit of Lizzie Washington's account in this office but under existing authority, I, as disbursing officer, have no authority to disburse same, in-as-much-as the matter is in controversy.

For the information of the Office you are advised that Walter Washington, as well as several of the other apparent heirs, have made frequent inquires as to the disbursements of these funds and they have been informed that same could not be disbursed as long as the matter was in dispute.

At the present time there is to the credit of the estate the amount of $471.87 derived from lease rentals.

Very respectfully,

J. L. Suffecool,
Superintendent.

JLR:EV.
Walter Washington's letter
is returned herewith.

ED-Ind
39195-23
ESS

Shawnee Indian Agency,
Shawnee, Oklahoma,
May 21, 1923.

The Commissioner
of Indian Affairs,
Washington, D. C.

Dear Mr. Commissioner:-

This is to acknowledge receipt of carbon copy of Office letter addressed to Honorable Joe J. Manlove, House of Representatives; also carbon copy of letter written Mr. Manlove from Mr. Charles M. Fear of Joplin, Missouri, making inquiry concerning funds to the credit of his deceased wife, Mrs. Marie A. Fear; and in reply to same I have to advise the Office that no hearing has been held to determine the heirs of Mrs. Fear, therefore, no disbursements of any funds to her credit may be made until the estate is probated.

Mr. Fear has been in correspondence with this office relative to such and I have informed him that until the hearing is held to determine the heirs that I have no authority under the law to make any disbursements.

Mr. Fear has also made inquiry as to whether he and his daughter, Mrs. H. E. Carter, of 838 Putnam Ave., Detroit, Michigan, might prepare affidavits as to their relationship to Mrs. Fear, and forward same here to the Examiner of Inheritance in order that they may not be put to the expense of coming to Shawnee during the hearing. Mr. Fear has been advised that this matter will be left with the Examiner of Inheritance who would advise him whether such steps would be permissible. I understand that Mr. Fear has been in correspondence with the Examiner of Inheritance of this district, Mr. S. Y. Tutwiler, who is at present stationed at Anadarko, Oklahoma--who I presume has advised Mr. Fear in this matter.

At the present time there is a balance of $100 to the credit of Mrs. Fear on the books of this office.

Upon Mr. Tutwiler's arrival he will be requested to set a date to hold a hearing to determine the heirs to this estate.

Very truly yours,

J. L. Suffecool,
Superintendent.

JLR:EV.

Shawnee Indian Agency,
Shawnee, Okla.
May 22, 1923.

The Commissioner of Indian Affairs,
Washington, D. C.
Dear Mr. Commissioner:-

Transmitted herewith is my Heirship Report for the Third Quarter 1912, showing thereon collections made and a list of the estates against which the fees are still outstanding.

Every effort is being made to collect these fees from the delinquent estates or heirs.

Incls.   Very truly yours,

                                         J. L. Suffecool,
                                         Superintendent.

                              Shawnee Indian Agency,
                              Shawnee, Oklahoma,
                              May 24, 1923.

Mrs. Helen Rhodd,
   Marland, Oklahoma.

Dear Madam:-

This will reply to your letter of the 12th inst. regarding your inquiry concerning the allotment of Joseph Louis Acton.

You are informed that owing to a number of heirs the division of this allotment would be impracticable and on account of very low land-sales being made the sale of this allotment also cannot be made in the very near future. However, if arrangements can be made whereby a sale can be accomplished of the allotment a sale will be attempted and notice will be given you further at that time.

                              Very truly yours,

                                         J. L. Suffecool,
                                         Superintendent.
CD:EV.

Shawnee Indian Agency,
Shawnee, Oklahoma,
May 24, 1923.

Mr. Leo Wilmot,
R#3, Mayetta, Kansas.

Dear Mr. Wilmot:-

Further reference is made concerning Frank Wilmot estate of which you inquired on April 13, 1923.

You are kindly informed that the deed which you mentioned was handled by Mr. Snyder and of which I have no knowledge.

Further, I would not be in a position to advise you concerning this deed for the reason that it is a matter that was handled by Mr. Snyder. Mr. Snyder is the proper person to go to for advice concerning the deed.

All information concerning the Frank Wilmot estate, such as rentals, leasing matters, sale and etc, can be given you by this office.

Very truly yours,

J. L. Suffecool,
Superintendent.

CD:EV.

Shawnee Indian Agency,
Shawnee, Oklahoma,
May 8, 1923.

The Commissioner
of Indian Affairs,
Washington, D. C.

Sir:

Transmitted herewith if[sic] application of Alex Enokohn, for his share of Annuity of the estate of Pah nah wah, Probate 60326-17 JGMcG.

I respectfully recommend that this application be approved, and that his share be paid direct.

Very respectfully,

J. L. Suffecool
Superintendent

Probate
V A R

Shawnee Indian Agency,
Shawnee, Okla.
May 29, 1923.

The Commissioner of Indian Affairs,

Washington, D.C.

Dear Mr. Commissioner:-

This is to advise the Office that my report of heirship fees collected and uncollected for the Third Quarter, 1923, was submitted to the Office under date of May 22, 1923.

In the future these reports will be forwarded as soon, after the close of the quarter, as they can be properly prepared.

JLR.   Very respectfully,

J. L. Suffecool,
Superintendent.

Shawnee Indian Agency,
Shawnee, Oklahoma,
May 31, 1923.

Mr. Billy Williams,
R#6, Norman, Oklahoma.

Dear Mr. Williams:-

Sac & Fox – Shawnee Estates
1920-1924 Volume IX

I have your letter complaining of the use of the Inez Mann allotment by Scott Johnson You are kindly informed that these people are using this allotment through an arrangement with this office.

Your wife's share in this allotment amounts to so very little that it is considered un-necessary of further attention.

The timber matter you mention will be taken up with Scott Johnson the first time he comes into this office. Sometime in the near future, if any of the field force from this office happen to be in that vicinity, this matter will be given further attention.

Very truly yours,

J. L. Suffecool,
Superintendent.

CD:EV.

30713-23

Shawnee Indian Agency,
Shawnee, Oklahoma,
May 31, 1923.

The Commissioner
    of Indian Affairs,
        Washington, D. C

SIR:-

Agreeable with Office letter dated May 17th, 1923. bearing above caption concerning the sale of a portion of the allotment of Waw-pah-sose, Kickapoo allottee No. 21; the Office is informed that Pah-e-nah is dead and her heirs are determined under probate 79305-SYT, October 18th, 1921, therefore it is presumed proper for me to sign for the minor heirs of Pah-e-nah.

The Office is further advised that the un-named child of Waw-pah-sose died sometime in the year of 1918 in Mexico. The mother of this child came to Oklahoma in 1919. This statement was made by the mother in this office a few days ago. The heirs of the un-named child and Waw-pah-sose are un-determined and it is presumed proper for me to sign on behalf of the unknown heirs of this un-named child.

Very respectfully,

J. L. Suffecool,
Superintendent.

CD:EV.

Shawnee Indian Agency,

Shawnee, Oklahoma, June 2, 1923.

Mr. Roy D. Taylor, Asst. Cashier,
The Maud State Bank,
Maud, Oklahoma.

Dear Sir:

This will refer to your letter of the 26th ultimo, enclosing a cashier's check No. 19042 for $7.41, dated May 25, 1923, as rents received from cotton of the S. Pratt estate.

Please write on the bottom of the page of this letter and in-form me who paid this amount to the bank, so that this office can receipt to the proper person.

Very respectfully,

J. L. Suffecool,
Superintendent

TBA

Shawnee Indian Agency,
Shawnee, Okla.
June 8, 1923.

Mrs. Minnie Varner,

Cushing, Okla.
Route 4.

Dear Mrs. Varner:-

I have your letter of the 6th and note what you have to say and will try to make the matter clearto[sic] you.

The rental on the estate was paid 1921 year and amounted to $240.00 which was divided among the heirs in their proportionate shares. Robert received $37.33 for his share. He, also at that time had a small balance to his credit of $9.88, this amount plus the rental was made into one check and forwarded to him at Cushing last December 16, but same was returned unclaimed and I have held it waiting for his address. I am enclosing same to you for delivery to to[sic] him.

The rental on the estate was paid againin[sic] Dec. 1922 and amounted to $184.00 and Roberts[sic] share out of this is $30.66, which you have already received.

The $200 Bonus you speak of was paid only the first year of the lease and the other payments are made up of the advance royalty of 15 cents per acre for the second year and $1.00 per acre as rental, making $184.00 and Robert's share was the $30.66 you have received.

The next payment due on this lease will be Dec. 1923 and the amount will be $208.00 and Roberts share is 1/6 of this or $34.66, and will be sent you for delivery or to him as he may desire.

As regards the damages for the pipe line you state was constructed across the estate will take up with Mr. Collins and advise you later.

JLR.   Very truly yours,

                                              J. L. Suffecool,
                                              Superintendent.

Shawnee Indian Agency,
Shawnee, Oklahoma,
June 8, 1923.

Mr. S. Y. Tutwiler,
  Examiner of Inheritance,
    c/o Indian Agency,
      Anadarko, Oklahoma.

Dear Mr. Tutwiler:-

Replying to your letter of the 5th calling for further information in the matter of the heirs to the Phoebe Keokuk allotment, I have to advise that the file number of the finding is "La-H 55152-13, 62288-13 JBk. Mrs. Fear, according to the finding, holds 8/24ths interest in the Phoebe Keokuk estate and this is all of her interest in any estate under this jurisdiction. She has on hand at this time to her credit the amount of $100 derived from lease rentals.

Records show that Phoebe Keokuk died May 18th, 1893. It appears that Mrs. Fear's father was an Ottawa Indian by the name of King, who died previous to the time allotments were made.

Your reference to Mrs. Ruby Carter as being the daughter of Mrs. Fear was noted. I have made an investigation and find that this party is not a daughter but a niece---being a child of Mrs. Fear's sister.

Mrs. Fear, it appears, married several times. First she married a Mr. Shepprd[sic], I believe. The second time to a Mr. Leo Whistler, a Sac & Fox Indian; and the third marriage was with Mr. Fear. There were no children from any of the marriages.

I am inclosing herewith a certificate of appraisement on the allotment of Mrs. Phoebe Keokuk and some other data I have run across which may be of assistance to you.

Very truly yours,

JLR:EV.encls.

J. L. Suffecool,
Superintendent.

Shawnee Indian Agency,
Shawnee, Oklahoma,
June 13, 1923.

Dr. Jacob Breid,
    Supt. Indian School,
        Toledo, Iowa.

Dear Dr. Breid:-

I have your letter of June 8th making inquiry concerning the status of the estate of Emily Johnson, a Sac & Fox allottee of this reservation, and in reply have to state that the heirs were determined March 21, 1922 (Probate 10169-21) and were found to be Frank B. Davis and Harry Davis, Grand-Nephews of the deceased.

It appears that for sometime[sic] some of the Indians living under your jurisdiction who claim to be related to Emily Johnson have from time to time presented petitions in which they claim that they had a right to inherit in this estate, but after looking over the findings in the matter, I am of the opinion that no one who is legally entitled to share in the estate has been excluded. The proceedings were lengthy and thorough, I believe.

Sometime last year, one, Joe Mitchell from your reservation presented to the Office through this Agency a petition requesting that the heirship matter of this estate be re-opened, and I am of the opinion that the Office returned to him said petition and advised him of the findings; and that his claims would not be considered. These papers, I think, were mailed to him through your office.

I would suggest that you inform the Indians who pretned[sic] to be relatives of the deceased Emily Johnson that the matter of determining her heirs has been given very thorough consideration by the Department, and that any further petitions on their part would be useless and a needless expense, as according to the law of descent in Oklahoma, the proper persons were determined as heirs.

Very truly yours,

J. L. Suffecool,
Superintendent.

JLR:EV.

Land-Allot
33858-13
96904-22
H V C

Shawnee Indian Agency,
Shawnee, Oklahoma,
June 28, 1923.

The Commissioner
of Indian Affairs,
Washington, D. C.

Dear Mr. Commissioner:-

Reference is made to cancellation of allotment of Eugenia Tah-ho-ka-le-tha, Absentee Shawnee allottee No. 467.

The Office is advised that there is on file in this office Court Order concerning $400 required to insure payment to James Gibson for his interest in this allotment.

It is further reported that this office has in escrow $400; also Superintendent Victor M. Locke, Muskogee, Oklahoma is holding $400 as evidenced by letter, copy of which is herewithinclosed[sic].

There are inclosed certified copies of Court Order authorizing sale of a portion of the allotment of Wantay Davy, described as S/2 of the NE/4 and the NW/4 of the SE/4 of Section 2, Twp. 14 North, Range 8 East, Creek County, Oklahoma; also order concerning said sale. There is also inclosed certified copy of warranty deed made by Jim Gibson covering the portion of the allotment of Wantay Davy mentioned before. These instruments are submitted for the information of the Office in order that a determination of the heirs of Wantay Davy, Creek allotee[sic], may be made.

It appears that there is no further matter that this office can furnish in the matter of a settlement of this estate. However, the Office is respectfully advised that immediate action will be made in the matter of determination of the heirs of Wantay Davy. Any further reports, papers, or matter pertaining to this estate will be immediately furnished by this office, if requested.

Very truly yours,

CD:EV encls.

J. L. Suffecool,
Superintendent

41086-23

Shawnee Indian Agency,
Shawnee, Oklahoma,
July 6, 1923.

The Commissioner
of Indian Affairs,
Washington, D. C.

Dear Mr. Commissioner:-

Reference is made to Office letter dated June 27, 1923 bearing above reference regarding competency of Eliza Colvin, Nancy Fehlig, and Nellie Wiley.

The Office is advised that these heirs have very little Indian blood; and that Nancy Fehlig lives in Kansas City and her husband who is a white man is a business man of that City; Eliza Colvin lives at Maud, Oklaho ma[sic]; and Nellie Wiley also lives near Maud, Oklahoma. These three heirs are fully competent to transact any business in connection with all of their trust estates.

Very respectfully,

J. L. Suffecool,
Superintendent.

CD:EV.

Shawnee Indian Agency,

Shawnee, Okla.

July 9, 1923.

Mr. S. Y. Tutwiler,

Examiner of Inheritance,
Anadarko, Okla.,

Dear Mr. Tutwiler:-

I have your letter of the 5th making inquiry as to the number cases pending at this agency.

In reply I have to advise that we have thirty eight cases that should be probated at the earliest possible date. Twelve of these are especially urgent- some of these estates have quite a balance to their credit and as some of the heirs are needy,- the hearings should be held at a very early date.

JLR,

Very truly yours,

J. L. Suffecool,
Superintendent.

41687-23

Shawnee Indian Agency,
Shawnee, Oklahoma,
July 12, 1933.

The Commissioner
  of Indian Affairs,
    Washington, D. C.

Dear Mr. Commissioner:-

    Re-submitted herewith are deeds executed by George Oliver Morton and Andrew Conger to each other, and one by George Oliver Morton in favor of his two minor children which were returned to this office for correction and further report.

    The correction as to description in the deed from George Oliver Morton to Andrew Conger covering the Hattie Conger allotment has been inserted.

    Referring to the deed in favor of George Morton's minor children covering the allotment of Jasper Conger, an agreement was reached between George Oliver Morton and me that if patent in fee was issued to him covering the Sarah Bear allotment that he would deed some of his inherited interests to his children.

    The inherited interests of George Oliver Morton are as follows:

Jack Bear	Allot. No.	2
Silas Conger	" "	381
Jasper Conger	" "	383
Wm. Conger	" "	384
Jay Conger	" "	380
Hattie Conger	" "	386
Rachel Davis	" "	348
Clifford Morton	" "	305
Oliver P. Morton	" "	303
Sarah Bear	" "	3

    Some of these have been sold but the greater amount of them are still held in trust so that it appears George Oliver Morton can very well afford to deed the Jasper Conger allotment to his two children.

    I recommend that it be approved.

Very truly yours,

J. L. Suffecool,
Superintendent.

ENCLS.
CD:EV.

102

Shawnee Indian Agency,
Shawnee, Oklahoma,
July 13, 1923.

Supt. George A. Hoyo,
Ponca Indian Agency,
Whiteagle, Oklahoma.

Dear Mr. Hoyo:-

This will acknowledge receipt of carbon copy of your letter to Mr. Arza B. Collins and foot note in which you request that we furnish you with the Indian Office file number of the correspondence which determined the heirs of Maggie M. Burgess and Charles Mohee.

The Indian Office file numbers requested [illegible] as follows: "L-H 6698-15 FWS", in the case of Charley Mohee; and "L-H 117763-13 FE" in the case of Maggie Burgess nee Mohee,

Roy Burgess has a 2/9ths interest in the estate of Maggie Burgess, nee Mohee; and a 1/6th interest in the estate of Charley Mohee.

Very truly yours,

J. L. Suffecool
Superintendent.

EV.

Shawnee Indian Agency,

Shawnee, Okla.

Dr. Jacob Breid, Supt.,

Sac & FOx[sic] Sanatorium,

Dear Dr.:-

I have your letter of the 9th inst., relative to the payment of the lease rental of George Black Cloud.

I concur in your opinion as to the payment of this to George until the other heirs receive their shares. In a separate communication I enclosing checks for the other heirs for credit to their accounts. These were drawn at about the time George's check was but were not mailed until our accounts were completed.

I also acknowledge receipt of your letter advising me of the names of the Indians who live within your jurisdiction and are heirs to estates at this place. In the regular course of business any fund which may be to their credit will be forwarded to you for delivery. We thank you for the list of heirs and the same will be of assistance to use in disposing of funds belonging to them.

JLR.   Very truly yours,

                                                  J. L. Suffecool, Supt.

DEPARTMENT OF THE INTERIOR

UNITED STATES INDIAN FIELD SERVICE

RECEIVED
JUL 20 1923
SHAWNEE INDIAN
AGENCY

Potawatomi Indian Agency,
Mayetta, Kansas,
July 18, 1923.

Mr. J. L. Suffecool, Supt.,
Shawnee Indian Agency,
Shawnee, Okla.

Dear Mr Suffecool:

Inclosed please find form for the signature of the heirs of Ke-wah-ko-uck and Pam-ah-to-quah allotment No. 1 and 2 Kickapoo Reservation Kansas. This land sold for $4400 to Herman Beaman, Whiting, Kansas.

The following is a schedule of bids received:

Herman Beaman,		$4,400.00
Simont[sic] Smith,		4,000.00
W.A. Pendlebury,	3,750.00	
DE. Deutcher,		3,755.00
Thomas Smith,		3,300.00

The land was appraised at $3300 and consists mostly of scrub timer. I believe it to be the best interests of those concerned to sign the acceptance.

Very truly yours,

A. R. Snyder
LLS   Supt. & Spl. Disb. Agent.
Encls.

Shawnee Indian Agency,
Shawnee, Oklahoma,
July 23, 1923.

Mr. Peter McCoonse,
  Algonace[sic], Michigan,
    Box 86.

Dear Sir:-

      I have your letter of the 18th inst., making inquiry about the property of your father-in-law, Joseph M-a-zhm-qua, deceased Pottawatomie allottee No. 55; and in reply I have to advise that he was allotted the NW/4 of Section 36-7-4 E which land was sold August 25, 1905, and at that time passed from under the jurisdiction of this office.

      Peter Soldier was declared the sole heir of Ketumwah, and since Peter is dead, his heirs are his wife and daughter, and funds derived from this estate have been forwarded to them through the Superintendent of the Indian Agency at Mayetta, Kansas.

      In the future all funds derived from this estate will be so handled.

      Mr. Ira C. Deaver's present address is Bristow, Oklahoma.

Very truly yours,

J. L. Suffecool,
Superintendent.

JLR:EV.

Shawnee Indian Agency,
Shawnee, Oklahoma,
July 23, 1923.

Mr. Mitchell We-wa-sah,
Mayetta, Kansas.

Dear Sir:-

Replying to your letter of the 20th inst., in which you
make inquiry about the estate of Peter Shb-znah, a deceased
Pottawatomie allottee; I have to advise that the allotment of the above
was described as follows: NE/4 of NE/4, and Lot 2 of the NE/4--all in
Section 4, Township 5, Range 1 East; and the W/2 of the SE/4 of Section
33-6-1.

The records disclose that a patent in fee was issued for this
land February 24, 1908. Since that time the land passed from under the
jurisdiction of this office, we have nothing more to do with it.

Very truly yours,

J. L. Suffecool,
Superintendent.

JLR:EV.

Shawnee Indian Agency,
Shawnee, Oklahoma,
July 23, 1923.

Mr. John Blackcloud,
Montour, Iowa.

Dear Sir:-

This will acknowledge receipt of your letter under date of July 21, 1923
in which you ask information concerning an inherited interest you have in some land
belonging to your mother.

In reply I have to advise that your interest in this inherited interest of
your mother is 1/27th. The amount of bonus paid is $2,400. Your share of this
amounts to $89.77, which has been sent to Dr. Breid.

Any other information you desire, you may get from Dr. Jacob Breid at Sac & Fox Sanatorium, Toledo, Iowa.

Very truly yours,

J. L. Suffecool,
Superintendent.

ev.

Shawnee Indian Agency,
Shawnee, Oklahoma,
July 24, 1923.

Mr. A. R. Snyder,
  Supt. Potawatomi Ind. Agency,
    Mayetta, Kansas.

Dear Mr. Snyder:-

Mrs. Elmer Walker (Wah tho quah) recently called at this office and made inquiry concerning the heirs of Ke-wah-ko-uk, a Kansas-Kickapoo allottee. She claims that she should inherit in this estate by will as the old man made a will sometime prior to his death naming her as beneficiary.

I know nothing of the merits of the case, and it is requested that you forward to this office a copy of the approved hearing so that we may inform Mrs. Walker as to who were determined the legal heirs. Or, in the event the hearing is too voluminous just furnish this office a statement giving the file number and the names of the heirs, and the circumstances showing why Mrs. Elmer Walker was not determined one of the heirs.

Mrs. Walker states that Mr. Ford A. Harvey, of Omaha, Nebraska was the legal guardian for her, and that he knows the circumstances surrounding this case.

Very truly yours,

J. L. Suffecool,
Superintendent.

JLR:EV.

Shawnee Indian Agency,
Shawnee, Oklahoma,
July 30, 1923.

Mrs. Me She Morgan,
   Montour, Iowa.

Dear Madam:-

I am in receipt of your letter of the 27th inst., referring to George E. Kapayon, an Indian boy adopted by Mrs. Morgan.

From the information given in your letter, I am unable to ascertain who this boy is, and in what allotment you may think he is interested. I would suggest that you refer the matter to Dr. J. Breid, Supt. of the Sac & Fox Sanatorium, Toledo, Iowa, who will be in a position to give you the information desired, and if the boy is entitled to an interest, have Dr. Jacob Breid write this office concerning such.

Very truly yours,

J. L. Riley,
Clerk in Charge.

JLR:EV.

Ed-Ind
57125-23
ESS

Shawnee Indian Agency,
Shawnee, Oklahoma,
July 31, 1923.

The Commissioner
   of Indian Affairs,
      Washington, D. C.

Dear Mr. Commissioner:-

This will acknowledge receipt of Office letter of above reference under date of July 28, 1923; regarding a complaint made by Louis Sullivan; and the original of his letter addressed to the Office.

In reply I have to advise that previous correspondence has been had with the above names Indian concerning this matter and he has been told several times by this office, and also by the Office, reference "Ed-Ind 4102-23 12566-23 ESS" that as yes no hearing has been held to determine the heirs.

Louis Sullivan is lazy and takes no interest whatever in farming. He is not competent to handle his own affairs sufficiently to keep from being swindled by unscrupulous white people.

Louis Sullivan's letter is returned herewith, as requested.

Very truly yours,

J. L. Suffecool,
Superintendent.

EV.
encl. 1.

Shawnee Indian Agency,
Shawnee, Oklahoma,
August 3, 1923.

Mr. A. R. Snyder,
Supt. Potawatomi Indian Agency,
Mayetta, Kansas.

Dear Mr. Snyder:-

A letter was received in this office this morning from Thomas Lightfoot of Rulo, Nebraska requesting that a sale be made of the John Moses allotment which is under the jurisdiction of this office.

In connection with this estate, sometime last summer you were requested to submit petitions for sale covering this same land, and due to the fact that the heirs of Martha Lightfoot were undetermined at that time, it appears that no action was taken. However, notice was given this office by you that immediately upon determination of the heirs of Martha Lightfoot that this office would be notified. There is no record that a declaration of the finding of the Secretary in the matter of the heirship of this estate was ever furnished by you.

If the heirs of Martha Lightfoot, who is one of the heirs of John Moses are determined, please have all of the heirs of John Moses and Martha Lightfoot residing within your jurisdiction execute petitions for sale of this allotment, which is described as the W/2 of the NE/4 of 24-17-2 East, Payne County, Oklahoma.

The heirs of Martha Lightfoot residing within your jurisdiction are:

Daniel Whitecloud
Sarah Whitecloud
Louise Whitecloud

all heirs of John Moses.

Very truly yours,

J. L. Suffecool,
CD:EV.   Superintendent.

Land-Sales
60714-23
JTH

Shawnee Indian Agency,
Shawnee, Oklahoma,
August 8, 1923.

The Commissioner
of Indian Affairs,
Washington, D. C.

Dear Mr. Commissioner:-

Receipt is acknowledged of carbon copy of Office letter of August 2nd, 1923 addressed to Mrs. Angeline Williams, Port Cobb, Oklahoma, and her letter to the Office.

Replying to the same, I have to advise that Mrs. Williams is making inquiry relative to the estate of Wa-tho-pe-wes-ka-ka--deceased Shawnee allottee, whose heirs are Angeline Williams and Polecat, each sharing equally.

Polecat died something like a year ago and up to the present time his heirs are undetermined, and in view of such no action can be taken towards partitioning to Mrs. Williams her share of the land and have the same sold.

At the present time land values in this locality are low. It is not probably that a sale of the original allotment could be effected.

110

After the heirs of Polecat have been determined and Mrs. William[sic] still desires to partition the estate, steps will be taken towards that end.

Very truly yours,

J. L. Riley,
Clerk-in-Charge.

JLR:EV.

Shawnee Indian Agency,
Shawnee, Oklahoma,
August 17,1923.

Mr. C. F. W. Felt,
Chief Engineer System,
Railway Exchange,
80 East Jackson Bld.,
Chicago, Illinois.

Dear Sir:-

This will acknowledge the receipt of your letter under date of July 31st, 1923 in further reference to the settlement of heirs of Cora Smith, nee Bass, for 2.26 acres of right-of-way over the NE/4 of Section 31, Twp. 18, R. 6--the same being the allotment of the said Cora Smith, nee Bass, now deceased.

The contents of your letter have been noted and this office acknowledges the fact that the amount as set forth in your letter has been paid to the heirs of the said Cora Smith, nee Bass, the same being the assessment of a damage. This damage was assessed against the Cushing Traction Company on account of securing right-of-way across this allotment upon representation that the line would be an interurban electric road. Whereas, when completed it was a standard gauge steam railway.

It is a fact established by court records that suit was brought against the A. T. & S. F. Ry. Company by the white property land owners adjacent to the land owned by the Indians, and that additional damages were secured for the reason that this line was changed, as noted above, from an interurban to a standard gauge steam railway.

It is noted in reading the brief that was prepared by the Attorney who represented the white people that more that 60% additional damage was secured through the court--in many cases this was more than 60%.

There is due the heirs of Cora Smith, nee Bass, if a settlement is effected on a 60% basis of the original assessment, the sum of $76.80, and if this additional amount is tendered in settlement it is believed that this office can secure the necessary deed to the two and twenty-six hundredths acres; and if your Company sees fit to settle on this basis an effort will be made by the representative of this office to close the matter.

I am in receipt of a letter from the Commissioner of Indian Affairs, under whose jurisdiction this land is held, to the effect that if this office is unable to receive from your Company a settlement that would appear to be fair to the parties concerned, that I furnish the Office with certain data in order that same may be presented to the Department of Justice. It is hoped that a settlement may be made at an early date and my representative, or myself in person will meet with a representative of the Company at any date and place designated. However, if the place of settlement is designated at some other point than this office it will be necessary that the expenses incident to the trip be borne by your Company.

Very truly yours,

J. L. Suffecool,
Superintendent.

JLS:EV.

Shawnee Indian Agency,

Shawnee, Okla.

Aug. 20, 1923.

Mr. George A. Hoyo, Supt.,

Whiteagle, Okla.

My dear Mr. Hoyo:-

Replying to your letter of the 18th. concerning the estate of Nannie Hollowell, I am enclosing herewith a certificate of appraisement of the eighty acres and a card showing the heirs, file number etc.

Incls.   Very truly yours,
JLR.

J. L. Suffecool,
Superintendent.

Shawnee Indian Agency,
Shawnee, Oklahoma,
August 24, 1923.

Mrs. Zella Marie Graham,
Emmett, Kansas.

Dear Madam:-

This is in reply to your letter of the 13th inst. and another letter of earlier date with reference to the estate of your grandfather, Joseph Welch.

You are informed that this matter has been taken up with Mr. Wm. Moutaw and that he has been requested to submit all claims he has against the estate of said Joseph Welch.

Mr. Dushane of this office called upon Mr. Moutaw and discovered that Mrs. Carrie Moutaw had just recently died. This may in part explain the reasons for Mr. Moutaws[sic] not taking any earlier action, however, he assured Mr. Dushane that he would immediately take action towards completing this matter and submit his claims to the estate so that they may receive proper consideration; and that until they[sic] it will be impossible to make any settlements with the other heirs.

You will re-call your mother deeded to you her one-fifth interest in the allotment of said Joseph Welch, and that from the date of this deed forward, you will be entitled to the revenue from the allotment covered by your deed. Previous to the date of the approval of this deed any revenue that has accrued will be made to the credit of your mother for her one-fifth interest.

On July 30th a letter was mailed to Mr. Frank Welch, Bellvue[sic], Kansas, who was requested to have such heirs of Lucius A. Darling living in that vicinity to sign sale papers for the allotment of Lucius A. Darling. It was noticed that you signed these sale papers when instead your mother should have signed for the reason that she is the heir and not yourself of Lucius A. Darling.

Please have your mother sign the Lucius A. Darling papers inclosed herewith.

Very truly yours,

J. L. Suffecool,
Superintendent.

CD:EV.
encls.

Shawnee Indian Agency,
Shawnee, Oklahoma,
Sept. 8, 1923.

Mr. Ed. Brown,
Montour, Iowa.

Dear Sir:-

Replying to your letter of the 1st inst. regarding money due you from the estate of Cora Shaquequot; I have to advise that all money belonging to the Indian heirs living in Iowa has been transferred to Dr. Breid at Toledo, and you may call there and receive your share. I am unable to advise you what your share amounts to as the decedent through which you heir was under the jurisdiction of the Toledo office, and the records are there.

Very truly yours,

J. L. Suffecool,
Superintendent.

JLR:EV.

Shawnee Indian Agency,
Shawnee, Oklahoma,
Sept. 8, 1923.

Dr. Jacob Breid,
Sac & Sanatorium[sic],
Toledo, Iowa.

Dear Doctor Breid:-

In replying to your letter making inquiry concerning funds due George E. Kapaiou, and Indian boy living with Mrs. Mameche Morgan; I have to advise that I am inclosing herewith my official check No. 16825 on the

Shawnee National Bank, payable to your order for $51.95, drawn against the account of Ke-wa-sa-no-qua, which represents all funds now to the credit of this estate. The division of the funds will be made by you and distributed among the proper heirs.

I am also inclosing herewith my official checks made payable to your order, as follows:

Ck. No.	Amt.	Acct. of
16828	$96.00	Pa phia na
16829	32.00	Pone wya tah
16830	5. 14[sic]	Phia pau maha

which please place to the credit of the proper Indians.

These mounts represent lease rentals due from estates under this jurisdiction in which Indians living near Toledo are interested.

Very truly yours,

J. L. Suffecool,
Superintendent.

JLR:EV.
encls. 4.

Shawnee Indian Agency,
Shawnee, Oklahoma,
Sept. 10, 1923.

Messrs. Frank & Harry Davis,
Cushing, Oklahoma.

Dear Friends:-

I am in receipt of your letter of the 5th inst., making inquiry concerning the estate of your deceased mother, Flora McClellan; and in reply you are advised that the records of this office disclose that this allotment was sold back in 1905 to Mr. Lee Patrick, and the proceeds were properly disposed of.

As regards your grandmother's estate which was in Kansas, you say, I can give you no information as the same was under the jurisdiction of Mayetta, Kansas office.

Very truly yours,

J. L. Suffecool,
Superintendent.

JLR:EV.

Shawnee Indian Agency,
Shawnee, Oklahoma,
Sept. 10, 1923.

Mr. J. L. Suffecool,
  Supt. Shawnee Indian Agency,
  Shawnee, Oklahoma.

Dear Mr. Suffecool:-

I have the honor to report concerning claims made by one, John Pettit, to the estate of Charley Mohee on account of said Charley Mohee living with and being cared for by John Pettit for 16 years from 1893 to 1909.

I have examined thoroughly the office files concerning Charley Mohee and find that the attention of the claim of John Pettit has been thoroughly presented to and considered by the Indian Office, and it appears to have been satisfactorily settled. It appears that John Petit has been paid at various times from funds belonging to Charley Mohee for such care and maintenance during the period mentioned before. There is also on file carbon copy of an affidavit submitted by Osmond Franklin according to Office request forwarded by former Supt. Horace J. Johnson with a request that if the Office required any further information to so advise Mr. Johnson, and that the information called for would be furnished. It appears that the Indian Office at Washington was satisfied that John Pettit has received sufficient pay for his claims against the estate of Charley Mohee.

I recommend that no further action be taken in this matter unless directed by the Commissioner in accordance with the status of the claim at the time correspondence ceased between the Office and former Supt. Horace J. Johnson.

Very respectfully,

Charles Dushane
Charles Dushane.

CD:EV.
cc to Indian Office
  & John Pettit

Shawnee Indian Agency,
Shawnee, Oklahoma,
Sept. 20, 1923.

Standard[sic] & Ennis,
Attorneys & Counselors,
Shawnee, Oklahoma.

Gentlemen:

Enclosed herewith official check payable to the order of Mrs Emma Griffinstine for $344.03, from the account of Catherine Griffinstine.

This check represents a part payment on a claim that Mrs. Emma Griffinstine has against the estate of Catherine Griffinstine, and is all the funds to the credit of the estate at the present time.

Very truly yours,

J. L. Suffecool
Superintendent

MPG-encls.

****

Shawnee Indian Agency,
Shawnee, Oklahoma,
Sept 20, 1923.

Mrs Emma Griffinstine,
206 Lawrence Ave.,
Wichita, Kansas.

Dear Madam:

Enclosed herewith official check No 16942, payable to your order for $344.03, from the account of Catherine Griffinstine.

This check represents part payment on a claim you have against the estate of Catherine Griffinstine, and is all these is[sic] deposit at the present time.

Very truly yours,

J. L. Suffecool
Superintendent

MPG-encl.

Shawnee Indian Agency,
Shawnee, Oklahoma,
Sept 26, 1923.

Miss Bessie Wilson,
R#2, Box 70,
Shawnee, Oklahoma.

Dear Madam:-

This has reference to the carbon copy of Office letter addressed to you under date of August 6, 1923 which had reference to your letter to the Office under date of April 19th.

You will note in the Office letter that they say that it will be necessary to get a statement from you relative to the matter and that you should call on me at Shawnee for that purpose.

I will be pleased to see you at any time it may be convenient for you to come and will be glad to take the matter in hand and do what I can for you.

Your friend,

J. L. Suffecool,
Superintendent.

JLS:EV.
cc to
Indian Office
(Land-Probate-F. C. T.
33028-23
60804-23
O'N)
CC TO
Mr. R. B. Drake
Supervising Probate Attorney,
            Muskogee, Oklahoma.

Shawnee Indian Agency,

Shawnee, Oklahoma, Sept. 30, 1923.

Messrs. Bell & Fellows,
        Attorneys & Councilors,
            Tulsa, Oklahoma.

Gentleman:

Reference is made to your letter of the 14th ultimo, enclosing an assignment covering the allotment from the heirs of Pea skah wa se, deceased, the S/2 of the NW1/4 of section 26, township 11 north, range 4 east.

This is to advise you that the filing fee in each assignment is $11.00. This Office have[sic] your check for $6.00. Please remit me a cashier's check for $5.00 to cover the balance of the filing fee.

Very respectfully,

J. L. Suffecool,
Superintendent

TBΛ

Shawnee Indian Agency,
Shawnee, Oklahoma,
Oct. 2, 1923.

Mr. P. W. Cress,
Attorney at Law,
Perry, Oklahoma.

Dear Mr. Cress:-

Reference is made to your letter of the 28th of September regarding the claim of Mr. John Pettit against the estate of Charley Mohee.

In accordance with your request the records in this office upon which was based our conclusion with reference to the attitude of the Indian Office have been referred to and copies of certain correspondence regarding this matter are inclosed herewith for your information.

Very truly yours,

J. L. Suffecool,
Superintendent.

CD:EV.
encls.

Shawnee Indian Agency,
Shawnee, Oklahoma,
Oct. 2, 1923.

Mr. John A. Bourbonnais,
R#1, Box 69, Pryor, Okla.

Dear Mr. Bourbonnais:-

I have your letter of recent date making inquiry as to when the Examiner of Inheritance will be here to hold hearing to determine the heirs of your deceased mother's estate.

In reply you are advised that we have received no definite information as to when Mr. Tutwiler will arrive but he is expected sometime this fall. When he arrives and sets a date to hold the hearing you will be sent a notice.

Very truly yours,

J. L. Suffecool,
Superintendent.

JLR:EV.

Shawnee Indian Agency,

Shawnee, Okla.

Oct. 4, 1923.

The Commissioner of Indian Affairs,

Washington, D.C.

Dear Mr. Commissioner:-

I am enclosing herewith report of heirship fees collected by me during the First Quarter 1924.

Attached hereto is a list showing the estates on which the fees remain uncollected. Efforts are being made to collect these fees and when funds become available the collection is made.

Incl.   Very truly yours,
JLR.

J. L. Suffecool,
Superintendent.

Shawnee, Oklahoma,
October 5, 1923.

Mr. John A. Buntin, Supt.,
   Kiowa Indian Agency,
      Anadarko, Oklahoma.

Dear Mr. Buntin:

    Little Fish, a deceased Shawnee allotee[sic] of this jurisdiction, has several heirs living near Anadarko and, has from time to time they have small lease rentals derived from this estate, I am requesting that you advise me of the status of each.

    The heirs as determined are as follows:

```
George Ki-o-nut K-26----------------------------Share------66/1440
Jack Ki-o-nut  K-27------------------------------Share-----114/1440
(Dec'd)Thomas Worcester  W-26-----------------------Share---  80/1440
Michael Martin M-27------------------------------Share---  160/1440
Nancy Longhat L-17------------------------------Share---  180/1440
Ne-ko-ty (Grover Inkimah)  I-1-----------------Share---   90/1440
Cinda Inkinish I-2-------------------------------Share---   30/1440
Samuel Inkinish I-3------------------------------Share---   30/1440
Ruth Inkinish  I-4-------------------------------Share---   30/1440
Charles E. Adams A-25----------------------------Share---  120/1440
Robert Adams  A-26------------------------------Share---  120/1440
Joseph Edmonds  E-4-----------------------------Share---   60/1440
Scipio Edmonds  E-5-----------------------------Share---   40/1440
Houston Edmonds E-6-----------------------------Share---   40/1440
Taylor Edmonds  E-7-----------------------------Share---   40/1440
Charles Williams  W-27--------------------------Share---  120/1440
Lydia (Lida) Penn  P-34-------------------------Share---  120/1440
Mary Deer Worcester, wife-----------------------Share---    1/3
Thomas Keys, son-------------------------------Share---    2/9
Michael Martin, son----------------------------Share---    2/9
Ira Deer Worcester, son-------------------------Share---    2/9
```

    This information is desired so that proper disposition of lease rentals may be made.

                        Yours truly,

JLR/FB   [No Signature]

Shawnee Indian Agency,
Shawnee, Oklahoma,
Oct. 6, 1923.

Mr. Wm. Moutaw,
  Lexington, Oklahoma.

Dear Mr. Moutaw:-

  We have received repeated requests from the heirs in Kansas with reference to the settlement of the estate of Joseph Welch. You will remember from two or three months ago representatives of this office called upon you for the purpose of making arrangements with you with reference to the settlement and submittal of claims on your part against the estate of said Joseph Welch.

  It was understood at that time that you would submit your claims in writing sometime soon thereafter. In as much as this settlement has now been so long delayed that it appears necessary that you be given a definite stated time to make this settlement or reduce your claims in writing. For that reason you will be given until October 16th which falls on Tuesday, one week from next Tuesday to make your settlement. After that day, I will make my final report and recommendation to the Indian Office and request for instructions appropriate in this case. I sincerely hope that you will come up to this requirement and submit your claims as requested.

       Very truly yours,

       J. L. Suffecool,
       Superintendent.

CD:EV.

Shawnee Indian Agency,
Shawnee, Oklahoma,
Oct. 10, 1923.

The Commissioner
  of Indian Affairs,
    Washington, D. C.

Dear Mr. Commissioner:-

  Inclosed herewith are papers and correspondence relative to the claim of one, John Pettit against the estate of Charley Mohee, deceased Iowa allottee.

In response to a letter from the attorney representing John Pettit, this office submitted certain correspondence and an affidavit signed by Osmond Franklin on which we based our reasons for concluding that the Office considered this claim of no merit. The attorney was cited to Office letter dated June 6, 1918 bearing reference "Probate 6698-15, 19929-18 TDM" wherein Superintendent H. J. Johnson made a complete report to the Office and copy of this letter was mailed to the Attorney. Also, copy of the affidavit was mailed him--closing with a letter to the Office by Horace J. Johnson requesting that if further evidence was required that he be notified immediately. No response being made to Supt. Johnson, it was concluded by this office as mentioned before.

Very truly yours,

J. L. Suffecool,
Superintendent.

CD:EV
encls.

Shawnee Indian Agency,
Shawnee, Oklahoma,
Oct. 17, 1923.

Mr. Jacob Dole,
    Perkins, Oklahoma.

Dear Mr. Dole:-

This is in reply to your letter of the 9th inst. regarding heirship matter in connection with the estate of Lee Patrick Tohee. It appears that wen the hearing was held in this matter your wife was unable to be present on account of sickness, and for that reason you would like to have the heirship hearing re-opened.

It is the opinion of this office that any evidence you might be able to submit would not materially change the findings of heirship by the Department; however, it is probably that your wife has a right to request for a re-opening of this hearing and it will be required of you that you submit proper affidavits and submit your request for a re-opening of a hearing to determine the heirs of Lee Patrick Tohee.

Very truly yours,

J. L. Suffecool,
Superintendent.

CD:EV.

****

Shawnee Indian Agency,
Shawnee, Oklahoma,
Oct. 17, 1923.

Mr. David Tohee,
Perkins, Oklahoma.

Dear Mr. Tohee:-

With reference to your request for information regarding the estate of Edward Tohee, you are requested to give further information as to just what you want. From the letter you wrote, the information given is not sufficient to establish whether the estate you have reference to has been probated by the Department, or whether it is an estate yet to be probated.

However, write us again more fully so that we may be enabled to give you the information desired.

Very truly yours,

J. L. Suffecool,
Superintendent.

CD:EV.

Shawnee Indian Agency,
Shawnee, Oklahoma,
Oct. 19th, 1923.

Mr. Edward Rice,
Cushing, Oklahoma.

Dear Friend:-

You will remember that at the last time I was in Cushing that you asked me to write to the Superintendent of the Quapaw Indian Agency, Miami, Oklahoma with reference to some of your inherited interests there.

I have to advise that I have a letter from Mr. Chandler, the Superintendent, with reference to the matter, and it is inclosed herewith for your information.

If there is anything further that can be done in this matter, I will be glad to communicate with you upon your request.

Very truly yours,

J. L. Suffecool,
Superintendent.

JLS:EV.
encl. 1 let.

30116-23

Shawnee Indian Agency,
Shawnee, Oklahoma,
Oct. 20, 1923.

The Commissioner
of Indian Affairs,
Washington, D. C.

Dear Mr. Commissioner:-

Reference is made to Office letter dated May 3, 1923, captioned as above, regarding disposition of the allotment of Priscilla Bayliss and land inherited by her from her mother, Elmira Bayliss, for the purpose of making payments for her care at a Sanatorium in Kansas.

If the Office will permit the sale of this 240 acres of land included in the allotment of Priscilla Bayliss, and the share partitioned to her of her mother's allotment, for the sum of about $3,000 or $3,500, with a provision that payment of the assessment be deferred which is against this land on account of the Little River Drainage Ditch being constructed across these two tracts of land, a sale may be concluded. If consent is given for a deferred payment of the assessment mentioned before, instructions should be given as to the manner to be pursued in the sale. Owing to the demoralized condition of farming interests at the present time, it appears necessary that action of some nature be pursued as to relieving the purchaser of the necessity of making a payment of the sum of money required to purchase the land.

Any suggestions which the Office may make in connection with the disposition of these lands will be very greatly appreciated.

Very truly yours,

J. L. Suffecool,
CD:EV   Superintendent.

60751-23

Shawnee Indian Agency,
Shawnee, Oklahoma,
Oct. 20, 1923.

The Commissioner
of Indian Affairs,
Washington, D. C.

Dear Mr. Commissioner:-

Reference is made to Office letter dated Sept. 19th, captioned as above regarding Absentee Shawnee land-sales to E. T. Carson and Hal Johnson.

Due to the fact that Departmental findings of heirships do not correspond with the shares disposed of according to Federal court Decree, I would respectfully request that I be given specific instructions as to whether I should make divisions of rentals from the Shawnee lands involved according to Departmental findings of heirships, or according to Federal Court Decree.

Very truly yours,

J. L. Suffecool,
Superintendent.

CD:EV.

Land-Sale
75351-12
99530-22
JTH

Shawnee Indian Agency,
Shawnee, Oklahoma,
Oct. 27, 1923.

Sac & Fox – Shawnee Estates
1920-1924 Volume IX

The Commissioner
  of Indian Affairs,
    Washington, D. C.

Dear Mr. Commissioner:-

This will comply with Office letter captioned as above regarding final papers in the sale of the Samuel Cummings allotment to one J. R. Thorn, dated January 19, 1923.

In connection with this sale there are transmitted herewith the following papers:

General Inventory and Appraisement of the Samuel Cummings land.

The final decree.

Annual report of the Guardianship of Helen Cummings, incompetent, by Guardian, A. J. Cummings of Pottawatomie County.

Final Account of Guardian in the matter of the guardianship of the persons and estates of Clarence, Florence and Biroha Shives, minors of Modoc County, California.

Decree approving final account of guardian in the matter of the guardianship of the persons and estates of Clarence, Florence and Biroha Shives, minors of Modoc County, California.

The final report and petition for discharge of the guardian in the matter of the guardianship of Christina O'Bright, Edith and Andy O'Bright, by Harry Johnson, Guardian.

It appears that this about complies with the foregoing mentioned Office letter which tends to show the disposition of the entire proceeds of the land-sale of the Samuel Cummings, allotment.

Very truly yours,

J. L. Suffecool,
Superintendent.

CD:EV.
encls.

Shawnee Indian Agency.

Shawnee, Oklahoma.

October 30, 1923.

Commissioner of Indian Affairs,
Washington, D. C.

Dear Mr. Commissioner:-

Reference is made of the Office Letter dated September 12, 1912, to the Honorable Secretary of the Interior, bearing reference as above 62903-23, J. T. H., regarding the sale of 1/24 interest in the allotment of Martha Mullen, deceased allottee number 803, by Rena Smith Richardson, in favor of Frank Smith.

According the same Office Letter, the respective interests of Eliza Colvin, Zoa Denton, Nancy Fehlig, a 2/24 each; Rena Richardson and Birdie Smith, a 1/24 each; and Frank Smith, 16/24. After the approval of Rena Richardson's deed to Frank Smith, it was stated, Frank Smith then owned 17/24. This is not true for the reason that Frank Smith purchased a 2/24 interest of Eliza Colvin's by deed, approved December 15, 1922. Records in the book of inherited Indian lands, volume 44, Page 116. Therefore Frank Smith's interest of the Martha Mullen allotment amounts to 19/24.

Very respectfully,

J. L. Suffecool,
Sup't.

CD:VB

Shawnee Indian Agency.

Shawnee, Oklahoma.

October 30, 1923.

Commissioner of Indian Affairs,
Washington, D. C.

Dear Mr. Commissioner:-

There are submitted herewith, papers in the sale of the undivided 1/6 interest of the land belonging to Frank Poncho, of the allotment of Paw-kaw-kah, Kickapoo allottee number 205, sold to Pah-pah-thah-peah, for the sum of $800. There are also submitted; two deeds signed by the heirs of Paw-kaw-kah, for the purpose of completing this sale and the partition of the allotment and of the heirs.

Papers in this sale appear to be regular and I recommend there[sic] approval.

Very respectfully,

J. L. Suffecool.
Superintendent.

CD:VB

79854-23

Shawnee Indian Agency.

Shawnee, Oklahoma,
November 2, 1923.

The Honorable,
The Commissioner of Indian Affairs.

My Dear Mr. Commissioner:

This will acknowledge receipt of office letter of above reference under date of October 20th concerning the allotment of Fredrick Chouteau, deceased Shawnee Allottee No. 87. In accordance with your instructions the entire file has been forwarded to Superintendent Snyder of Mayetta, Kansas.

Very Respectfully,

J. L. Suffecool,
Superintendent.

JLS:SMS

****

[The letter above given again.]

****

October 30, 1923.

79854-23

The Honorable Commissioner of Indian Affairs,

Dear Mr. Commissioner:

This will acknowledge receipt of office letter of the above reference, under date of October 20, with reference to the allotment of Fredrick Chouteau, deceased Shawnee #87. In accordance with office instructions, the trial file has this day been forwarded to Superintendent A. R. Snyder, of Mayetta, Kansas.

Very Respectfully,

J. L. Suffecool,
Sup't.

JLS:B

****

[The letter above given again.]

J. A. BUNTIN
SUPERINTENDENT

MAKE ALL CHECKS PAYABLE TO
A. G. WILSON, SPEC. DISB. AGENT

DEPARTMENT OF THE INTERIOR

UNITED STATES INDIAN SERVICE
KIOWA INDIAN AGENCY
ANADARKO, OKLAHOMA

RECEIVED
NOV 5 1923
SHAWNEE INDIAN
AGENCY

November 2, 1923.

Mr. J. L. Suffecool, Supt.,
Shawnee Indian Agency,
Shawnee, Oklahoma.

Dear Sir:

In compliance with your request of October 5, I am furnishing you the following information on the heirs of Little Fish, who reside on this reservation. The following heirs as listed in your letter are deceased. Their heirs, together with their interests are given below:

W26 -   Thomas Worcester, deceased. Heirs--

Mary Deer Worcester   1/3
Thomas Keys   2/9
Michael Martin   2/9
Ira Deer Worcester   2/9

Mrs. F See if any of these dead or alive, have friends Place address on accounts

Nancy Longhat, deceased. Heirs---

	Little Kahnoosty	1/4
	Simon Black Star	1/4
	Nellie Black Star	1/4
L 51	Rachel Long Hat	1/4

a 26   Robert Adams, deceased. Heirs---

a 25   Charles E. Adams   all

I 1   Nah co ta ty (Grover Inkanish) deceased. Heirs---

	Hyacinth Inkanish	1/3
	Samuel Chisholm	1/3
I 4	Ruth Nah co ta ay	1/3

All of the heirs as listed in your letter, together with the heirs of the deceased heirs live on this reservation and are of age. Checks in payment of their share of the estate could be drawn direct to them and sent to this office for delivery.

Very respectfully,
JA Buntin
Superintendent.

102

82[??]0-23

Office of Indian Affairs,

Washington.

Nov. 3, 1923.

Mr. J. L. Suffecool,
Sup't, Shawnee Indian Agency,

My dear Mr. Suffecool:

Your letter of October 20, 1923, relative to the estate of Joseph Welch has been received and considered,

As to the alleged claim which Mrs. Amelia Moutaw, now deceased, had against the estate but which she never filed with you or[sic] attempted to substantiate, and which her husband failed to file after being requested by you, this is a matter which it is believed should now be considered closed.

The record shows that Mrs. Moutaw and her husband collected the entire rental from the allotment from the year 1910 to 1921, although Mrs. Moutaw was entitled to only one-fifth of such rental as an heir. It is shown that William Boler, lessee, paid Mr. Moutaw, during the period from 1910 to 1921, the total sum of $3,958.00 as rental for the allotment. The exclusive use of this rental, it is believed, would more than justly compensate them for the funeral expenses and care of the allottee during his last illness, which you report was the nature of the claim of Mrs. Moutaw. If the other heirs of Joseph Welch desire to put in a claim against the estate of Mrs. Moutaw, now deceased, on account of the rentals wrongfully received by her from the lease of the allotment of Joseph Welch, they are at liberty to do so.

Hereafter, so long as the allotment is restricted, the rentals should be collected through your office and divided among the heirs according to their inherited interests in the allotment.

Very truly yours,

E. B. Meritt,
Assistant Commissioner.

****

Shawnee Indian Agency,

Shawnee, Oklahoma,
November 7, 1923.

Mr. William Moutaw,
Lexington, Oklahoma.

Dear Mr. Moutaw:

Further reference is made to the settlement of the Joseph Welch estate concerning which you wrote under date of October 16th last. The letter was not received in this office until the 24th of October. On the 20th of October report was made to Indian Office as to the progress made in this settlement. In reply to the report the Indian Office at Washington gives its instructions by letter, copy of which is here enclosed.

Very Truly Yours,

_____

J. L. Suffecool,
Superintendent.

CD:AMS

****

Shawnee Indian Agency,

Shawnee, Oklahoma,
November 7, 1923.

Mrs. Gelah[sic] Marie Graham,
Emmett, Oklahoma.

Dear Madam:

Further reference is made with reference to the settlement of the estate of Joseph Welch wherein instructions were given under date of Nov. 3, 1923 directing that the rentals from the allotments of Joseph Welch as fast as they are collected be divided among the heirs according to their inherited interest in the allotment.

Due to the fact that Mrs. Carrie Moutaw, one of the heirs of Joseph Welch recently died and on account of the fact that Mrs. Moutaw's husband collected rentals from the Joseph Welch estate amounting to the sum of $3958.00 that it will be necessary for all of the heirs interested to make claims against the estate of Mrs. Moutaw. For the further information rentals amounting to something like eight or nine hundred dollars since this office began to make collection of rentals following Mr. Moutaw's administration of the allotment. The funds now held will be apportioned to each heir and placed to such heirs credit and checks will be made accordingly and forwarded to the heirs within the next few days. You of course understand Carrie Moutaw's interest will be held on special deposit until such time as her heirs are determined and the claims of the other heirs against Mrs. Moutaw's share have all been duly approved, when settlement will be finally made in accordance with the determination of heirship and approved of claims. Please notify your mother Mrs. Deleye of such action.

Very Truly Yours,

_____

J. L. Suffecool,
Superintendent.

CD:AMS

133

Sac & Fox – Shawnee Estates
1920-1924 Volume IX

****

Shawnee Indian Agency,

Shawnee, Oklahoma,
November 7, 1923.

Mr. John L. Welch,
Belvue, Kansas.

Dear Sir:

Further reference is made with reference to the settlement of the estate of Joseph Welch wherein instructions were given under date of Nov. 3, 1923 directing that the rentals from the allotments of Joseph Welch as fast as they are collected be divided among the heirs according to their inherited interest in the allotment.

Due to the fact that Mrs. Carrie Moutaw, one of the heirs of Joseph Welch recently died and on account of the fact that Mrs. Moutaw's husband collected rentals from the Joseph Welch estate amounting to the sum of $3958.00 that it will be necessary for all of the heirs interested to make claims against the estate of Mrs. Moutaw. For the further information rentals amounting to something like eight or nine hundred dollars since this office began to make collection of rentals following Mr. Moutaw's administration of the allotment. The funds now held will be apportioned to each heir and placed to such heirs credit and checks will be made accordingly and forwarded to the heirs within the next few days. You of course understand Carrie Moutaw's interest will be held on special deposit until such time as her heirs are determined and the claims of the other heirs against Mrs. Moutaw's share have all been duly approved, when settlement will be finally made in accordance with the determination of heirship and approved of claims. Please notify your mother Mrs. Deleye of such action.

Very Truly Yours,

_____

J. L. Suffecool,
Superintendent.

CD:AMS

****

Shawnee Indian Agency,

Shawnee, Oklahoma,
November 7, 1923.

Mr. Frank M. Welch,
Belvue, Kansas.

Dear Sir:

Further reference is made with reference to the settlement of the estate of Joseph Welch wherein instructions were given under date of Nov. 3, 1923 directing that the rentals from the allotments of Joseph Welch as fast as they are collected be divided among the heirs according to their inherited interest in the allotment.

Due to the fact that Mrs. Carrie Moutaw, one of the heirs of Joseph Welch recently died and on account of the fact that Mrs. Moutaw's husband collected rentals from the Joseph Welch estate amounting to the sum of $3958.00 that it will be necessary for all of the heirs interested to make claims against the estate of Mrs. Moutaw. For the further information rentals amounting to something like eight or nine hundred dollars since this office began to make collection of rentals following Mr. Moutaw's administration of the allotment. The funds now held will be apportioned to each heir and placed to such heirs credit and checks will be made accordingly and forwarded to the heirs within the next few days. You of course understand Carrie Moutaw's interest will be held on special deposit until such time as her heirs are determined and the claims of the other heirs against Mrs. Moutaw's share have all been duly approved, when settlement will be finally made in accordance with the determination of heirship and approved of claims. Please notify your mother Mrs. Deleye of such action.

Very Truly Yours,

_____

J. L. Suffecool,
Superintendent.

CD:AMS

Shawnee Indian Agency,

Shawnee, Oklahoma,
November 8, 1923.

Mrs. Irene Cadue,
Powhattan, Kansas.

Dear Madam:

I have your letter of the 5th inst. making inquiry concerning lease money derived from the estate of which your deceased husband Peter Soldier was an heir. At the present time there is no money here derived from that estate. Any money belonging to you and your child has been transferred to the Pottawatomie Agency at Mayetta, Kansas the first part of the past July. If you have not received the same call on Mr. Snyder at that place who can give you information concerning such.

Very Truly Yours,

J. L. Suffecool,
Superintendent.

JLR:AMS

Shawnee Indian Agency,

Shawnee, Oklahoma,
November 27, 1923.

Mrs. Millie Dole,
R. F. D.,
Perkins, Oklahoma.

My Dear Friend:

This will acknowledge the receipt of your letter of November 23, 123[sic] in which you write me about the estate of Lee Patrick Tohee and that you still think that you are one of the heirs. The law providesthat[sic] in reopening an heirship case that those who desire to have it reopened must furnish the Superintendent affidavits setting forth their reasons in detail as to why the case should be reopened. I do not feel that it would be proper for me to take the initiative in this matter. That is I do not believe it would be proper for me to start this action. If I did, the other Indians who were declared the heirs would be likely to accuse me of being partial and not looking after their interest.   If you will furnish me with the necessary affidavits I will forward the same to the Indian Office with such recommendations as the case may warrant.

It is noted in your letter that if I would do this for you that you will give me $50.00. Now Mrs. Dole, that is a proposition that I will have absolutely nothing to do with. I am paid a salary by the Department for looking after the interest of the Indians and can not and will not consider a proposition of this kind. In the future please do not mention a thing of this kind in your letters. It is not right and honest.

There will be an examiner of inheritance at this agency about March 1st., 1924, and I would advise you to bring this matter up to his attention at that time. If there is anything further I can do to help you, please let me know.

Very Truly Yours,

J. L. Suffecool,
Superintendent.

JLR:AMS

Shawnee Indian Agency,

Shawnee, Oklahoma,
November 30, 1923.

Mr. Anthony Bourbonnais,
607 W. Reno Ave.,
Oklahoma City, Oklahoma.

My Dear Friend:

This will acknowledge the receipt of your letter of November 27. I note what you say. Yes Jingo is in rather bad circumstances. Yet I can see no one to blame but himself for this condition. However, we all make mistakes in life and I will be glad to help him in any way I can. With reference to the determining the heirs of your deceased mother, I have to advise that I am in receipt of a letter from the examiner of inheritance in which he states that he will be at this agency some time in the near future at which time he will take up the matter of probating your mother's estate. The local force here at the agency have been so busy that it has been impossible to reach this matter.

Very Respectfully,

_____

J. L. Suffecool,
Superintendent.

JLS:AMS

Shawnee Indian Agency,

Shawnee, Oklahoma,
December 1, 1923.

Mrs. Julia A. Reed,
In Real 2211 Brown St,
Milwaukee, Wisconsin.

Dear Madam:

Enclosed herewith is my official check No. 17682 for $3.00 payable to your order. This represents all you share of the money derived from the Joseph Louis Acton estate.

Yours Very Truly,

_____

J. L. Suffecool,
Superintendent.

AMS

Shawnee Indian Agency,

Shawnee, Oklahoma,
December 7, 1923.

Mr. Frank Welch,
Wamego, Kansas.

Dear Mr. Welch:

This will reply to your letter of the 2nd., inst., concerning matters in the Joseph Welch estate you inquired about in your letter. There is enclosed my official check No. 17915 under date of Dec. 6, 1923 for $155.99. With reference to the sale of the Joseph Welch allotment you and the other heirs could submit claims against the proceeds of the sale that would be placed to the credit of Mrs. Moutaw, the same as you now have in the matter of rentals being collected at this time. On November 7th., last a letter was written Mrs. Zella Graham of Emmett, Kansas, carbon copy of which was mailed you covering the matter of submittal of claims against Mrs. Moutaw's estate. If the carbon copy did not reach you, you can be supplied by this office with another copy.

With reference to the amount of rental that is being collected now I have to advise you that rentals in this vicinity have so depreciated that it is very improbable that the rental in this case could be increased. A further reason, as you are well aware, the improvements of the Joseph Welch land are in a deplorable condition. You visited this land something like a year ago and know this to be a fact. However, if you feel and are willing to find the party who will give more than Mr. Boler pays, the matter of the increase in rental will be considered. I must say that Mr. Boler is a very good lessee and a good man to have on the place and should have due consideration. A lessee might be procured who would be willing to pay a little more money and at the same time run the risk of getting a scalawag instead of a man like Mr. Boler. Let us hear from you further with reference to this matter.

Yours Very Truly,

_____

J. L. Suffecool,
CD:AMS   Superintendent.

Probate
92350-13
90389-23
CET   Shawnee Indian Agency.

Shawnee, Oklahoma,
December 8, 1923.

The Honorable,
The Commissioner of Indian Affairs.

Sac & Fox – Shawnee Estates
1920-1924 Volume IX

My Dear Mr. Commissioner:

I have the honor to acknowledge the receipt of Office communication of above reference under date of December 4, 1923, in which there was enclosed a letter from Millie Tohee Dolce of Perkins, Oklahoma, in reference to the allotment of Lee Patrick Tohee, Iowa Allottee Number 5. In reply I have to advise as follows. That the records of this office indicate that under date of September 3, 1923, reference 69788-21, the Department declared Annie Perry Tohee to be the sole heir of David Tohee, deceased Iowa Allottee No. 8. The heir as mentioned above is living upon and occupying the allotment of her deceased husband, David Tohee. This allotment is leased and the rentals are deposited to and paid to Annie Perry Tohee. The writer of the letter enclosed, Mrs. Dolce, has frequently taken this matter up with me and I have explained it several times, giving her the full history of the case.

Lee Patrick Tohee, Iowa allottee No. 5, was the son of David Tohee. This allottee died June 20, 1891, unmarried and without issue and his allotment was inherited by his father, David Tohee. David Tohee died February 2, 1920, without issue or issue of deceased issue, leaving surviving, his wife, Annie Perry, who would inherit his entire estate according to the succession laws of Oklahoma. Mrs. Dolce's letter is enclosed herewith as requested by the Office.

Yours Very Truly,

_____
J. L. Suffecool,
JLS:AMS   Superintendent

encl.

Ed-Ind.
91703-23
ACH

Shawnee Indian Agency,

Shawnee, Oklahoma,
December 12, 1923.

The Commissioner of Indian Affairs,
Washington, D. C.

Dear Mr. Commissioner,

140

This is to acknowledge receipt of carbon copy of Office letter addressed to Mr. Mark Smith Hayton, Colorado, and his letter to the Office in which he makes inquiry concerning any right he may have with the Shawnee Indians.

In reply I have to advise the Office that Mr. Mark Smith's mother, Jane Delaware Smith, a Shawnee Allottee died the past summer and up to the present date no hearing has been held to determine her heirs. Mr. Smith is an apparent heir and it is expected that Mr. Smith will be determined an heir when the hearing is held, some time this spring, and he will be entitled to his proportionate share of his mothers[sic] restricted allotment. At the present time there are no funds to the credit of his Deceased mother's account.

Returned herewith is Mr. Smith's letter.

Yours Very Truly,

_____

J. L. Suffecool,
Superintendent

encl.

JLR:AMS

Shawnee Indian Agency.

Shawnee, Oklahoma,
December 11, 1923.

Supt. A. R. Snyder,
Pottawatomie Indian Agency,
Mayetta, Kansas.

Dear Mr. Snyder:

Replying to your letter of the 7th., inst., onclosing[sic] acceptances of sale by the heirs of John Moses, allottee No. 101, you are advised as follows. These papers do not appear to have been submitted directly to you rfom[sic] this office but that they were submitted to you by Thomas Lightfoot, one of the heirs in the estate, for your transmittal to this office when theheirs[sic] in Kansas referred to signed the sale papers. The papers were intended to be used by the heirs of John Moses who resided in Kansas. These heirs inheriting through Martha Lightfoot of your agency. These papers will not be returned for the reason that recently there were transmitted like papers to Dan Whitecloud of Rulo Nebraska who has consented to submit to these heirs for their signatures. However, it will be appreciated, when convenient, to call their attention to the necessity of returning those papers to this office at a very early date.

Very truly yours,

_____

J. L. Suffecool,
Superintendent.

J.
CD:AMS

Shawnee Indian Agency.

Shawnee, Oklahoma,
December 12, 1923.

Mr. John A. Buntin, Supt.,
Kiowa Indian Agency,
Anadarko, Oklahoma.

Dear Mr. Buntin:

I am enclosing herewith my official check No. 17958 payable to your order for $31.40 which please place to the credit of the following named Indians, who are heirs of Thomas Worcester.

Thomas Worcester	$6.32
Ruth Inkinish	$1.77
Grover Inkinish	$6.99
Charles E. Adams	$9.41
Robert Adams	$6.91
	$31.40

This represents the lease money derived from the estate of Little Fish a deceased Shawnee allottee. This amount is forwarded to you in order that the accounts of the above named Indians may be cleared.

Sac & Fox – Shawnee Estates
1920-1924 Volume IX

Very truly yours,

_____
J. L. Suffecool,
Superintendent.

JLR:AMS

Shawnee Indian Agency.

Shawnee, Oklahoma,
December 13, 1923.

County Clerk, Payne County,
Stillwater, Oklahoma.

Dear Sir:

There is enclosed herewith Indian Deed Inherited Lands covering the S1/2 of NE1/4 of Section 4, Township 17 North, Range 6 East of the Indian Meridian, conveying by Lelia Bigwalker in favor of Robert Charles Pate and Harry Samuel Pate of Cushing, Oklahoma, together with my official check No. 17930 dated Dec. 8, 1923 in your favor in the sum of $1.00 for the recording of the deed.

Very truly yours,

_____
J. L. Suffecool,
CD:AMS   Superintendent.

Shawnee Indian Agency.

Shawnee, Oklahoma,
December 12, 1923.

Mr. John A. Buntin, Supt.,
Kiowa Indian Agency,
Anadarko, Oklahoma.

Dear Mr. Buntin:

I am enclosing herewith my official check No. 17958 payable to your order for $31.40 which please place to the credit of the following named Indians, who are heirs of Thomas Worcester.

Thomas Worcester ---	$6.32
Ruth Inkinish --	$1.77
Grover Inkinish ---	$6.99
Charles E. Adams --	$9.41
Robert Adams --	$6.91
	$31.40

This represents the lease money derived from the estate of Little Fish a deceased Shawnee allottee. This amount is forwarded to you in order that the accounts of the above named Indians may be cleared.

Very truly yours,

_____

J. L. Suffecool,
Superintendent.

JLR:AMS

Shawnee Indian Agency.

Shawnee, Oklahoma.
December 21, 1923.

Mrs. Amelia Dole.
Route #1.
Perkins, Okla.

My dear Friend:

This will acknowledge receipt of your affidavit with reference to your claim in the estate of Lee Patrick Tohee. I have this day written to the Office asking for specific instructions and am inclosing for your information a copy of my letter.

Your friend,

Inc.

J. L. Suffecool,

JLS-Mo   Superintendent.

Shawnee Indian Agency.

Shawnee, Oklahoma,
December 15, 1923.

Mr. Arthur Pratt,
R. F. D. #2.
Maud, Oklahoma.

My Dear Friend:

On my return to the office this morning Mr. Dushane, one of the employees, brought tomy[sic] attention that Mrs. Powell and Mrs. Amanda Pratt and yourself were in the office and seemed to be some what peeved because no action has been taken in the settlement of the Pratt estate. Now, Arthur, I do no blame you very much for being peeved. In fact I think you people have some cause and it appears that this office has not done all that could be done in effecting a settlement. Yet I believe that you understand the condition as well, if not better than I do. I believe that this office has done all that could be reasonably expected considering the conditions under which we have been obliged to act. There is an action that can be taken that will settle the entire matter and I have advised you and your brothers and sisters about the same but it looks rather hard for one to take such action. What I mean is that the Department could be asked and it is believed that the request would be granted, that a Patent in Fee [illegible] in the name of the heirs and this of course would put the whole matter in the hands of the estate and if this was done and after you people got through I fear that there would be very little left to divide, and I hesitate very much in taking this action.

You will remember that I was at your place with Mr. Riley and from there we sent over to the old place with your brother from Oklahoma City, and that we thought at that time we would be able to make some distribution of the personal effects of your father. Within a very few days after that visit I was called to account for my action and somewhat criticized for going over to the place. Now all you people know that the personal effects that are in that house is not worth a quarrel and I doubt the expediency of drawing this off into a settlement of the same.

It seems to me that the best course to take would be to submit all papers in the case that has heretofore been prepared and I had the intention of doing that and had asked Earnest in person to submit his objection in writing but I failed to receive any response from him and it is my purpose if possible to do justice to all concerned. I trust that you will not be too prone to criticize the action of this office in the matter and on the occasion of my next visit in your section I am going to call at your house and talk the matter over in person. I want to say, Arthur, that I am exceedingly sorry that this matter has reached such a complicated and unsatisfactory status.

Thanking you for past consideration, I am

Very respectfully,

_____

J. L. Suffecool,
Superintendent.

JLS:AMS

Shawnee Indian Agency,
Shawnee, Oklahoma,
Dec. 15, 1923.

Mr. Arthur Pratt,
R F D #2,
Maud, Oklahoma.

Dear Mr. Pratt:

This is according to promise made you during my absence yesterday in the matter of the settlement in the estate of your deceased parents.

In connection with this you are advised that there can be nothing done in this till all of you heirs can come to an agreement of some kind. There is no question about the deterioration of the property but it appears that the heirs should come to an agreement if they wish this to stop. When the heirs have reached an agreement and have a proposition to submit to the Indian Office at Washington the matter will again be given further consideration.

Very truly yours,

Carbon Copy: J. L. Suffecool, Supt.
Mrs. Jessie Powell,
Mrs. Elmer Pratt,
R F D # 2,
Maud, Oklahoma.

Shawnee Indian Agency,

Shawnee, Oklahoma,
December 17, 1923.

Mrs. H. E. Carter,
838 Putnam St.,
Detroit, Michigan.

Dear Mrs. Carter:

This has further reference to the determination of the heirs of your foster mother, Mrs. Mary A. Fear, which matter is now pending in the Indian Office awaiting further information from you as to who was your natural parents, whether both were Indians, the maiden name of your mother, the tribe which she belonged to and the number and description of her allotment if she received one. Also if you natural mother is deceased and if you were recognized as one of her heirs. It appears that you have submitted an affidavit showing that you were adopted by Mrs. Marie Whistler or Marie A. Fear and her husband Charles W. Fear, a white man, in Omaha in the presence of Justice of the Peace Pritchard, Frank Kennedy and John Quinn. It has been inferred from your testimony that some sort of written agreement was entered into. If so and this instrument is still in existence it is requested that the same be forwarded to me so that I may send the same to the Indian Office at Washington for its consideration in determining Mrs. Fear's heirs.

I am also sending a copy of this letter to your foster father, Mrs[sic] Charles W. Fear at Jefferson City, Missouri, for him to supply the information requested herein if he has the same available. However I shall expect a reply from you giving me all the information you possess relative to this matter. Mr. Fear is also requested to give me this and any other information he may think will be pertinent to the case. A prompt reply from each of you will be appreciated.

Very truly yours,

_____

J. L. Suffecool,
Superintendent.

JLR:AMS

147

Shawnee Indian Agency.

Shawnee, Oklahoma,
December 17, 1923.

The Commissioner of Indian Affairs,
Washington, D. C.

My Dear Mr. Commissioner:

There are transmitted herewith partition papers in the petition of the allotment of Big Jim, Absentee Shawnee No. 500, whose allotment is described as the W1/2 of Section 28, Township 9 North, Range 1 East I. M., in Oklahoma. The partition in this matter is being affected in accordance with Office instructions under date of January 23, 1923, bearing reference 101173. It will be noted that the Big Jim allotment was effected in the decision of the Circuit Courts of Appeals of the 8th Circuit in cases No. 5813 and 5814, September 10, 1922. Under paragraph five of Office letter mentioned the Office directs where it is possible and advisable, land may be partitioned and you may report such cases for instructions.

These papers are being submitted for the purposes of advancing the settlement by partition to as an advanced stage as is possible under the circumstances. The papers in the case consists of partition for petition signed by the two heirs whose shares are still restricted and the purchase of the unrestricted portion at one time owned by Charley Bob. There are aloo enclosed with the papers two deeds covering the entire interest of allotment unconveyed at the time of the rendering of the decision by the Court of Appeals. It was therefore necessary for Mr. E. T. Carson, purchaser in this case to procure the second deed covering the remaining portion held by Charley Bob.

Upon examination of these papers it will be noted that Mr. Carson holds an undivided 19/72 interest which was at one time owned by Charley Bob and that it does appear that it might be necessary that Mr. Carson, in order to convey his interest, should execute either a Quit Claim deed or an instrument of some nature in order that he may convey to the other two heirs the portion that is being partitioned to them in accordance with the petition submitted. It would also appear that in as much as the other two heirs hold undivided interests in the entire allotment that it wouldlso[sic] be necessary that these heirs convey to Mr. Carson by deed or like instrument for this purpose. If the petition papers as submitted are not sufficient for the conveying of the undivided parts of this allotment to the three parties interested the Office will please direct or instruct as to the nature of instruments to be executed for the proper convenancing[sic] for the parts of this allotment.

The petition shows that the portion assigned to each of the three are not of equal value, hence, it wil[sic] necessary that a sum of money be made part of a consideration in the partition in the case of Mr. Carson who is being assigned to a tract valued at something like $475.00 above an equal partition. This $475.00 is to be paid Little Jim or To-to-mo in order that he may be given an equal share or division in the partition. The attention of the Office is called to the part assigned to Sallie Bob who is being given the N1/2 of the NW1/4 of 28-9-1, consisting of one-fourth of the entire allotment but which is held at a value about equal to her share in the allotment amounting to 17/72. The appraisal papers covering the three tracts of land on form 5-110-a are enclosed herewith. After examination of these papers I respectfully request that further instructions with reference to the best method for the settlement of this proposition be given.

Very respectfully,

_____

J. L. Suffecool,
Superintendent.

CD:AMS

Shawnee Indian Agency.

Shawnee, Oklahoma,
December 17, 1923.

The Honorable Commissioner of Indian Affairs,
Washington, D. C.

My Dear Mr. Commissioner:

This will reply to Office letter dated December 11, 1923, to Honorable Tom D. McKeown, Congressman, bearing reference Land Sales J. T. H. carbon copy of which was mailed to this office for immediate report. The Office is respectfully advised that on account of the great number of heirs interested that considerable delay necessitated on account of procuring consent to the same from at least a majority of said heirs. However, the papers in the sale were recently transmitted and no doubt will be in the Office within a short time.

Trusting this will be satisfactory, I am

Very respectfully,

_____

J. L. Suffecool,
Superintendent.

CD:AMS

Shawnee Indian Agency.

Shawnee, Oklahoma,
December 21, 1923.

The Honorable
    The Commissioner of Indian Affairs,
        Washington, D. C.

My dear Mr. Commissioner:

There is inclosed herewith an affidavit subscribed and sworn to by Amelia Falls Dole. The affidavit fully explains itself hence do not think that it needs comment. However, for the information and convenience of the Office I am giving the probate reference of Lee Patrick Tohee and David Tohee.

David Tohee: Probate No. 69788
                dated September 3, 1923.

Lee Patrick Tohee:
                Probate No. 91387-13;
                     92350-13
                     F E
        Dated August 13, 1913.

I do not feel that it is proper for me to take this matter up without specific directions from your Office. If the Office is of the opinion that Amelia Falls Dole has a valid claim I will be pleased to comply with such instructions as may be given.

Incl.   Very respectfully,

JLS-Mc   J. L. Suffecool
Copy to   Superintendent.
Amelia Dole
R. #1, Perkins, Okla.

Shawnee Indian Agency.

Shawnee, Oklahoma,
December 24, 1923.

Mrs. Rena Smith Richardson
Kiowa, Oklahoma.

My Friend:

This will acknowledge the receipt of your letter of December 18, concerning the leasing of 120 acres of land in which you are interested as an heir for oil and gas and that you are unwilling to sign a lease at $1.50 an acre for the reason as you state that you have been offered $2.50 per acre. In your letter you ask for my advice in the matter. Of course if you can get $2.50 per acre that would be the proper thing to do but are you certain that your offer of $2.50 per acre is from a reliable source and that the man who offered it would pay that much? This is wild-cat territory and as stated above if you can receive more perfectly good and all right but this I doubt very much for the reason that practically all lands in wild-cat territory do not bring more than $1.50 and some even lower, and in a number of cases people donate their acreage in order to procure a lease and have the territory developed. Now Mrs. Richardson this is a matter for you to decide yourself. I would be glad if you could get $2.50 an acre but I do not believe that I would wait too long as you might not get anything. The other heirs have signed and it does not seem exactly right that they should be kept out of their money because you are unwilling to sign. I do no seek to use undue influence in this matter yet I believe we oew[sic] something to the other heirs.

With reference to the rent money on the land, you are advised that the lessee has not turned in the proceeds for the sale of the share of the crop, which is according to the lease contract. As soon as this is done and the money properly accounted for your share of the proceeds will be forwarded to you.

Very respectfully,

J. L. Suffecool,
Superintendent.

JLS-Mc

Shawnee Indian Agency.

Shawnee, Oklahoma,
December 24, 1923.

Mrs. Rachel V. Offett
    Miami, Oklahoma.

Dear Mrs. Offett:

I have your letter of the 22d making inquiry concerning lease money due you from the estate of your grandfather and in reply I have to advise that the check for $5.14, which was recently forwarded you, represented the distribution of proceeds which had accumulated to the estate of Mta na pa ha e we; your share of the distribution being $4.25 and the balance of $.89 represented your share of the lease money which has been paid in to the office this year on this land.

All money that has been paid in to this office for you from the above estate has been forwarded to you as well as all of the other heirs. You are aware that you are one of the numerous heirs to the estate therefore your share is necessarily small. You may advise any of the other heirs whom you happen to come in contact with that all funds belonging to them have been sent to them.

Very truly yours,

J. L. Suffecool,
JLR-Mc   Superintendent.

Shawnee Indian Agency.

Shawnee, Oklahoma,
December 24, 1923.

Mr. George A. Hoyo,
    Supt. Ponca Agency,
        Whiteagle, Oklahoma.

Dear Mr. Hoyo:

Referring to your letter of the 20th instant concerning the will of Frances O. English and her interest in the Kirwin and Murray estates. I would be pleased if you would send this office the Office file number of the will for our use in connection with the above named estates.

Very truly yours,

J. L. Suffecool,
Superintendent.

JLS-Mc

Shawnee Indian Agency.

Shawnee, Okla.
Dec. 24, 1923.

Mr. Monroe LaClair
Vetal, Bennett County, S.D.

Mr. dear Friend:

This will acknowledge receipt of your letter of the 19th instant. I am inclosing herewith check No. 15553 for $37.50, payable to your order. This represents rent from the lease of the Ozetta Trombler estate. We have been holding this check for some time as we did not know your address. Please send us Oliver's address as soon as possible as we wish to communicate with him.

Very truly yours,

Inc.

J. L. Suffecool,
Superintendent.

Mc

Shawnee Indian Agency.

Shawnee, Oklahoma,
December 26, 1923.

Mr. A. B. Collins,
Cushing, Oklahoma.

My dear Mr. Collins:

Replying to your letter of the 24th I inclose herewith check #18090 for $25.00 payable to Nancy Barker. This leaves her a balance of $944.09.

I also inclose check #18094 for $205.00 payable to Gilbert Gibbs. This represents proceeds from agricultural lease on his land. Kindly deliver the checks to the proper parties.

Very truly yours,

Incl-2

J. L. Suffecool,

XXX-Mc   Superintendent.

Shawnee, Oklahoma
January 3, 1924

Mrs. Matilda Wind
Chilocco, Oklahoma

Dear Mrs. Wind:

In determining the heirs of your half sister Mrs. Marie A. Fear the question has arisen as to whether Mrs. Carter was legally adopted by Mr. and Mrs. Fear.

If you know anything regarding the adoption of Mrs. Carter by Mr. and Mrs. Fear please have prepared a statement and sign the same by a notary public and forward to me so that I may in turn give the information to the examiner of inheritance, who is awaiting such information.

Yours very truly,

J. L. Suffecool

JLR/LB   Superintendent.

Shawnee, Oklahoma
January 3, 1924

Mr. S. Y. Tutwiley[sic]
Indian Agency
Concho, Oklahoma

Dear Mr. Tutwiley:

I am inclosing herewith a list of deceased Indians whos[sic] heirs are undetermined, also the list which is the names of prospectious[sic] heirs. This is in compliance with a request made in your letter of recent date.

We have endeavored to give you the proper attention of your prospectous[sic] heirs and I would suggest that when you mail the notice to these people that you make your letter address Shawnee so that we will know what persons did not receive the notices and that we may make other attempts regarding them. The following list contains the names deceased Shawnee, Pottawatomie, Kickapoos, Indians. The list of the Sac & Fox deceased Indians is being prepared and will be sent to you at a later date.

When do you expect to proceed to Shawnee for inheritance work.[sic]

Yours very truly,

J. L. Suffecool
JLR/LB   Superintendent.

Shawnee Indian Agency.

Shawnee, Oklahoma,
January 7, 1924

Mr. A. R. Pugh
    323 West 8th. St.
    Bristow, Okla.

Dear Sir:

This is to acknowledge receipt of your letter of the 4th. making inquiry concerning the S.E.-4 section 11-12-4.

You are advised that this land was originally allotted to Maggie Sullivan, a Sac and Fox Indian, who is now deceased. There is no oil and gas lease on the land and one cannot be made at this time, for the reason that the heirs of the deceases[sic] allottee are still un-determined. The department regulations prohibit the making of an oil and gas lease on lands where the heirs are undetermined. Within six months[sic] time it is hoped to have the hearing on this matter and determine the heirs.

Very truly yours,

J.L.Suffecool
Superintendent.

JLR:IEP

Shawnee Indian Agency.

Shawnee, Oklahoma,
January 11, 1924

Mrs. Matilda J. J. Stultz
Miami, Oklahoma.

Dear Mrs. Stultz:

Replying to your letter of January 1, concerning the estate of your Grandfather, whom you said was Tom Tascawe, I have to advise you that we do not have any account by this name, but it is presumed that you are refering[sic] to M-ta-na-ka-ka-we's estate, in which you are an heir. The rentals have been accumulating to the credit of this estate for several years and the total amounting to $358.38, which was recently distributed among the heirs and your share, as well as all the others, was placed to the credit of yours and their accounts, and checks have been drawn payable to the ones whose addresses are known.

You no doubt are aware there are numerous heirs to this estate and shares would of course be small. You make the statement that you do not understand how it is that Della Evans and Eliza Jane Jones shared in this estate. The heirs were determined according to the law [sic] descent in Oklahoma and if you will determine the relation of these parties through blood or by marriage and will familiarize yourself with the laws of descent of Oklahoma you will see how these parties came to be heirs to the estate of your Grandfather. In the future the money belonging to you from this estate will be sent you as soon as sufficient amount is placed to your credit to justify the drawing of a check.

Yours truly,

J.L.Suffecool

JLR:IEP   Superintendent.

Shawnee Indian Agency.

Shawnee, Oklahoma,
January 11, 1924

Mrs. Jane Edwards,
    Miami, Oklahoma.
        Box 79

Dear Mrs. Jones:

I am in receipt of your letter of the 28th, making inquiry concerning funds from the estate of Tom Pasonwe.

In reply, you are advised that our records do not show that we have had any funds, carried under the name of that given, by you. But it is presumed that you are refering[sic] to the M-ta-na-ka-ka-we estate, in which you and the other Jones are interested. Your balance to date derived from the estate is only $1.16. You no doubt are aware that your interest in the estate is very small. Your fractional share being 88/5566600. Up to a few months ago the accumulated rentals on the estate amounted to $358.38 and this has been divided among the respective heirs, then your share of this and the recent rentals equaled the $1.16.

The land is not sold and there is no prospect of an early sale. In the future your money will be sent to you, when such an amount has been placed to your credit, as will justify the drawing of a check.

Very truly,

J.L.Suffecool
JLR:IEP   Superintendent.

Shawnee Indian Agency.

Shawnee, Oklahoma,
January 11, 1924

Mr. O.K. Chandler
Miami, Oklahoma.

Dear Mr. Chandler:

I am advised that Frank Posecawe, an Indian lives under your jurisdiction and who was an heir to the estate of M-ta-ma-ka-ka-we, under this jurisdiction is dead. If his heirs had been determined and hearing was held at your Office please supply me with a copy of the signings so that I may distribute a small balance held to Frank's credit in this Office.

Very truly yours,

J.L.Suffecool
Superintendent.

JLR:IEP

Shawnee Indian Agency.

Shawnee, Oklahoma,
January 11, 1924

Mrs. Amelia Dole
Perkins, Oklahoma
Route #1.

My dear friend:

I am in receipt of a letter from the Indian Office under date of January 5, in further reference to claim to the estate of David Tohee, deceased Iowa allottee No. 8. I understand that the Office has, this day mailed you a letter explaining the home situation. This will definitely settle this question and it will not be necessary to bring it to the attention of the Office for further consideration

I regret that I did not find you and your husband at home when I was there on the 8th., We had a very nice little meeting. I note that the Children are not in school, it is not right for you to take them off visiting and keep them out of school so long. There are no

objections for the short visit but one extending over a period to two
weeks is entirely too long.

Your friend,

J.L.Suffecool
JLS:IEP   Superintendent.

Shawnee Indian Agency.

Shawnee, Okla.
Jan. 12, 1924

Mrs. Nancy Pratt
Route #1, Box 88
Yale, Oklahoma.

Dear Mrs. Pratt:

Replying to your letter of recent date in which you made
inquiry concerning the estate of Joe Epeteska, a deceased
Pottawatomie Indian. You are advised that you may appear either at
Shawnee or at Mayetta Kansas before the examiner of inheritances,
concerning the above named estate. However, I would suggest that
if you wish to have an early determination of the heirs that you
appear at Shawnee, before the Examiner of Inheritances, who
expects to be here some time in May or April, for the purposes of
determining heirs of deceased Indians.

Notices will be sent you at such time the hearing is to be held.
Will your address continue to be Yale, Oklahoma? IF not notify me
so that we will know where to mail the notices. The description of
the land still in trust is E1/2 of NW1/4 24-6-4.

There is no Government lease on this land of record. I do not
know whether Mrs. John Laracy is using it or not.

Very truly yours,

J.L.Suffecool
Superintendent.

JLR:IEP

Shawnee Indian Agency.

Shawnee, Oklahoma,
January 12, 1924

Mr. John C. Wabahaquin
    Planet, Wisconsin.

Dear sir:

I have your letter of the 8th, making inquiry about the Pamdosh land, and in reply you are advised that the James Pamdosh land was sold in 1918.

I do not know who your mother is but I presume you are asking about the estate of No-ne-ke-kat, whose heirs are Nancy and Anna Kahdot.   All money derived from this estate has been distributed among the heirs.

I am unable to ascertain who your Grandpa and Grandma were, as you do not give their names in your letter.

Very truly,

J.L.Suffecool
Superintendent.

JLR:IEP

****

Shawnee Indian Agency.

Shawnee, Oklahoma,
January 12, 1924

Mrs. Mary Matche
    Mayetta, Kansas.

Dear Mrs. Matche:

I have a letter from Mr. Snyder at Mayetta, returning Anna's check unsigned. I have signed same and it is returned to you for delivery to Anna. You also made inquiry as to the sources of the funds you and Anna recently received. The last amount sent you two were derived from small accumulations of interests, credited to the estate of No-ne-ke-kat. This money represented the interest earned on lease rentals, which had been credited to No-ne-ke-kat. The lease money you have received some time ago.

The Agriculture lease money on this estate will be sent you shortly. The Oil and Gas lease money is not due until the first part of May 1924. When the same has been paid into this Office and properly accounted for, yours and Anna's share will be sent to you.

Very truly yours,

J.L.Suffecool
Superintendent.

JLR:IEP

Carbon copy to Mr. A. L[sic]. Snyder,
Mayetta, Kansas.

Shawnee Indian Agency.

Shawnee, Oklahoma,
January 12, 1924

Mr. A.R. Snyder, Sup't
Mayetta, Kansas.

Dear Mr. Snyder:

I am in receipt of a letter from Mr. Angell requesting that I give him information concerning the inherited interests of Shawnee, deceased Kansas Sac and Fox allottee No. 70.

I failed to find any inherited interests belonging to a Kansas Sac and Fox the name of Shawnee. Possibly you could give me some information which would help identify the Indian's interest in question. If so kindly mail me such, at your earliest convenience so that I may give Mrs. Angell the information requested.

Thanking you I am,

Very truly yours,

J.L.Suffecool
Superintendent.

JLR:IEP
Carbon Copy to Mr. B.O. Angell, Examiner of Inheritances,
Winnebago, Nebraska.

Shawnee Indian Agency,
Shawnee, Oklahoma,
January 14, 1924.

Mrs. Matilda Wind
Indian School
Chilocco, Oklahoma.

Dear Mrs. Wind:

I have received your affidavit recently made in connection with the adoption of Mrs. Ruby Carter by Mr. and Mrs. Charles Fear and the same has been sent to the Examiner of Inheritance. To-day I am in receipt of a further request from him concerning the mother of Mrs. Ruby Carter.

At your earliest convenience please advise me if Mrs. Kittie Lee, the mother of Ruby Carter, was an Indian and if so of what tribe and if she had an allotment the description and number of same and where allotted. Thanking you for this and sorry that I have to bother you again for further information, I am

Very truly yours,

J. L. Suffecool,
JLR:Mc   Superintendent.

Copy to
S. Y. Tutwiler
    Concho, Oklahoma.

Shawnee Indian Agency.

Shawnee, Oklahoma,
January 11, 1924

Mr. S.Y. Tutwiler
Indian Agency
Concho, Oklahoma.

Dear Mr. Tutwiler:

With further reference to your letter of recent date concerning the adoption of Mrs. Ruby Carter by Mr. and Mrs Charles W. Fear, I have to state that I am in receipt of a sworn statement made by Mrs. Matilda Wind of Chilocco, Oklahoma, a sister of Mrs. Fear. I am enclosing the statement and hope the same may be of some benefit to you in advising the Office concerning the matter.

Very truly yours,

J.L.Suffecool
Superintendent.

JLR:IEP

Shawnee Indian Agency,
Shawnee, Oklahoma,
January 15, 1924.

Mrs. Sarah Roubidoux
Rulo, Nebraska.

Dear Mrs. Roubidoux:

This will acknowledge receipt of your letter of January 7, in which you make inquiry about the John [Illegible] estate. In reply I have to advise that the papers have all been sent to Washington and just as soon as the money is received we will be glad to send it to you direct. I note what you say about Louise. I think your plan is a good one and will try and carry it out as you suggest. I saw Dan, your brother, at Red Rock early in December. Was sure glad to see him again. I remember your folks well when I taught in the little old day school there. I often think of the many people there that I knew. Hope that I will be able to get to see you some day.

Your friend,

J. L. Suffecool,
Superintendent.

JLS-Mc

Sac & Fox – Shawnee Estates
1920-1924 Volume IX

Shawnee Indian Agency,
Shawnee, Oklahoma,
January 15, 1924.

Mr. S. Y. Tutwiler,
   Examiner of Inheritance,
     Concho, Oklahoma.

Dear Mr. Tutwiler:

     This will acknowledge receipt of your letter of January 15, 1924 in which you include a copy of a letter of W. S. Pratt, of Maud, inquiring about the estate of Harriett Pratt. In reply I have to advise that the estate of Harriett Pratt has been probated and the heirs determined. According to the probate proceedings 1/3 of the estate, I believe, went to the husband, Sevellon Pratt. Sevellon Pratt died on the 5th day of July, 1922, and left surviving him the following:

     Ernest O. Pratt
     Walter S. Pratt
     Arthur R. Pratt
     Jessie L. Powell
     Charlie O. Pratt
     May Wilmett
     Louis W. Pratt, who is dead, and left surviving him Gertie Pratt, wife, and four children.
     Elmer T. Pratt, who left surviving him Amanda Pratt and one child.

     All of these heirs live in and around Maud, Oklahoma, and a letter addressed to Maud will reach them.

     On the 14th of October, 1922, an attempt was made by this office to probate the estate but the papers in the case were never completed for the reason that the heirs shortly after the hearing got into a jangle which has not been settled to date.

     I trust that the above information will be sufficient to enable you to proceed.

     Very respectfully,

     J. L. Suffecool,
JLS-Mc   Superintendent.

Shawnee Indian Agency,
Shawnee, Okla.
January 17, 1924.

Mr. Arthur Bourbonnais
c/o Bair Oil Co.
Rawlins, Wyoming.

Dear Sir:

Answering your letter of the 13th instant inquiring about the estate of Mrs. Mary Bourbonnais. I have to advise that the heirs are as yet undetermined.

We expect to hold a hearing on this and other estates during the coming spring and I will advise you just when it will be held.

Very truly yours,

J. L. Suffecool
Mc   Superintendent.

Copy to
S. Y. Tutwiler, Ex. of Inheritance
Indian Agency
Concho, Oklahoma.

DEPARTMENT OF THE INTERIOR

UNITED STATES INDIAN FIELD SERVICE

RECEIVED
JAN 24 1924
SHAWNEE INDIAN
AGENCY

Mayetta, Kansas,
January 22, 1924.

Mr. J. L. Suffecool,
Shawnee, Oklahoma.

Dear Mr. Suffecool:

This will refer to your letter of January 12, a copy of which I enclosed to Mr. Angell, concerning the inherited interests of Shawnee, deceased Kansas Sac and Fox allottee No. 70.

We are in error in this matter, as Shawnee's interests were sold down there before you took charge and the inheritance was transferred to this agency. I personally told Mr. Angell that she had interests there, having that in mind, but the horse is on me. The office force tells me that there are no records here showing such interests.

Very truly yours,
A. R. Snyder
A. R. Snyder, Superintendent.

ARS/AM

Land-Sales
285-24
 N R

Shawnee Indian Agency,
Shawnee, Oklahoma,
January 22, 1924.

The Commissioner of Indian Affairs.
Washington, D. C.

Dear Mr. Commissioner:

This is to acknowledge receipt of carbon copy of Office letter written to Mr. Albert Moore of Tama, Iowa, and his letter written to you concerning the lease on the alotment[sic] of Watt Grayson, deceased Sac and Fox Indian, and call for my report as to the property of Mrs. Sarah Thompson, a deceased heir of the above named Indian.

The Office is advised that Sarah Thompson died a couple of years ago and up to the present time her heirs have not been determined. Mr. Moore seems to think that her husband, John Thompson, should not be determined an heir but according to the laws of succession in the state of Oklahoma, I do not see how he can be excluded. The hearing will be held some time this spring as the Examiner of Inheritance is expected here at that time.

Mr. Moore states in his letter that I know John Thompson's record. I will also state that I know Mr. Albert Moore's record and can not say anything very favorable for him.

Very truly yours,

Incl.

J. L. Suffecool,

JLR-Mc   Superintendent.

Shawnee Indian Agency,
Shawnee, Oklahoma,
January 22, 1924.

Mr. O. K. Chandler, Supt.
    Indian Agency,
      Miami, Oklahoma.

Dear Mr. Chandler:

      In determining the heirs of Mrs. Marie A. Fear, a adopted member of the Sac and Fox tribe of Indians in Oklahoma, the question of whether the adoption of Mrs. Ruby Carter, daughter of Mrs. Kittie Lee an Ottawa Indian living under your jurisdiction, was according to legal procedure has arisen and in order to determine this it is necessary that certain information be had. I have been informed that Mrs. Kittie Lee was allotted with the Ottawa people and that she is the mother of Mrs. Ruby Carter. Please advise Mr. S. Y. Tutwiler, Examiner of Inheritance, at the Indian Agency, Concho, Okla., if such is the case, giving him the description of her allotment and if same is still held in trust.

      Please mail me a copy of your letter to Mr. Tutwiler.

Very truly yours,

J. L. Suffecool,

JLR-Mc   Superintendent.

Copy to Mr. Tutwiler

****

Shawnee Indian Agency,
Shawnee, Oklahoma,
January 22, 1924.

Mr. S. Y. Tutwiler,
    Examiner of Inheritance.
        Indian Agency
        Concho, Oklahoma.

Dear Mr. Tutwiler:

　　With further reference to your letter of recent date concerning the adoption proceedings connected with the Marie A. Fear matter, I am inclosing herewith a certificate furnished by Mrs. Matilda Wind, a sister of Mrs. Fear, in which she states that Mrs. Carter is a daughter of Mrs. Kittie Lee, an Ottawa Indian under the Miami, Oklahoma office.

　　I am writing Supt. Chandler and requesting that he give you any information he can connected with this case.

Very truly yours,

Incls.

JLR-Mc

J. L. Suffecool
Superintendent.

Shawnee Indian Agency,
Shawnee, Oklahoma.
January 22, 1924.

Supt. A. R. Snyder
    Pottawatomi Indian Agency
        Mayetta, Kansas.

Dear Mr. Snyder:

　　I am in receipt of a letter from James Lasley who informs me that James Blandin died July 17, 1922. James Blandin was an heir to certain lands in Oklahoma and if his heirs have been determined kindly advise me so that I may make proper distribution of any funds that may come into this office for him.

Very truly yours,

J. L. Suffecool,
JLR-Mc
Superintendent.

Shawnee Indian Agency,
Shawnee, Oklahoma.
January 22, 1924.

Mr. James Burnett
Hardy, Oklahoma.

Dear Sir:

Replying to your letter of January 17 concerning your interest in the Acton estate, you are advised that your share of the last rental paid was only $3.00. The rent was only $75.00 and from this amount $15.00 was deducted for the probate fee and your share, 6/120, was $3.00.

You state that you have been drawing $9.00 and some odd cents for your share. I have examined the record and I do not find that you have drawn lately at one time the amount of $9.00. Your payment before the last was only $3.75. You no doubt have confused the amounts.

Very truly yours,

J. L. Suffecool,
JLR-Mc   Superintendent.

Shawnee Indian Agency,
Shawnee, Oklahoma.
January 23, 1924.

Mr. Thos. H. Owen
224 American National Bank Bldg.
Oklahoma City, Okla.

My dear Mr. Owen:

This will acknowledge the receipt of your letter of January 21, making inquiry concerning certain funds presumed to be held in the Treasury of the United States for Mrs. Fannie Foote, deceased. In reply you are advised that the records of the Washington office would indicate that there is was $1132.15 due

Mrs. Foote at the time of her death. You inquire as to the necessary procedure, etc., to secure this fund. In reply you are advised that it will first be necessary to have the estate of Fannie Foote probated. We expect to have the Probate Attorney at this office sometime this spring and this case will be taken up and disposed of at that time. After Mrs. Foote's heirs have been declared by the Secretary of the Interior then it would be proper to take the matter up. I saw Robert Keokuk of Ripley, Oklahoma, a few days ago and brought this matter to his attention and he told me that he would write your bank. Will be pleased to give you further information if desired.

Very respectfully,

JLS Mc
Copy to
Robert Keokuk
Ripley, Okla.

J. L. Suffecool,
Superintendent.

Shawnee Indian Agency,
Shawnee, Oklahoma,
January 24, 1924.

Mrs. Alice W. Wapshineh
Hominy, Oklahoma.

Dear Mrs. Wapshineh:

I have your letter of the 18th inquiring about the Frank Wilmot land. You are advised that no hearing to determine the heirs in this estate has been held but expect there wull[sic] be one held this sring[sic] sometime. When the Examiner of Inheritance arrives and sends out notices to the prospective heris[sic] you will be notified.

Very truly yours,

J. L. Suffecool,
Superintendent.

JLR-Mc

Shawnee Indian Agency,
Shawnee, Oklahoma,
January 26, 1924.

Mr. John C. Wabshagin
Planets[sic], Wisconsin.

Dear friend John:

Replying to your letter of January 20, making further inquiry about the Pamdosh land in which your deceased mother Teresa Kee wac ko chee was an heir, you are advised that this land was sold several years ago and the land of your mother was also sold several years ago and the funds derived from same disbursed to the parties entitled thereto.   There are no interests whatever here belonging to the Pamdoshes[sic] or your mother, therefore, you have no interest here as an heir to your mother.

Very truly yours,

J. L. Suffecool,
JLR-Mc   Superintendent.

Shawnee Indian Agency,
Shawnee, Oklahoma,
January 26, 1924.

Mrs. Alice Hunter
    Route 4
        Cushing, Okla.

Dear Mrs. Hunter:

This will acknowledge the receipt of your letter of January 24, in which you tell me about the trouble George Gibbs is having with his father Gilbert Gibbs and that he wants Gilbert to pay him because he did not take care of him. In reply you are advised that I have talked to George about this several times and told him that there was absolutely nothing that could be done by this office that would furnish him any relief. I think he is making a mistake in getting a lawyer to look into this matter for him. He will have to pay for this service and I do not believe that he would be able to get anywhere with it. After the land is sold that you speak of in which

Gilbert is one of the heirs, it would be a good time to take this matter up and see whether he would not be willing to help George. Until that time there is nothing that can be done. I would be pleased to talk this matter over with you personally on the occasion of my next visit to Cushing.

Your Friend,

J. L. Suffecool,

JLS-Mc   Superintendent.

Shawnee Indian Agency,
Shawnee, Oklahoma,
January 26, 1924.

Mr. J. E. Smith
  Box 55, Capitol Hill Station,
    Oklahoma City, Okla.

Dear Mr. Smith;

I am in receipt of your letter of the 24th in which you make inquiry as to any interests the heirs of John B. McKee, a citizen Pottawatomi Indian, may have here in the way of funds. In reply you are advised that I am unable to locate just who these heirs are and I doubt very much whether they would have any interest here whatever as Mr. McKee disposed of his land prior to his death You no doubt are referring to a payment the Pottawatomie Indians are trying to obtain from the Government in the form of a settlement for an old claim they are contending for but up to the present time no definite action has ever been taken in the matter and do not know that the claim will ever materialize as information upon which the claim is based in needed.

Very truly yours,

J. L. Suffecool,

JLR-Mc   Superintendent.

Shawnee Indian Agency.
Shawnee, Oklahoma,
January 26, 1924.

The
    Commissioner of Indian Affairs.
      Washington, D. C.

My dear Mr. Commissioner:

      It appears according to records in this office that report in
the heirship case of Willie Gibson, Absentee Shawnee, un-allotted,
was submitted under date of February 24, 1919 by Examiner of
Inheritance E. A. Upton. If decision has been rendered in this case this
office has no record of such. The decision as to the heirs is now
desired. Please advise this office as to the action taken.

                Very respectfully,

                J. L. Suffecool,
CD-Mc   Superintendent.

Shawnee Indian Agency,
Shawnee, Oklahoma.
January 28, 1924.

Mr. S. Y. Tutwiler,
    Examiner of Inheritance.
      Concho, Oklahoma.

Dear Mr. Tutwiler:

      I am inclosing herewith an additional list of deceased Indians
and their probably heirs under this jurisdiction which you requested
several weeks ago. A partial list was sent you recently of Shawnee,
Kickapoo and Pottawatomi deceased Indians. There are some others
whose prospective heirs I am unable to locate but am corresponding with
other parties to see if I can obtain such information. After your arrival
here these scattering cases will be discussed.

                Very truly yours,
Incl.

                J. L. Suffecool,
JLR-Mc   Superintendent.

Shawnee Indian Agency,
Shawnee, Oklahoma,
January 28, 1924.

Supt. George A. Hoyo
Ponca Indian Agency,
Whiteagle, Oklahoma.

Dear Mr. Hoyo:

I am preparing a list of the probably heirs of deceased Indians under this jurisdiction for the benefit of Mr. Tutwiler, the examiner of inheritance.

Mary Vetter, who died a few months ago near your place, has several heirs but I am not familiar with their location and I am requesting that you give me a list of the probable heris[sic] and their addresses so that notice may be mailed them.

Thanking you, I am

Very truly yours,

J. L. Suffecool,
JLR-Mc   Superintendent.

Shawnee Indian Agency,
Shawnee, Oklahoma.
February 2, 1924.

Mr. Buddise D. Godkey

Rulo, Nebraska.

Dear Sir:

I have your letter of the 22d inquiring as to whether you have any funds here to your credit derived from the Tessie Roubideaux estate. You are advised that we do not have any funds here for you and I do not find any record showing that you were recognized as a legal heir of Mrs. Roubideaux.

Very truly yours,

J. L. Suffecool,
JLR-Mc   Superintendent.

Shawnee Indian Agency,
Shawnee, Oklahoma,
February 2, 1924.

American National Bank
    Oklahoma City, Okla.

    Attention Mr. Thos. H. Owen

Dear Mr. Owen:

This is to acknowledge receipt of your letter of January 28, concerning the matter of probating the estate of Fannie Foote, in which you advise me that you have been appointed administrator of the estate. As you were informed in my former letter we expect the probate attorney at our office some time this spring and the matter of determining the heirs will be taken up. After the approval of the findings by the Secretary of the Interior the funds belonging to Mrs. Foote will then be ready for disbursement.

Very truly yours,

J. L. Suffecool,
JLR-Mc   Superintendent.

Shawnee Indian Agency.
Shawnee, Oklahoma.
February 13, 1924.

Mr. James W. Rodgers
    Attorney at Law
        Hodenville[sic], Oklahoma.

Dear Sir:

This is to acknowledge receipt of your letter of February 7, written in behalf of Thomas Deer, a Seminole Indian, who claims that his father was a Shawnee Indian and that his grandmother was Nancy Wilson, a Shawnee Indian, and that he wonders whether he inherited any of her estate.

You may advise Mr. Thomas Deer that the findings as made by the Department of the Interior did not determine him an heir as his relationship to the deceased was too far removed for him to participate. Mr. Deer has been advised of this a time or two in the past. The hearing was held by an Examiner of Inheritance appointed by the Department of the Interior and the findings approved by the Secretary of the Interior. Before the approval of such the matter was thoroughly reviewed and if some heir had been excluded the findings would not have received Departmental approval.

Very truly yours,

J. L. Suffecool

R-Mc

Superintendent

Ed-Ind.
6409-24
ESS

Shawnee Indian Agency.
Shawnee, Oklahoma.
February 13, 1924.

The Honorable
    The Commissioner of Indian Affairs.
        Washington, D. C.

My dear Mr. Commissioner:

Sac & Fox – Shawnee Estates
1920-1924 Volume IX

     This is to acknowledge receipt of carbon copy of Office letter written to Frank L. Williams of Tama, Iowa, concerning money due him from the estate of Andrew Barker.

     The Office is advised that at the present time Mr. Williams, or Ka ka que na, has a small balance of $5.94 to his credit. This amount is being transmitted to him through Dr. Jacob Breid, Superintendent of the Sac and Fox Sanatorium, for delivery. His interest in the estate is rather small as he inherited through Phia taw na ha. In the future his shares will be forwarded to him immediately along with the shares of the other heirs. Sometimes the small amounts are held to the credit of the account pending the receipt of other lease money before drawing the check so that the drawing of the check may be justified, as it frequently happens that when a check is written for a small amount the same is never cashed apparently being lost or torn up. This causes considerable trouble in reconciling my bank accounts. The funds belonging to Indians who live at Toledo are forwarded as soon after their receipt in this office, where the amount involved is several dollars, as can conveniently be done.

     Mr. Williams' letter is returned herewith.

     Very truly yours,

     J. L. Suffecool,
R-Mc   Superintendent.

Probate
42139-21
M H W

     Shawnee Indian Agency.
     Shawnee, Oklahoma.
     February 13, 1924.

The Honorable
     The Commissioner of Indian Affairs,
        Washington, D. C.

My dear Mr. Commissioner:

     This is to acknowledge receipt of Office letter of February 7, bearing reference as shown above, calling my attention to a request made in Office letter dated November 2, 1923 with

177

reference to the case of Franklin Wilamette, deceased Pottawatomi allottee #11881.

In reply I have to advise that a search of this allottee's folder has been made and I am unable to locate the office letter in question. I do not remember having received the same. Please mail me a copy of the letter in question so that I may comply with instructions contained therein.

Very truly yours,

J. L. Suffecool,
R-Mc   Superintendent.

Shawnee Indian Agency.
Shawnee, Oklahoma.
February 13, 1924.

Mr. Andrew J. Whipple,
    c/o Field Clerk
    Muskogee, Oklahoma.

Dear Sir:

Replying to your letter of the 4th in which you make inquiry as to whether you have any funds here derived from your father's estate, you are advised that you have no money here from such estate. You will remember you disposed of your interest in this estate several years ago.

Very truly yours,

J. L. Suffecool,
R-Mc   Superintendent.

Sac & Fox – Shawnee Estates
1920-1924 Volume IX

Shawnee Indian Agency,
Shawnee, Oklahoma,
February 13, 1924.

Dr. Jacob Breid,
    Supt., Sac & Fox Sanatorium
      Toledo, Iowa.

Dear Dr. Breid,

      This is to acknowledge receipt of your letter of January 31, written in behalf of William Davenport, an heir to the John McKuk estate, making inquiry concerning rent money which has been paid to him. You state that William understood that he was to receive $180 per annum and that he received only $117. Please advise William that he received his correct proportionate share and that no change has been made on the lease. The entire rental last year was $270; the cost ($36.00) of a well was taken from this leaving $234 to be divided among the heirs, William getting one-half of this or $117.

      You also state that William contemplates visiting this agency in the near future regarding the division of this estate. When he comes I shall be glad to take the matter up with him.

Very respectfully,

J. L. Suffecool,
Superintendent.

R-Mc

Shawnee Indian Agency,
Shawnee, Oklahoma,
February 15, 1924.

Supt. A. R. Snyder,
    Pottawatomi Indian Agency
      Mayetta, Kansas.

Dear Mr. Snyder:

      Enclosed is application signed by Mary Tecumzee for her pro rata share of annuity payment.

179

Very truly yours,

**Mc

J. L. Suffecool
Superintendent.

Shawnee Indian Agency.
Shawnee, Oklahoma.
February 16, 1924.

Mr. Andrew Denton
c/o Hotel Akron

Akron, Colorado.

Dear Mr. Denton:

Replying to your letter of February 6, concerning the amount of $33.00 which is due you, you are advised that this matter is being adjusted by the Department at Washington and payment will be made you as soon as possible. However, I can not state whether it will be a few days or a few months.

In regard to the selling of your interest in the original estate in which you are interested, you are advised that there is no market for lands at the present hence nothing can be done along that line.

Very truly yours,

R-Mc

J. L. Suffecool,
Superintendent.

Fy. 264

Shawnee Indian Agency,
Shawnee, Oklahoma.
February 16, 1924.

Ozark Pipe Line Corporation
Arcade Building
St. Louis, Mo.
Attention: Mr. Carl Banker, Claim Dept.

Gentlemen:

Replying to your letter of February 12, concerning damages to be paid the heirs of Henry Myers, whose land is described as the N/2 of NW/4 of Sec. 3-5-1, on which you have constructed anchors for a telephone pole, our records show that the heirs to this estate are Mrs. Dollie R. Slavin and John A. Myers, a minor, both of Lexington, Oklahoma.

Inasmuch as the damages for such will be small and as Mrs. Slavin in the guardian of the minor John A. Myers, you may make remittance to her direct, provided an amicable agreement can be reached. I will request that you obtain from her a signed receipt and forward me a copy of the same so that I may attach it to my files.

Very truly yours,

J. L. Suffecool,
R-Mc   Superintendent.

Shawnee Indian Agency,
Shawnee, Oklahoma,
February 16, 1923.

Mr. J. R. Thorn

Maud, Oklahoma.

Dear Mr. Thorn:

I am inclosing herewith my official check #18830, payable to your order for $937.40, also a voucher which you will please sign on the dotted line marked 'X.' and return to me in the inclosed penalty envelope. This covers the original amount of $943.40, less $6.00 paid for quit-claim deeds, which you placed here about 10 years ago to protect the interests of the minor heirs to the Samuel Cummings estate, which allotment you purchased through the county courts. The matter is almost completed now and I have been authorized by the Indian Office at Washington to return the original deposit.

I am also inclosing a voucher covering the interest on the original amount for the period of 10 1/2 years at the rate of 4% per annum. Under instructions from the Indian Office I am not permitted to pay to you at this time this interest. I have been instructed to prepare the voucher, obtain your signature and send to Washington for the Department's consideration and if it thinks the interest should be allowed a check will be sent toyou[sic] direct from the Washington office. It is not customary to allow interest on such deposits but as this is such an unusual case the Department has stated that the payment of interest would be considered. You will be advised later as to what definite action is taken towards such.

I am very glad, and I know you are too, that this matter is drawing to a successful conclusion. It has been a source of such worry and work to this office, yourself and the Indian Office in Washington. Please return the inclosed vouchers signed with ink at the earliest possible date.

Very truly yours,

r-mc

J. L. SUFFECOOL, SUPT.

Probate
75398-12
7517-24
C E T

Shawnee Indian Agency,
Shawnee, Oklahoma,
February 16, 1924.

The Honorable
The Commissioner of Indian Affairs,
Washington, D. C.

My dear Mr. Commissioner:

This will acknowledge receipt of Office communication of above reference under date of February 8, 1924, in which was inclosed a letter from Mrs. Gertie Pratt of Maud, Oklahoma, in reference to the estate of Harriett Pratt, deceased Pottawatomi allottee No. 1328, whose heirs were determined December 16, 1912.

The probate finding which is on file in this office shows that Sevellon Pratt, husband of the above, was entitled to 1/3 of the estate. He was a white man and died the 5th day of July 1922 and left surviving him several children and grand-children. The files of this office disclose that on the 15th day of March 1919 Sevellon Pratt made a will. This will apparently has been duly executed but has not been probated in the local court. I am inclosing a copy of the will for the information of the Office. The funds to the credit of Sevellon Pratt, deceased husband of above allottee, amount to $306.60. According to the terms of the will he gave his entire property, both inherited and personal, to his son Charlie Orville Pratt.

There has been a great deal of controversy with reference to the settling of this estate. This is due to the fact that one of the heirs, Ernest Pratt, son of Sevellon Pratt, deceased, had opposed all actions taken by this office looking toward the settlement of the estate since October 14, 1922. Shortly after the death of Sevellon Pratt the heirs came to the office and requested that I hold a hearing. This request was granted, duly advertised, and a hearing called to be held on the 14th day of October, 1922. All of the interested heirs were present. Testimony was taken and is now on file in this office and it appeared at that time that an amicable settlement would be soon made. However, shortly after this date they apparently began to disagree among themselves. An attempt was made by this office to partition the land and to send the partitionment in with the papers concerning the determination of the heirs. A visit was made to the land in question, an appraisment[sic] made and steps taken toward partition. Earnest[sic] Pratt, one of the participants in the estate, immediately objected claiming that he was not receiving what was justly due him, yet every effort was made to divide the estate as equally as possible. Since that date the matter has come up for discussion in this office by the various heirs from time to time. Unable to reach any settlement before the opening of the farming season for the year of 1923 it became necessary to lease the land. Sealed bids were called for and Ernest Pratt had the highest bid and it was leased to him, using the regular Departmental form of lease. Another lease has been executed on this land for the year of 1924. Sealed bids were called for and received on the 7th of February, 1924. Ernest Pratt again had the highest bid and a lease has been executed in his favor.

The Examiner of Inheritance, Mr. S. Y. Tutwiler, reports that he will be at this unit early in the month of March and it has been decided to refer this matter to him on his arrival and such instructions as he may issue concerning the same will be carried out as far as possible.

Mrs. Gertie Pratt's letter is returned herewith as requested.

Very respectfully,

Incls.   J. L. Suffecool,
S-Mc   Superintendent.

Shawnee Indian Agency,
Shawnee, Oklahoma,
February 19, 1924.

Mrs. Mary Wabskie Wamego

Mayetta, Kansas.

Dear Madam:

This is in reply to your letter of the 13th instant concerning the estate of Myra Nahkasa. It appears that you are under the impression that the heirs in this estate have not been determined. This is to notify you that they have been determined and that you and Pimo Kahdot are the two heirs and now own the remainder of the allotment described as the

NW/4 of NW/4 of Sec. 3, T. 5, R. 4E
and the
NE/4 of NW/4 of Sec. 4, T. 5, R. 4E.

You are further advised that no party can come into this office and by mere statements convince us that they are the owners of this allotment until regularly disposed of by you[sic] heirs through the Department.

Very truly yours,

J. L. Suffecool,
CD-Mc   Superintendent.

Shawnee Indian Agency,
Shawnee, Oklahoma,
February 19, 1924.

Hon. K. C. McMichael,
Attorney at Law,

Sapulpa, Oklahoma.

Dear Sir:

This will reply to your letter of the 11th instant regarding the estate of Alex Gibson wherein Willie Gibson is an heir and concerning which Mary Gibson, now Thompson, your client wishes to be informed. This office recently addressed the Indian Office at Washington regarding the status of the heirship in the estate of Alex Gibson. The Office states that the heirs of Willie Gibson, who is an heir of Alex Gibson, have never been determined and now the Office wishes to know whether Mary Gibson, now Thompson, and the son Willie Gibson, Jr., are still living. Please furnish us with the information as to whether Willie Gibson Jr., is still living. Upon furnishing the office with such information no doubt the heirs of Willie Gibson will be determined in a very short while. Let us hear from you at your earliest convenience.

Very truly yours,

j[sic]. L. Suffecool,

CD-Mc Superintendent.

Shawnee Indian Agency,
Shawnee, Oklahoma,
February 20, 1924.

Mrs. Vestina M. Mohee
  Red Rock, Oklahoma.
  (Through Supt. Hoyo, Whiteagle, Okla.)

Dear Mrs. Mohee:

With further reference to the matter of check #15576, dated May 22, 1923, for $10.28 which was sent you last May as your share of the lease rental from the Charles Murray estate, you are advised that the records shoe[sic] that this check has never been paid by the bank and evidently the same has never been cashed by the party receiving it. In order that you may have a duplicate check issued to you it will be necessary that you make a statement and swear to same before a notary public or some other person qualified to take oaths and sent to me so that I may take proper action towards having the duplicate check issued.

I am inclosing a form giving instructions that you may follow in making such statement. Please return the form with your letter to me.

Very truly yours,

J. L. Suffecool

R-Mc Superintendent.

Shawnee Indian Agency,
Shawnee, Oklahoma,
February 20, 1924.

Mr. S. Y. Tutwiler,
   Examiner of Inheritance,
      Indian Agency,
         Concho, Oklahoma.

Dear Mr. Tutwiler:

   This is to acknowledge receipt of the several notices to be
posted and served on certain Indians in connection with holding hearings
here of deceased Indians. Some of these Indians' whereabouts are known
but the majority do not live within tis vicinity and can not be reached.

   Those that can not be served with notices are as follows:

   Mesquah and Tom Smith, probable heirs of Thy-ka-to-ke,
      Mexican Kickapoo unallotted. These heirs are living in
      Old Mexico and we will be unable to reach them.

   Pay-ko-ne-hah and Nah-me-pay-she-quah, probable heirs of
      Tah-pah-she. Living in Old Mexico.

   Frank Reed or Me-na-miesh, probable heir of Soh-kah-tah--
      Jennie Reed. He lives in Old Mexico at the present time
      but will probably return before your arrival, in which case
      the notice will be served on him.

   Pah-nah-keth-tho, Kee-nah-ko-thet, Kee-ah-tha-com-cke-quah
      and No-ah-ke-peah, probable heirs of Ah-kie-kuck,
      Mexican Kickapoo. All live in Old Mexico. One of the
      probable heirs Peme-pah-ho-neah-quah lives in Oklahoma
      and the notice will be served on her as soon as we can get
      in touch with her.

   The probable heirs of Jane Delaware are scattered. Grace Smith
was last heard of in Shawnee and we will try and reach her. Mark
Smith is in Hayton, Colorado, and we will send a notice to the
Postmaster and request him to serve the notice. Billie Johnson is at
Shawnee, Route 3, and we will try to reach him. Olney, John and Ada
Smiths' whereabouts are unknown but inquiry will be made concerning
them.

Very truly yours,

J. L. Suffecool,
R-Mc   Superintendent.

Shawnee Indian Agency,
Shawnee, Oklahoma,
February 20, 1924.

Mrs. Stella Curtin

Holdenville, Okla.

Dear Mrs. Curtin:

This is to call your attention to a new proposition made by one Mr. Weir, who lives near the Sam Deer allotment, offering to purchase said Sam Deer allotment for the sum of $1,000. It is understood that Mr. Weir will need to purchase this allotment through Hal Johnson, who purchased an interest in the allotment, and that the sum derived from the sale will be equally divided between you and your brother and Hal Johnson; Mr. Johnson taking 1/2 and your brother and yourself taking the other half. This appears to us a better proposition than the first one offered by the purchasers. However, your wishes in this matter will be considered.

I would appreciate your attention to this at as early a date as possible.

Very truly yours,

J. L. Suffecool,
CD-Mc   Superintendent.

Shawnee Indian Agency,
Shawnee, Oklahoma,
February 20, 1924.

Mr. James W. Rodgers,
    Attorney at Law,
        Holdenville, Okla.

Dear Mr. Rodgers:

This is to acknowledge receipt of your letter of February 16, with further reference to the matter of the heirs of Nancy Wilson, a deceased unallotted Shawnee Indian. In compliance with your request I am giving you the names of the heirs as determined by the Department, which are as follows:

Tonely Worth, husband)	1/3
or)	
Toney Wentworth)	
Ida Sloat, Grand-daughter	1/3
Daniel Chisholm, grand-son	1/3
(son of Garfield Ellis)	

Nancy Wilson at the time of her death held 1/2 interest in the W/2 of SW/4 of 21-10-3, Laura Wilson allotment, and 1/2 interest in the SW/4 of NW/4 of 20-10-3, Jerry Wilson allotment. I reviewed the papers on file pertaining to this hearing and do not find that the names of Thomas Deer or Thompson Deer were submitted as possible heirs. I have made inquiry among several of the older Indians as to whether they knew that these boys were sons of Garfield Ellis and none of them seemed to be able to give much information regarding the matter. I am unable to state whether they have any claim in the Nancy Wilson estate or not. At the time the hearing was held testimony was taken from the Shawnee Indians who were in a position to know the family history of Nancy Wilson. Inasmuch as the hearing has been held and the heirs determined, the burden of the proof as to whether Thomas and Thompson Deer were grandsons of Nancy Wilson rests with them and they would be required to submit the necessary papers in showing such if they care to push the matter. The file in the case is here in the office and may be examined by you here and copies of the same may be had if you wish to come here and make the same.

Very truly yours,

J. L. Suffecool,
R-Mc   Superintendent.

Shawnee, Oklahoma

Feb. 25, 1924

Mr. A. R. Snyder
　　Mayetta, Kansas

Dear Mr. Snyder;

　　　　Enclosed my official checks which you will please deliver.
These amounts represents each persons[sic] share in the Lucius A. Darling
Estate which was recently sold for $ 4,111.00[sic] .

18966	Maggie Darling	$177.63
18967	Louis O. Darling	50.75
18968	Anna M. Konkoskie	50.75
18969	Frances E. Steward	50.75
18970	Louise Darling	50.76
18971	George P. Darling	50.76
18972	Lucius J. Darling	50.76
18973	Ernest C. Darling	50.76

Very truly,

Superintendent
J. L. Suffecool

CF

_____

Shawnee Indian Agency,
Shawnee, Oklahoma,
February 25, 1924.

Mr. Wm. H. Layton
　　Route 2
　　Stroud, Oklahoma.

Dear Mr. Layton:

I have received your letter of February 23d with reference to the matter we discussed concerning the south eighty of Irene Jefferson allotment which has been deeded to the minor heirs of Mose Jefferson. I note what you say and of course can not help but agree with your recommendation. You are there on the grounds and have had an opportunity to thoroughly familiarize yourself with the conditions. I therefore request that you see Mr. Regan and advise him that under the existing circumstances it will be necessary for all parties that are now occupying that part of the allotment conveyed to the children[sic] to vacate at once and that no future trespass of this kind be permitted. If this action is not taken by Mr. Regan to cause said premises to be vacated within a reasonable time please report the matter and it will be referred to the United States Attorney.

Very respectfully yours,

J. L. Suffecool,

S-Mc

Superintendent.

Shawnee Indian Agency,
Shawnee, Oklahoma,
February 25, 1924.

Atlantic Oil Producing Co.
Commercial Building,
Tulsa, Oklahoma.

Attention: Mr. Charles B. Ellard

Dear Sir:

This is to acknowledge receipt of your letter of February 19, 1924 with further reference to the matter of furnishing you with proof of death and heirship of Waw such che, also known as Anna Sanache. The employee who was to furnish this information has made diligent search of the records and he has failed to find anything which would be of use to you. He says, after failing to find anything pertaining to the matter, that he had neglected advising you. In view of the circumstances it will not be possible for this office to furnish you the desired information but it is suggested that you take the matter up with the Indian Office at Washington stating what you desire and it may be possible that it can furnish you a copy of the proof of death and heirship records. A nominal fee will be charged for this by the Indian Office at Washington, the amount of which you will be advised if the information can be obtained there.

Very truly yours,

J. L. Suffecool,
R-Mc   Superintendent.

Shawnee Indian Agency,
Shawnee, Oklahoma,
February 25, 1924.

The Postmaster,

Hayton, Colorado.

Dear Sir:

I am inclosing herewith a notice to determine the heirs of Jane Deleware[sic][sic], the mother of Mark Smith, who was formerly a patron of your office. If Mr. Smith is still a patron of your office please have him sign this paper and return to me in the inclosed penalty envelope.

Also please ascertain from Mr. Smith the addresses of Grace, Olney and John Smith so that they may be sent notices.

Thanking you for your assistance, I am

Very truly yours,

j[sic]. L. Suffecool,
R-Mc   Superintendent.

****

Shawnee Indian Agency,
Shawnee, Oklahoma,
February 25, 1924.

The Postmaster,

Hominy, Oklahoma.

Dear Sir:

I am inclosing herewith a notice to determine the heirs of Jane Deleware, the mother of Mark Smith, who was formerly a patron of your office. If Mr. Smith is still a patron of your office please have him sign this paper and return to me in the inclosed penalty envelope.

Also please ascertain from Mr. Smith the addresses of Grace, Olney and John Smith so that they may be sent notices.

Thanking you for your assistance, I am

Very truly yours,

J. L. Suffecool,
R-Mc   Superintendent.

****

Shawnee Indian Agency,
Shawnee, Oklahoma,
February 26, 1924.

Mr. Billy Johnson
    Route #3
        Shawnee, Okla.

Dear Mr. Johnson:

I inclose herewith notice of hearing to be held in April to determine the heirs of Jane Deleware[sic], absentee[sic] Shawnee allottee No. 226.

Please sign this notice and return same to me.

Very truly,

J. L. Suffecool,
--Mc   Superintendent.

Shawnee Indian Agency,
Shawnee, Oklahoma,
February 27, 1924.

Mr. Charles W. Fear
  c/o Charles U. Becker
    Jefferson City, Mo.

Dear Mr. Fear:

This is to acknowledge receipt of your letter of the 23d in which you make further inquiry regarding the heirship or your deceased wife. You state that some weeks ago Mr. Tutwiler has recommended that Mrs. H. E. Carter and yourself be recognized as the legal heirs of Mrs. Fear. As to this I am unable to give information as the approved Departmental findings have not been received by this office to date. When this notice has been received you will be advised as to the heirs of Mrs. Fear. Immediately upon the approval of these findings the money accumulated as rental to the credit of Mrs. Fear will be disbursed to the proper heirs.

The farm and oil and gas lease rentals for the year 1922 were paid to Mrs. Fear prior to her death. There is at present on hand the amount of $208.69 which is derived from leases as follows:

Agricultural lease for 1923, her share-	$100.00
Oil and gas lease for 1923, her share-	106.66
Interest-	2.03

The agricultural lease for 1924 has been prepared for a consideration of $125 but up to date the lease is incomplete but no doubt will receive approval. The next payment on the oil and gas lease is due July 31, 1924 and Mrs. Fear's share of that will be $106.67. I suppose the oil and gas company will continue to keep the oil lease on the land as I have heard nothing to the contrary.

I am unable to give you the present address of John Keokuk. However, his last address as given us is Shamrock, Oklahoma.

You may rest assured that after the hearing to determine Mrs. Fear's heirs has received Departmental approval that any funds to her credit will be immediately disbursed to the heirs. You will remember though that there will be a fee due the Government for holding this hearing and the same will be deducted from her balance here before disbursing the funds.

Very truly yours,

J. L. Suffecool,
Superintendent.

R-Mc

Probate
42139-21
71947-23
M H W

Shawnee Indian Agency,
Shawnee, Oklahoma,
March 4, 1924.

The Commissioner of Indian Affairs.
Washington, D. C.

Dear Mr. Commissioner:

With further reference to Office letter of recent date concerning a petition which was to be prepared by the heirs of Franklin Wilamette concerning a claim against the Wilamette estate presented by Mrs. Anna M. Linescum, the Office is advised that the letter in question has been located and steps are now being taken to ascertain from the heirs their desires in the matter.

After as many signatures as can be secured to the land sale petition are obtained the petition with the statement of objections, if any, by the heirs will be forwarded to the Office for consideration and action.

Very truly yours,

J. L. Suffecool,
Superintendent.

JLR-Mc

Sac & Fox – Shawnee Estates
1920-1924 Volume IX

Ed-Ind.
11289-24
ESS

Shawnee Indian Agency,
Shawnee, Oklahoma,
March 4, 1924.

The Commissioner of Indian Affairs.
Washington, D. C.

Dear Mr. Commissioner:

This is to acknowledge receipt of carbon copy of Office letter of the 28th of February, bearing file as above, to Nah-mah-tuck-ke of McLoud, Oklahoma, regarding the distribution of funds derived from the estates of Okemah and Thi-the-quah, both deceased.

In reply the Office is advised that the allotments of both of these deceased Indians had patents in fee issued thereon in 1907, prior to the death of the allottees, hence no interest will be conveyed to the heirs from these estates. O-ke-mah was declared the sole heir of the estate of Paw-ka-tuck (L-H 48344-14 EGT) and O-ke-mah's heirs were determined according to Probate 828-19 L.S. Nah-mah-tuck-ke is an heir to one-sixth interest of the Paw-ka-tuck estate through O-ke-mah. At the present time there are no funds to the credit of the account of O-ke-mah and a the Thi-the-quah estate has no interest whatever under this jurisdiction it has no account here.

Several years ago the estate of Ke-she-she was sold and the funds derived from this sale were distributed among the heirs as then determined. O-ke-mah being one of the parties determined as heirs, but it later developed that George Kish-ke-ton, a grand-nephew of the decedent was the sole heir and the distribution of the funds was erroneous. After the error was discovered steps were then taken to have the parties who had received the funds erroneously to reimburse George Kish-ke-ton. Some collections have been made and steps are being taken to make collections whenever debtor Indians have funds to their credit. As a result of this erroenous[sic] distribution O-ke-mah received $338.67 and under authority (Probate 77850-20, 107295-14, LAP) issued for the payment of funds from O-ke-man's account to George Kish-ke-ton this amount has been set up as an obligation against the O-ke-mah account and any funds placed to the credit of the account will be held for the purpose of liquidating this long-standing obligation.

It is noted that Nah-mah-tuck-ke seems to be under the impression that money is being held here belonging to the estate of O-ke-mah and Thi-the-quah but at the present time no funds are here to the

195

credit of either of the accounts as the funds derived from the estate in which O-kemah was interested have been divided and paid out to the proper heirs immediately upon receipt of the same. Thi-the-quah, as stated above, has no interest here now. It is the intention however, in the future, to hold funds that may belong to the heirs of O-ke-mah for the purpose of liquidating the account of George Kish-ke-ton.

Returned herewith is Nah-mah-tuck-ke's letter.

Very truly yours,

J. L. Suffecool,
JLR-Mc   Superintendent.

Ed-Ind.
95829-14
11106-24
E S S

Shawnee Indian Agency,
Shawnee, Oklahoma,
March 4, 1924.

The Commissioner of Indian Affairs.
Washington, D. C.

Dear Mr. Commissioner:

This is to acknowledge receipt of carbon copy of Office letter of February 25th to Mr. George H. Lybarger of Fort Scott, Kansas, in reply to his communication making inquiry about the estates of Hellen Cook and Peter the Great.

In reply the Office is advised that Mr. Lybarger is an heir to the estate of Hellen Cook, which is not leased for the present year, and as there is not much demand for lands of the character at the present there is not much possibility of either a lease or the sale of this estate for the coming year. Funds derived from the rental of this estate have been forwarded to Mr. Lybarger after the same have been properly accounted for in this office.

I am unable to give any information as regards the estate of Peter the Great as it appears that this land was sold in 1901 and is not now under Governmental restrictions.

Returned herewith is Mr. Lybarger's letter.

Very truly yours,

J. L. Suffecool,
JLR-Mc   Superintendent.

Shawnee Indian Agency,
Shawnee, Oklahoma,
March 4, 1924.

Mr. A. R. Snyder,
    Supt. Potawatomi Agency,
        Mayetta, Kansas.

Dear Mr. Snyder:

I have your letter of February 27th in which you request the
addresses of the below names[sic] Indians who are heirs to the M-ko-k-gih-
maw estate:

ah-then-a-ah[sic] or Ah-sene-he-ah; in Old Mexico.
Ah-nah-thote; deceased. Heirs live here.
Come-so-quah or Ke-ma-si-quah; Old Mexico.
Kup-pah-ke-quah or Kah-pah-pe-ko-quah; lives here.
Mat-ti-ah; Old Mexico.
Wab-sose or Wah-pah-sose; deceased.
Pah-ah-kuk-koke; No information concerning him.
Ne-mah-ko-wah; Has account here; whereabouts unknown.
Nam-ah-tho; deceased.

All of the above have accounts here except Pam-ah-kuk-koke,
and he may have an account here under some other name but I am unable
to determine that as none of our Indians here seem to know him. It also
appears that Mat-ti-ah is under the name of Mah-ti-yot here, if the person
is one and the same. I will make inquiry from the Kickapoo or
Potawatomi Indians concerning this last again and see if they can help me
identify this party.

Very truly yours,

J. L. Suffecool,
R-Mc   Superintendent.

Shawnee Indian Agency,
Shawnee, Oklahoma,
March 5, 1924.

Mr. Leo Whistler

    Lynch Hotel
    Stroud, Oklahoma.

Dear Mr. Whistler:

    This is to acknowledge receipt of your two letters of March 3d, the first asking about the determination of the heirs of Marie A. Fear, your former wife, and the other about lease money due you from the Phoebe Keokuck[sic] allotment.

    In reply you are advised that the heirs of Marie A. Fear's estate have just been recently determined and they are Charles W. Fear and Ruby Lee Carter, each receiving one-half of the estate. I note in your letter that you state you were never divorced from Mrs. Fear but according to information obtained from the hearing it appears that a court decree was granted February 15, 1893 in Lincoln County divorcing you and Mrs. Fear.

    In regard to the lease money from the Phoebe Keokuk land will state that the lease up to the present time for the year 1924 has not been approved but the same is being placed in line for early action. It appears that some trouble has been had in the preparation of the lease this year, but I believe it will be signed up and approved shortly.

Very truly yours,

J. L. Suffecool,
R-Mc   Superintendent.

Shawnee Indian Agency,
Shawnee, Oklahoma,
March 5, 1924.

Mr. Ben F. Coon

Maud, Oklahoma.

Dear Mr. Coon:

This is to acknowledge receipt of your letter of the 3d concerning the heirs of Margaret Bedell. You state in your letter that you do not wish the funds derived from the rental of this estate to be disbursed or distributed to Leonard H. Coon.

Since Mr. Leonard H. Coon has been determined an heir and you feel that there is some doubt as to his right in inheriting in this estate it will be up to you to produce evidence that the findings approved by the Department are erroneous. If you can produce such evidence and have the same properly supported you may present same to me at this office and I will in turn take the matter up with the Department at Washington. The share belonging to Leonard H. Coon is being held here until something definite has been established as to whether he was erroneously declared an heir.

Very truly yours,

J. L. Suffecool,
R-Mc   Superintendent.

Shawnee Indian Agency,
Shawnee, Oklahoma,
March 6, 1924.

Mrs. Ruby L. Carter

838 Putnam Street
Detroit, Michigan.

Dear Mrs. Carter:

I incolse[sic] herewith my official check No. 19142 for $9.85, payable to your order.

You no doubt are aware that you and Mr. Charles W. Fear have been determined heirs to the estate of Mrs. Marie A. Fear, each of you inheriting one-half of the same.

The inclosed check represents one-half of the balance Mrs. Fear had to the credit of her account, after $25.00 had been deducted for paying the hearing fee.

Very truly yours,

J. L. Suffecool,
--Mc   Superintendent.

Shawnee Indian Agency,
Shawnee, Oklahoma,
March 6, 1924.

Mr. Morris Welch

Box 83
Bartlett, Kansas.

Dear Mr. Welch:

Enclosed herewith are checks in your favor as follows:

#18983   -- $91.35
 189931   --   1.34

The check for $91.35 represents your share in the Lucius A. Darling estate. This allotment was sold for $4,111.00 and your interest, according to the heirship findings, was 54/2430.

The check for $1.34 represents the balance of your account here.

Very truly yours,

J. L. Suffecool,
--Mc   Superintendent.

Shawnee Indian Agency,
Shawnee, Oklahoma,
March 6, 1924.

Stanard & Ennis,
     Attorneys.

     Shawnee, Oklahoma.

Gentlemen:

     Referring to your letter of the 5th instant I inclose my
official check #19150 for $215.00 payable to Emma
Griffenstein. This is to apply on her claim against the estate
of Catherine Griffenstein and represents the balance to the
credit of said estate.

                              Very truly yours,

                              J. L. Suffecool,
--Mc   Superintendent.

Shawnee Indian Agency,
Shawnee, Oklahoma,
March 6, 1924.

Mrs. Charles N. Darling

     Whitman County
     Palouse, Washington.

Dear Madam:

     It has been reported to us that your husband recently died. In case
this is true please advise us if the estate has been probated and if so give
the names of the heirs.

     Mr. Darling has an interest in the Lucius A. Darling estate. This
land was sold some time ago and your husband has to his credit the sum
of $532.90, as his share in the land sale.

Very truly yours,

J. L. Suffecool,
--Mc   Superintendent.

Shawnee Indian Agency,
Shawnee, Oklahoma,
March 6, 1924.

Mr. A. R. Snyder,
    Supt. Potawatomi Agency,
        Mayetta, Kansas.

Dear Mr. Snyder:

I am inclosing herewith my official check #19154 drawn on the account of Ida Nullake and payable to your order for $166.60 which is transferred to you to apply on the Jessie Lee estate funds from which were erroneously divided.

Your letter of May 13, 1922 states that Frank Smith is sole heir to the estate and that any funds which had been paid to Ida Nullake and Philip Lee should be returned to your office to be credited to Frank Smith's account. Mrs. Nullake's account has been credited at different times with small amounts until she received the inclosed amount. You will note that the check is for $166.60, whereas her indebtedness of $166.66. This small balance of six cents will be forwarded to you when she has more funds to the credit of her account. The amount owed by Philip Lee was taken up on your ledgers under your official receipt #493059, November 8, 1923.

At your convenience please return this amount to me so that Frank Smith's account may be credited with it.

Thanking you, I am

Very truly yours,

J. L. Suffecool,

R-Mc   Superintendent.

Probate
18376-19
C E T

Shawnee Indian Agency,
Shawnee, Oklahoma,
March 6, 1924.

The Commissioner of Indian Affairs,
Washington, D. C.

Dear Mr. Commissioner:

Reference is made to Office letter, dated February 7, 1924, reference as above, regarding the estate of Willie Gibson, whose heirs are undetermined.

Complying with the above Office letter I have to advise that Mary Gibson, now Mary Thompson, and Willie Gibson, Jr., widow and son of said Willie Gibson and his probable heirs, are still living and now reside at Sapulpa, Oklahoma.

The appraisements called for in said Office letter covering the allotment of Alex Gibson and Quah-qua-che-qua are inclosed herewith.

The Office will please refer to Probate bearing reference 71675-21 S Y T. In this finding it appears that Willie Gibson is not an heir to the estate of said Quah-qua-che-qua.

The amount of $77.27 is held to the credit of the Willie Gibson estate.

Very truly yours,

J. L. Suffecool,
D-Mc   Superintendent.

Shawnee Indian Agency,
Shawnee, Oklahoma,
March 6, 1924.

Mr. A. R. Snyder,
    Supt. Potawatomi Agency,
      Mayetta, Kansas.

Dear Mr. Snyder:

    A request has been made by Py-a-tho, Kickapoo Indian belonging here, regarding the estate of Pe-se-kah-kes-kuk, under your agency.

    Py-a-tho states that she is an heir in this estate and now wishes further information concerning the same.

Very truly yours,

J. L. Suffecool,
D/Mc   Superintendent.

Shawnee Indian Agency,
Shawnee, Oklahoma,
March 8, 1924.

Mr. A. R. Snyder,
    Supt. Potawatomi Agency,
      Mayetta, Kansas.

Dear Mr. Snyder:

    This is in reply to your letter of February 27, last, and willalso[sic] reply to a letter from Mary Wamego, under date of February 29, regarding the estate of Myra Nahkasa.

    As stated before, Mary Wamego and Pimo Kahdot were the heirs in this estate, therefore, after the death of Pimo Kahdot, the property may descend to Mary Wamego as sole heir but the heirs of said Pimo Kahdot have not yet been determined. Papers concerning the hearing are in the examiner's files in this office and further attention to the matter will be given by the examiner when he arrives here and your letter will be referred to him for whatever action he concludes is necessary.

The allotment of Myra Nahkasa consists of 80 acres described as the NW/4 of NW/4 of 3-5-4 and NE/4 of NW/4 of 4-5-5 still held in trust. This tract of land appears to be of little value and has not been leased through this office for years, therefore it appears that there are no funds to the credit of the estate.

Very respectfully,

J. L. Suffecool,
D/Mc   Superintendent.
Copy to
Mary Wamego
Mayetta, Kans.

Shawnee Indian Agency,
Shawnee, Oklahoma,
March 8, 1924.

Mrs. Irene Cadue

Powhattan, Kansas.

Dear Madam:

In reply to your letter of February 28th last requesting for information concerning land supposed to be allotted to Bennie Dick, I have to advise you that after careful search no party by the name of Bennie Dick appears enrolled in this office. Further your letter does not contain sufficient information to enable us to make a satisfactory search for the reason that Bennie Dick may be enrolled under some other name. If you will kindly give us further information such as description of the land we may be able to do better for you but it is not believed that there is such an estate under this agency.

Very truly yours,

J. L. Suffecool,
CD-Mc   Superintendent.

Shawnee Indian Agency,
Shawnee, Oklahoma,
March 10, 1924.

Mr, Milton Carter

Cushing, Okla.

My dear Friend:

This will acknowledge receipt of your letter of the 6th in which you speak of what you desire done with the allotment of your deceased wife Ella Carter, who died about two weeks ago.

In reply you are advised that I was in Cushing the day after your wife died with the deeds and expected to go down and have her sign them. When I suggested this to Mr. Collins he told me that your wife had died the night before. In view of the fact that Mrs. Carter is now dead it is not possible to deed the eighty to your son, as her estate will have to be probated and her heirs declared. I regret that I am not able to help you in this respect.

Very respectfully,

J. L. Suffecool,
Superintendent.

S/M

Shawnee Indian Agency.

Shawnee, Oklahoma,
March 10, 1924.

Miss Iola Powers,
407 N. Roosevelt St.,
Shawnee, Oklahoma.

Dear Miss Powers:

Enclosed herewith is my official check drawn on the Treasurer of the United States, payable to your order for $5.66, check No. 4529. This is the increase of compensation allowed by the Government after proper certification allowed by the Government after proper certification, due you for your work at this Agency from January 4, at noon to January 14, 1924.

Very truly yours,

_____

J. L. Suffecool,
Superintendent.

AMS.

DEPARTMENT OF THE INTERIOR

UNITED STATES INDIAN FIELD SERVICE

Potawatomi Indian Agency
Mayetta, Kansas
March 7, 1924.

RECEIVED
MAR 1 1924
SHAWNEE INDIAN
AGENCY

Supt. J. L. Suffecool,
Shawnee Indian Agency,
Shawnee, Oklahoma.

Dear Mr. Suffecool:

It is reported here that Pack-ta-neece who died on this reservation a few years ago, but who belonged under your jurisdiction, had certain interest down there at the time of his death. His nephew, Joe Turtle, has requested that I write you concerning this matter.

If you can give me any information that would be of interest to him, I would be pleased to pass it on to him.

Very truly yours,
    A. R. Snyder
A. R. Snyder
Superintendent
ARS:AW

****

207

Shawnee Indian Agency,
Shawnee, Oklahoma,
March 12, 1924.

Mr. A. R. Snyder,
    Supt. Potawatomi Agency.
      Mayetta, Kansas.

Dear Mr. Snyder:

Replying to your letter of March 7th in which you state that Pack-ta-neece died on your reservation a few years ago and who belonged under this jursidiction[sic] you are advised that I am unable to locate any allotment or inherited interest belonging to one by the name given.

It may be that he was known under some other name than that reported to you by Joe Turtle his nephew, who you state is making inquiry concerning the matter. If such be the case please advise me and I will look further into the matter.

Very truly yours,

J. L. Suffecool,
R/M   Superintendent.

Shawnee Indian Agency,
Shawnee, Oklahoma,
March 13, 1924.

Mr. A. R. Snyder,
    Supt. Potawatomi Agency.
      Mayetta, Kansas.

Dear Mr. Snyder:

I inclose herewith two letters received from Susan Masquas and Oliver LeClere representing claims against the estate of Kahdot Pemo[sic].

As these came from your agency I would ask that you kindly investigate same and if in your opinion they are authentic and just please place your approval upon them, and return to me. I will then file the claims and when the estate is ready for settlement will present them in behalf of these two parties.

Very truly yours,

J. L. Suffecool,
Mc/   Superintendent.

Shawnee Indian Agency,
Shawnee, Oklahoma,
March 13, 1924.

Mr. A. R. Snyder,
        Supt. Potawatomi Agency,
            Mayetta, Kansas.

Dear Mr. Snyder:

Referring to your letter of January 23d, I am inclosing herewith three sets of "Application for Tribal Payment Shares' form 5-172 signed by the heir or heirs in each case.

So far we have not secured Joe Murdock's signature as heir to Man-ah-quah, but as soon as same is secured we will forward the application to you.

Very truly yours,

J. L. Suffecool,
Mc   Superintendent.

Shawnee Indian Agency,
Shawnee, Oklahoma,
Mar. 15, 1924.

Mr. W. M. Williams,
New Hotel Alexander,
Tulsa, Oklahoma.

Dear Sir:

There is returned to you a cashier's check 73919 in the sum of $1.75 which you remitted to this office for a copy of proof of heirship to the estate of Nab-wah-kuk, in connection with title to land described as Lot. 1 of Sec. 5, Twp. 5 N., R. 5 E. I. M.

It will be necessary for you to address the Commissioner of Indian Affairs, Washington, D. C. as there is no copy on file in this office. We are indeed sorry we could not serve you. In a great number of cases we have the probate finding, especially the cases determined since the Act of June 25, 1910 was ~~pass~~ enacted.

Very truly yours,

J. L. Suffecool,
Supt. & Spl. Disb. Agt.

101173-23

Shawnee Indian Agency,
Shawnee, Oklahoma,
Mar. 15, 1924.

The Honorable
Commissioner of Indian Affairs,
Washington, D. C.

Dear Mr. Commissioner:

The Office will again refer, please, to my report dated Jan. 31, of the above reference relative to two allotments, viz, Alex Gibson and Ahl wa pa ma[sic], Absentee Shawnee allotments numbered 438 and 439 respectively.

Both of these allotments are within the Little River Drainage District, Pottowatomie[sic] County, Okla., and as shown on schedule of assessments bearing file No. 92052-12 dated Sept. 7, 1912 they are assessed at $297.75 against the Alex Gibson allotment and $180.00 against the Ahl wah pa ma allotment,

The owner of the unrestricted portion of the Ahl wah pa ma allotment (439) states that he is not willing to make an offer for the restricted part belonging to the other heirs but would be willing to have this office offer the land for sale. An offer was made by the owner of unrestricted portion of the Alex Gibson allotment as reported in my letter of Jan. 31, 1924, mentioned above, of $1000.00 for the remainder of this allotment or he will take $500, and 1/3 of the rents (the rents for the 5 year period amount $953.15), therefore they are asking over $800, for their 1/3 interest. We appraise the land and improvements at $2,500.00

In the Ahl wah pa ma estate the heirs who hold their interests are all minors. There are some minors in the Alex Gibson estate. After the Office has given consideration to the foregoing and other correspondence regarding these two allotments I will be pleased to be given such instructions as the Office deems proper.

Very respectfully,

3 od 15.

J. L. Suffecool,
Supt. & Spl. Disb. Agt.

Shawnee Indian Agency,
Shawnee, Oklahoma,
March 15, 1924.

Mr. Arley Burks
    Route 7
    Norman, Oklahoma.

My dear Sir:

I am referring to your lease on Potawatomi allotment #424, being the allotment of Oscar Little Doctor, deceased, covering the E/2 of the NW of Sec. 20-9-1, containing 80 acres, for a term of two years from the first day of January 1924.

Jean Little Doctor, one of the heirs in the allotment was in this office this evening and reported that you and she were having some little difficulty concerning chickens and cows, etc. From what I would gather from her conversation it would appear that you have ordered her to shut up her chickens and not allow them to have the range around the place where she lives. I regret that this condition has come about. It is not hardly possible for Jean to make a living and get along without her chickens and I think it would be rather cruel to cause her to have to keep the same shut up. You probably have a legal right to demand this but I doubt very much the wisdom of a course of this kind. I am writing you this letter with the hope that it may be possible for you and Jean to talk this matter over and reach some sort of an adjustment that will be agreeable to you both.   /[sic]

We are very much interested in the lessee and lessor in all of our leases and always wish that they get along together. Please let me hear from you at an early date and would be glad for you to go over and see Jean and see what can be done.

Very truly yours,

S/Mc
Copy to
Jean Little Doctor
Norman, Route 7.

J. L. Suffecool,
Superintendent.

Shawnee Indian Agency,
Shawnee, Oklahoma,
March 17, 1924.

Mr. A. R. Snyder,
　　Supt. Potawatomi Agency,
　　　Mayetta, Kansas.

Dear Mr. Snyder:

Enclosed herewith are checks as follows from the Mary Blandin estate lease to be taken up by you to the credit of the proper parties:

```
#19281  for $67.24, acct. of Samuel Blandin
    2   "    67.00,   "  "  Leonora      "
    3   "    67.00,   "  "  James V.     "
```

Very truly yours,

J. L. Suffecool,
Superintendent.

Mc/

Sac & Fox – Shawnee Estates
1920-1924 Volume IX

Shawnee Indian Agency,
Shawnee, Oklahoma,
March 17, 1924.

Mr. Charles W. Fear,
  c/o Secretary of State,
    Jefferson City, Mo.

Dear Mr. Fear:

      I am in receipt of your letter of the 12th making inquiry concerning funds which had accumulated as rental to the estate of your deceased wife Mrs. Marie A. Fear. You state that you are in receipt of my official check for $91.84 and that Mrs. Carter also has received my official check for $91.85 representing the interest due you two from this estate.

      You do not seem to understand why the $25.00 was deducted for hearing fee and request me to cite you the authority for retaining this amount for the purpose of paying the hearing fee. You are advised that under the Congressional Act of ~~January 24, 1923~~ Feb. 14 1889 (48 Stats. L. ~~1174, 1105~~ 40 413) all hearings hears by the examiner of inheritance from the Interior Department must be settled for from monies derived from that estate. You will readily see that the same was not deducted arbitrarily but done according to law. You further seem to think that such hearing was unnecessary but in order that the proper division of the estate may be had this was necessary under Departmental Regulations and the laws of the land. You further state that you did not request such a hearing. If I can understand your letters of the past few months it would appear that you were very anxious that the estate be probated at the earliest possible date and special efforts were made by this office, the Indian Office, and the Examiner of Inheritance to comply with your wishes in the matter. Quite a little time was spent by this office and Mr. Tutwiler in gathering the information so that a hearing could be held. There are quite a few cases to be determined at this agency. Several have been pending many months prior to your case and in order to accommodate you the matter of holding hearing on these cases was deferred so that Mrs. Fear's estate might be probated, All parties concerned have taken a special interest in this matter in order that you might be accommodated and I believe you have assumed an attitude in the matter which would give us reason to believe that you thought the proper attention was not been given the matter. You also state in your letter that you expect to go to Washington within the next two months and will try to secure a copy of the decree or decision regarding your rights to Mrs. Fear's property rendered by Mr. Tutwiler. No doubt the Indian Office will be very glad to give you this information and explain fully to you why $25.00 was deducted.

213

Very truly yours,

J. L. Suffecool,
R/M   Superintendent.

Shawnee Indian Agency,
Shawnee, Oklahoma,
March 22, 1924.

Mr. C. J. Greiffenstein[sic]

    c/o Tulsa Shirt Co.
    Tulsa, Oklahoma.

Dear Sir:

    I am in receipt of your letter written to Mr. Snake relative to the claim of Emma Greiffenstein against the estate of Katherine Greiffenstein. Against the claim of $800 there has been paid $599.03 leaving a balance still due of $240.97. This will be paid from the estate when funds accumulate to this amount. After this claim has been settled the money derived from the rental of the estate will be distributed according to the probate findings.

    Relative to the damage to the place done by the drainage ditch, I have to advise that this matter is still pending and is now in the hands of the U. S. Attorney for some action. I can not state just now what the outcome will be.

Very truly yours,

J. L. Suffecool,
R/Mc   Superintendent.

Shawnee Indian Agency,
Shawnee, Oklahoma,
March 26, 1924.

Mr. Charles W. Fear
   c/o Secretary of State.
     Jefferson City, Mo.

Dear Mr. Fear:

Replying to your letter of the 23d in which you ask further concerning the estate of your deceased wife Marie A. Fear I have to advise that the hearing held in the district court at Tecumseh is of little consequence concerning lands and estates still held in trust by the Government. Since the estate in which your wife was interested is still restricted the matter of determining the heirs was attended to by the Department of the Interior under the act of Congress quoted you in my previous letter. The Department does not recognize the probate matters as determined by county courts where trust lands are involved. I might say that you were put to a needless expense by having a hearing held here in the county courts.

I am inclosing herewith copy of departmental findings for your information as per your request.

Inasmuch as this land is still held in trust and there are several heirs to the Phorbe[sic] Keokuk allotment it will be necessary for you and your daughter and the other heirs to come to some agreement as to what you wish to do; whether to partition the land under Departmental regulations or all of you sign a petition for the Department to grant a patent in fee and then sell the land outright. There are several ways in which this may be done. The land could be partitioned as aforesaid or all heirs could sign a petition for the sale or make application for patent in fee. In either of the three cases you and your daughter will be given the control of your share or the proceeds derived from the sale in case the Department approves the request. In the event new leases are made on the land in the future you and your daughter will be requested to accept or reject the terms of the lessee. Since all of the heirs concerned are competent to transact their own business affairs I would suggest that all of you come to some agreement as to what you wish to do.

Sometime ago you asked me to furnish you the address of John Earl Keokuk. Just recently I received a letter from him at Shelby, Montana, and I suppose a letter addressed to him there would reach him.

Shawnee Indian Agency,
Shawnee, Oklahoma,
April 8, 1924.

Mr. George A. Hoyo,
    Supt. Ponca Agency,
        Whiteagle, Oklahoma.

Dear Mr. Hoyo:

      This has reference to your letter of March 25th regarding the interests of George and Charles Dailey and Miriam Dent in the estate of Kerwin Murray through Frances O. English.

      It appears that Robert Roubidoux will not be able to purchase the interests of these people and it also appears that it would not be advisable to sell the Kerwin Murray estate at this time for the reason that the Dailey's and Miriam Dent have only about 1/12 interest in the estate and that Robert Roubidoux's wife and her children own 1/2 of it. Roubidoux is making his home on this place and the farmer, Mr. A. B. Collins of Cushing, Oklahoma, advises that leasing arrangements have been effected by Roubidoux and the same has been transmitted to you for the signature of the heirs up there. I am taking the position that all of these inherited estates should be closed at as early a date as it can reasonably be accomplished and the estate of Kerwin Murray will be given further consideration and some arrangement made so that these shares can at least be reduced by the purchase by some of the heirs or the other heirs interests.

     Very truly yours,

     A. W. Leech,
D/Mc   Superintendent.

16054

Shawnee Indian Agency,
Shawnee, Oklahoma,
April 9, 1924.

The Commissioner of Indian Affairs,
    Washington, D. C.

S i r:

With further reference to the letter written by Mr. Thomas Ray Lybarger of Fort Scott, Kansas, under date of February 26, 1924, in which he makes inquiry concerning the Lybarger boys' interest in the estate of Peter the Great, the Office is advised that the matter was taken up with Mr. A. R. Snyder concerning the proceeds from the sale of this land which was sold many years ago and I am inclosing herewith a copy of a letter from Mr. Snyder, Superintendent of the Potawatomi Agency, Mayetta, Kansas, concerning these funds. This, I believe, gives as much information as this office is able to obtain.

Returned herewith is Mr. Lybarger's letter.

Very truly yours,

A. W. Leech,
R/Mc   Superintendent.

Shawnee Indian Agency,
Shawnee, Oklahoma,
April 9, 1924.

Mrs. Dave Anderson

Route #3, Box 6
Choctaw, Oklahoma.

Dear Madam:

This is to acknowledge receipt of your letter of the 8th in which you make inquiry as to why your mother did not come in as an heir on the Lucius Darling farm which was sold recently. You state that you wonder why she does not come in through her son William O. Darling.

From the information given me I am unable to answer your questions. You have not given me the name of your mother nor shown where she would have any connection with the Lucius Darling estate. Please advise me who William O. Darling was, what connection he had with the Lucius Darling estate, when and at what age he died and whether or not he had any children, and any other information concerning this matter. Upon receipt of this information the matter will be looked into thoroughly.

Very truly yours,

A. W. Leech,
Superintendent.

R-Mc

Shawnee Indian Agency,
Shawnee, Oklahoma,
April 9, 1924.

Mr. H. T. Riddle.

Shawnee National Bank.
Shawnee, Oklahoma.

Dear Mr. Riddle:

This is to acknowledge the receipt of your letter of the 5th in which you bring to my attention the Nallie[sic] Charley matter.

I have called this case to the attention of the Examiner of Inheritance and he informs me that any time Nellie Charley calls here the matter will be looked into. It appears that this case has been set for hearing a time or two but the Examiner has failed to get Nellie to testify. I have talked to her brother and he informs me that he will try to persuade Nellie to come to the office and give testimony in this matter. In the event that you see Nellie it might be well that you suggest that she come over and give testimony so that this matter may be closed up.

Very truly yours,

A. W. Leech,
Superintendent.

R-Mc

Shawnee Indian Agency,
Shawnee, Oklahoma,
April 9, 1924.

Mrs. Christine Tyner
  Skiatook, Oklahoma.

Dear Mrs. Tyner:

I have your letter of the 8th in which you make inquiry concerning lease money due you and the children derived from the estate of your deceased husband. In reply you are advised that at the present time no lease money has been paid into this office and there is no lease on the land. This matter will be brought to his attention soon. There is nothing that we can do to assist you since you have no funds here.

Very truly yours,

R/Mc

A. W. Leech,
Superintendent.

Shawnee Indian Agency,
Shawnee, Oklahoma,
April 9, 1924.

Mr. Davis Tyner

  Route #6
    Shawnee, Okla.

Dear Sir:

You are farming the Tyner land in which you are one-half owner. The other heirs are making inquiry as to the lease money due from this estate. Since you are one of the heirs and are living on the land I am requesting that you make a payment into this office at your earliest convenience for the share of the estate belonging to the other heirs as they are needing it badly they state.

Thanking you for your prompt attention, I am

Very truly yours,

A W. Leech,
R-Mc   Superintendent.

Shawnee Indian Agency,
Shawnee, Oklahoma,
April 10, 1924.

Hon. Mark Goode,
Goode and Diarker Lawyers,
Shawnee, Oklahoma.

Dear Mr. Goode:

This has reference to the rentals due the Indians heirs from the lessee on the allotment of James Bullfrog, described as the E/2 of the SW/4 of Section 35, Twp. 11 N., R. 2 East.

I note your letter to this office dated July 27, 1923 as to the position you take in this matter, viz., that no money wpuld[sic] be paid as rental from this land. There is being prepared a formal report to the United States Attorney for the collection of the rentals and before this was done Mr. Carson's attention was called to this and a promise was made to him that the formal report would not be made until we heard from him further. A promise was also made to him that a letter would be written to you stating at some length our position in the matter.

The action taken in this case is based solely in the manner the sale was approved of the Bullfrog land by the Department. The sale was made to A. L. Straughan[sic] upon an actual agreement by the Straughans that they would pay the Indians $8000.00 net. They would claim no back rentals, etc. The sale was approved May 25, 1923, therefore, there is due the Indians 5/12 of $500.00. The sum of $500.00 is the rentals for the entire allotment. The amount required to settle with the heirs owning the restricted portion of this land is $194.15.

I sincerely hope that a settlement can be effected so that it will not be necessary to again refer this case at this time to the United States Court. I will be pleased to have your decision in this at an early date.

Very respectfully,

od   A. W. Leech,   Supt. & S D A.
CC   E. T. Carson,
Shawnee, Oklahoma.

****

[The above letter given again, below, but with revisions.]

Shawnee Indian Agency,
Shawnee, Oklahoma,
April 10, 1924.

Hon. Mark Goode,
Goode and Dierker Lawyers,
Shawnee, Oklahoma.

Dear Mr. Goode:

This has reference to the rentals due the Indian heirs from the lessee on the allotment of James Bullfrog described as the E/2 of the SW/4, 38-11 N., R. 2 East.

I note your letter dated July 27, 1923 as to the position you take in this matter, viz., that no money will be paid as rental from this land. There is being prepared a formal submittal to the United States Attorney for the collection of the rentals and before this was done Mr. E. T. Carson's attention was called to this and a promise was made to him that the formal report would not be made until we heard from him further. A promise was also made to him that a letter would be written to you stating at some length our position in the matter.

The action taken in this case is based solely in the manner the sale of the Bullfrog land was approved by the Department. The sale was made to A. L. Straughan upon an actual agreement by the Straughans that they would pay the Indians $8000.00 net. They would claim no back rentals, etc. The sale was approved May 25, 1923, therefore, there is due the Indians 5/12 of $500.00. The sum of $500.00 is the rental for the entire allotment. The amount required to settle with the heirs owning the restricted portion of this land is $194.15.

The Bullfrog matter of the sale of the interest owned and the share sold by Charley Tyner was settled by the approval of the sale but this matter will have to be reopened in settling this rental matter. The question for decision on the part of Mr. Carson is as to whether he will direct the payment of the $194.15 by the lessee or have the interest he owns actually of the Bullfrog land given further attention of the United States Court. We will be pleased to have you decision in this at an early date .

Very truly yours,

A. W. Leech,   Supt.

CC, E. T. Carson,
        Shawnee, Okla.

Probate
24598-24
C E T

Shawnee Indian Agency,
Shawnee, Oklahoma,
April 15, 1924.

The Commissioner of Indian Affairs.
Washington, D. C.

S i r:

This is to acknowledge receipt of Office letter of the 12th instant having attached thereto a letter from Mr. Joe Tanwas of Horton, Kansas, making inquiry concerning the estate of John Sub-ne, or Sub-ne.

An examination has been made of the Citizen Band of Pottawatomie Indians and I am unable to locate an allottee by the name given. Neither am I able to locate any inherited interest that he might have held in trust estates. It may be that Mr. Tanwas ha confused the name with one similar to John Subne. Perhaps the Pottawatomie Indian Agency at Mayetta, Kansas, could give him information as to the proper name under which the party he is inquiring about was allotted.

Returned herewith is Mr. Tanwas' letter.

Very truly yours,

A. W. Leech,
R/Mc   Superintendent.

Shawnee Indian Agency,
Shawnee, Oklahoma,
April 15, 1924.

Miss Cecelia Dimbler,
c/o Fred H. Wood.
824 West Olive Street.
Herington, Kansas.

Dear Miss Dimbler:

223

This is in reply to your letter of recent date in which you make inquiry concerning your interest in the Elizabeth Dimbler estate and I will answer your questions as follows.

1. The location of the land is near Wanette, Okla.

2. There are 120 acres.

3. The valuation of the land is not to[sic] high at present due to the low prices on farm lands.

4. The annual rental is $150.

5. Forty acres are in cultivation.

6. Cotton and corn is raised on the land.

7. The prospect of oil on the land is uncertain.

The check you received in September 1923, No. 16915 for $18.75 was your share of the last rental paid. No rental will be due until July 1, 1924 and the same will be sent to the address given herein unless notified otherwise.

Very truly yours,

R/Mc

A. W. Leech,
Superintendent.

Shawnee Indian Agency,
Shawnee, Oklahoma,
April 16, 1924.

Mr. J. Harmon Lewis, Lawyer
Marmoth Building.
Shawnee, Oklahoma.

Dear Sir:

I am returning herewith, unsigned, the certificate that you had prepared in regard to the James Clark allotment, for the reason that I am unfamiliar with the circumstances connected with the case. It would appear that no regular departmental hearing was held to determine the heirs but that the findings were made as a result of affidavits of heirship being submitted to the Department at Washington.

I would suggest that you take the matter up with Mr. Thomas Alford, near Benson Park, who will be in a position to give the information desired as he is familiar with all these old cases and has in his possession records pertaining to old allottees, their circumstances, and so on.

Very truly yours,

A. W. Leech,
R/Mc   Superintendent.
Incl

Shawnee Indian Agency,
Shawnee, Oklahoma,
April 16, 1924.

Mr. R. I. Keator, Attorney.
Stangler Building, Room 24.
Pendleton, Oregon.

Dear Sir:

This is in reply to your letter of the 4th instant in which you make inquiry for Oscar Mahardy concerning his alleged interest in the estate of Alice Blanchard, Absentee Shawnee allottee #562.

The hearing to determine the heirs of Alice Blanchard was approved October 13, 1921, and under it the two children of Alice Blanchard inherited her entire estate. It appears from the testimony given at the time of the hearing that Oscar Mahardy was estopped from claiming as an heir in the estate. It would appear that his former wife, Alice Blanchard, lived with several men and that her relations with any of them would not constitute a valid common law marriage except with Oscar Mahardy, with whom she began living October 1907 and continued living with him until 1912, when they separated without a divorce. Shortly after the separation Oscar Mahardy began living with another woman as his wife and as a result of such action he was excluded as an heir. Alice Blanchard also began living with another man after the separation and this man was also excluded as a lawful heir. In view of such action none but her surviving children at the time of the hearing were determined heirs to her estate.

Very truly yours,

A. W. Leech,
R/Mc   Superintendent.

Probate
8805-18
W H G
L H
104178-13

Shawnee Indian Agency,
Shawnee, Oklahoma,
April 16, 1924.

The Commissioner of Indian Affairs.
Washington, D. C.

S ir:[sic]

The estate of Ke-she-she, Mexican Kickapoo allotment #215, was probated erroneously several years ago, the heirs having been determined as John Mine, O-ke-mah, Ah-the-pun, Pah-pe-ach, Ella Carter, and Mah-que-the-ech[sic].

A later hearing was held and it was decided that George Kish-ke-ton was the sole heir, inheriting through Mah-quo-the-eck. The Ke-she-she allotment was sold and the proceeds from the sale divided among the above named heirs as follows:

John Mine--------------------------------------$ 338.67
O-ke-mah------------------------------------- 338.66
Ah-the-pun----------------------------------- 677.33
Pah-pe-ach----------------------------------- 112.89
Ella Carter----------------------------------- 225.78
Mah-quo-the-eck----------------------------- 338.67

Under authority "Probate 77850-20; 107295-14; L. A. P." dated December 23, 1920, this land was sold. The amount that John Mine owed was paid to George Kisk-ke-ton[sic]. Pah-pe-ach's obligation was also settled and $50 has been paid on the amount owed by Ella Carter. George Kisk-ke-ton is the sole heir of Mah-quo-the-eck and, therefore, would not receive any refund from her estate. Under this authority an obligation of $338.67 has been set up against the account of O-ke-mah and will be paid as soon as this amount is credited to O-ke-mah's account.

The estate of Ah-the-pun was probated and Henry Murdock, a Kickapoo Indian, was determined as sole heir, "Land-80005-1916; 106530-1906.[sic] Mr. Murdock sold this inherited allotment and spent the proceeds for living expenses and so on. Ah-the-pun received from the Ke-she-she estate the amount of $677.33 which was spent during his lifetime, it is presumed. Since Henry Murdock is the sole heir of Ah-the-pun and has derived benefit from the sale of his allotment, and Ah-the-pun erroneously received proceeds from the Ke-she-she estate, it appears that Henry Murdock should reimburse George Kish-ke-ton, the sole heir of Ke-she-she, the amount of $677.33.

In view of such authority is requested to pay to George Kisk-ke-ton, from the account of Henry Murdock, after securing Henry's consent, this amount.

Very truly yours,

A. W. Leech,
R/Mc Superintendent.

Probate
12232-24
L a P

Shawnee Indian Agency,
Shawnee, Oklahoma,
April 17, 1924.

The Commissioner of Indian Affairs.
Washington, D. C.

S i r:

Reference is made to Office letter dated March 28, 1924, bearing file reference as above. The Office gives instructions in this letter that the date of death of the allottee be procured.

After inquiry among the older Kickapoo Indians it develops that Wah paw naw ke she no qua, Kickapoo allottee #81, died during the summer of 1893, sometime after receiving her allotment.

Mr. S. Y. Tutwiler, examiner of inheritance, is now working in this office and will hold hearing to determine the heirs on May 9, 1924, and it is believed that at that time the exact date or probable date of death will be developed by evidence from witnesses to be called then.

Very truly yours,

A. W. Leech,
D/Mc   Superintendent.

Shawnee Indian Agency,
Shawnee, Oklahoma,
April 17, 1924.

Mrs. Dave Anderson
Choctaw, Oklahoma.

Dear Madam:

I received your letter of April 14th in which you give me additional
information concerning your mother's relation to Lucius A. Darling,
whose land was sold several months ago. From the findings in the matter
of heirship it appears that Mrs. Esther T. Smith was decalred[sic] an heir of
William O. Darling and it appears that William O. Darling was entitled to
inherit in the Lucius A. Darling estate but for some reason that I am not
familiar with your mother was not determined an heir of the Lucius A
Darling estate.

The money derived from the sale of the Lucius A. Darling land has
been distributed among the heirs as determined by the Department of the
Interior and inasmuch as the funds have been paid out there is no recourse
for your mother in this matter apparently. If at any time she is in Shawnee
I would be pleased to have her call at the office and explain to me fully
her relationship to Lucius A. Darling.

Very truly yours,

A. W. Leech,
R/Mc   Superintendent.

Shawnee Indian Agency,
Shawnee, Oklahoma,
April 18, 1924.

Mr. A. R. Snyder,
Supt. Potawatomi Agency.
Mayetta, Kansas.

Dear Mr. Snyder:

In reply to your letter of the 15th calling for a list of the names of the heirs to the Pamdosh estate, I am inclosing herewith the names of the heirs to the estate of John Pamdosh, as well as those to the estate of his wife, Non ne ke kat. By this you will see that Seymour Kah-dot was not determined an heir.

Very truly yours,

A. W. Leech,
R/Mc   Superintendent.

Shawnee Indian Agency,
Shawnee, Oklahoma,
April 22, 1924.

The Commissioner of Indian Affairs.
Washington, D. C.

S i r:

In accordance with Office letter of recent date directing that a statement by Harrison Roubideau, or Whitehorn, of his acceptance of the partition of the allotment of Jennie Roubideau, described as the S.2 of NE.4 of Section 28, Twp., 17 North of Range 3 East, I. M., in Oklahoma, be procured, the same is herewith inclosed. There is also inclosed a letter from Harrison Whitehorn, who is also known as Harrison Roubideau, to the effect that he wants patent in fee to his 40 acres, whereas, in the petition it is stated that he does not want patent in fee. It appears that Mr. Roubideau, or Whitehorn, has changed his mind in that respect and now wishes patent in fee. It is understood that Mr. Roubideau had patent in fee issued to him for his own allotment.

Very respectfully,

A. W. Leech,
D/Mc   Superintendent.

Shawnee Indian Agency,
Shawnee, Oklahoma,
April 22, 1924.

The Commissioner of Indian Affairs.
Washington, D. C.

S i r:

      There is transmitted herewith a deed covering the N/2 of the NE/4 of Section 10, Twp., 11 North of Range 5 East of I. M., in Oklahoma, being the allotment of Henry Miller, Sac and Fox allottee #325, made by Ida Miller Spooner in favor of her four children, namely:

      Mary Elizabeth, age 12
      Bernice Henrietta, age 10
      Evangeline Miller, age 8
      Lenora Josephine, age 6

      Mrs. Spooner is also entitled to an interest in another allotment and now wants to make a deed covering that also in favor of her children but owing to the fact that the heirs are undetermined at this time it is therefore impossible for her to make this deed. The purpose of conveying the land to three children is that the parents want to use the funds allotted to them from trust funds of the tribe. The appraisment[sic] on form 5-110a is inclosed herewith and is a fair appraisment of the value, inasmuch as I was present when the appraisment was made, and I consider that the children are receiving full value for their money. Added to this fact these people intend to make improvements from the funds upon this and probably some of the other land.

      I recommend that the transaction be approved.

Very respectfully,

A. W. Leech,
D/Mc   Superintendent.

Shawnee Indian Agency,
Shawnee, Oklahoma,
April 22, 1924.

The Commissioner of Indian Affairs.
Washington, D. C.

S i r:

There is transmitted herewith the petition for partition of the allotment of [?]ire Gibson, deceased Absentee Shawnee allottee #415, described as the NW/4 and the W/2 of NE/4 of Section 31, Twp., 9 North, Range 2 East of I. M., containing 239.44 acres.

Very respectfully,

A. W. Leech,
D/Mc   Superintendent.

Shawnee Indian Agency,
Shawnee, Oklahoma,
April 25, 1924.

Mr. Charles O. Pratt,
2217 West Cedar Street,
Oklahoma City, Oklahoma.

Dear Mr. Pratt:

There is returned to you the will made in your favor by your deceased father bearing date of March 15th, 1919, which has been given consideration by the Department of the Interior.

In this connection the Indian Office, Washington, under date of April 18th, 1924, directs, " that in as much as Sevellon Pratt was a white man the Department has no authority to determine the heirs to the 1/3 interest inherited by him in the state[sic] of Harriet Pratt and no authority to approve his will disposing of this 1/3 interest.".

Therefore, it will be your duty to put the matter of approval of the will through the local probate court. You should wait no longer but record the will at Tecumseh at your earliest convenience.

Very truly yours,

A. W. Leech, Supt.

Shawnee Indian Agency,
Shawnee, Oklahoma,
April 25, 1924.

Mr. R. M. Tidwell,
Supt. Indian Agency,
Pawnee, Oklahoma.

Dear Mr. Tidwell:

I am in receipt of your letter of the 16th making inquiry as to the heirs of Joseph Springer. You advise me that you have been informed by Mr. Hoyo that Springer's heirs have been determined but in this apparently you are wrong as we have no record of a hearing having been held to determine Mr. Springer's heirs. He was an Iowa allottee and at the time of his death had a patent in fee status and left little, if any interest restricted. It appears that he died in the year 1921. At the present time he has the small amount of 60¢ to his credit here and if you have any amounts to his credit in your office it is suggested that you forward the same here.

Very truly yours,

A. W. Leech,
R/Mc
Superintendent.

Sac & Fox – Shawnee Estates
1920-1924 Volume IX

Shawnee Indian Agency,
Shawnee, Oklahoma,
April 26, 1924.

The Commissioner of Indian Affairs,
Washington, D. C.

My dear Mr. Commissioner:

My attention is called to certain deeds that were executed
during the year 1918, by the heirs of some of the estates of deceased
Shawnees under this jurisdiction, in favor of Hal Johnson and E. T.
Carson, of Shawnee, Oklahoma, and in going over the correspondence
relative to these I find that a report was made to your Office under date of
January 31, 1924, giving a list of these lands and the interests conveyed to
the above named parties. I also find that at the same time a schedule was
sent you showing the amount of rentals collected on these tracts and
giving the amount that should have been due the purchasers on a portion
of land deeded to them.

There appears to have been no reply made to these letters
and I would be pleased if the Office would consider and reply to them at
an early date as every few days some question arises as to a settlement in
some particular case.

I have had some correspondence with Mark Goode, an
attorney at Shawnee, relative to some of these cases and it appears that he
represents Mr. Johnson's interest. Mr. Goode seems rather inclined to not
agree with this office in our endeavors to effect a settlement in the matter
as he contends that his client has been put to a lot of unnecessary expense
and has been deprived of the rentals that were due him on the undivided
interest of the land that he had purchased. In a letter received from Mr.
Goode a few days ago, among other things referred to by him, is the
following paragraph:

"In the meantime what do you propose to do about the
rentals appropriated since and including 1918? I should be
pleased to find out about this."

Regardless of how this office or your Office may feel about
the conveyances of the interests above referred to, it appears that the
courts have decided that the grantors had a right to make them and if this
is the case it occurs to me that a portion of the rentals collected on these
lands were rightfully due the purchasers but it appears that these rentals
were paid through this office to the heirs who had conveyed their interests
to the purchasers. I believe there would be more probability of arriving at
a settlement if an understanding could be had as to these rentals and I

233

would be pleased if the Office would carefully consider this matter and advise me with reference to it.

These cases are of considerable annoyance here and will never be less the longer they continue in their present state. I am of the opinion that a decided effort should be made to settle up these estates either by the heirs owning the trust portions of the land buying out the interests of Johnson and Carson or their assigns or else permitting these parties to purchase the remainder of the land now held in trust. Failing in either of the above methods I would suggest that an effort be made for all parties to join in a conveyance to a third party. The interests involved are of such a nature that it is very difficult to partition the land, which would be a better plan it[sic] it could be done, but only a few of the tracts are in such a proportion as would make partition possible.

If the Office will advise me with reference to the rentals above mentioned, I will endeavor to work out a plan as to each particular case and submit it for approval. Trusting that I may be favored with an early reply, I am

Very respectfully,

A. W. Leech,
Superintendent.

L/Mc

Shawnee Indian Agency,
Shawnee, Oklahoma,
April 26, 1924.

Mr. Floyd W. Hobbs, Attorney
Holton, Kansas.

Dear Mr. Hobbs:

Further reference is made to the claim of Mrs. Masquat, of your county, with reference to the estate of John Shobznah. It appears that in former letters you were given notice to the effect that said John Shobznah was never allotted any land in this vicinity; that there is on Shobznah allotted here whose name was Peter Shobznah. Therefore, you are again notified that there is no estate here under the name of John Shobznah. If the party is an heir to any Shobznah it is probably that Peter Shobznah is the party but records show that Peter Shobznah parted with his land a number of years ago, therefore, it appears Mrs. Masquat has no inherited interest here.

Very truly yours,

A. W. Leech,
D/Mc   Superintendent.

Shawnee Indian Agency,
Shawnee, Oklahoma,
April 26, 1924.

Mr. John Shawneego
Indian School
Chilocco, Oklahoma

Dear Mr. Shawneego:

This is in reply to yours of the 23d instant regarding the Sam Deer and Amos Deer estates. Nothing has been completed so far for the reason that your sister Stella Curtin rejected the Amos Deer proposition. We wrote your sister again a day or two ago to the effect that you had approved of the proposition and that it might be proper for her to reconsider the matter and if possible to accept the proposition, inasmuch as you had done so.

It is to be hoped that these matters can be settle so that you people will be free from all annoyances in this connection. It will be some tome. perhaps at least sixty days, before we can expect much development but you will be notified of the progress of the matter from time to time.

Very truly yours,

A. W. Leech,
D/Mc   Superintendent.

Shawnee Indian Agency,
Shawnee, Oklahoma,
April 28, 1924.

Mr. E. H. Reese,
Vice-president Citizens National Bank.
Emporia, Kansas.

Dear Sir:

In going through the files of this office with reference to the estate of Margaret Bedell, a Shawnee allottee, I find that one of the heirs was Leonard Coon. It seems that this party is livening, or was living not long since, in Emporia.

Mr. Benjamin Coon, another heir in the above named estate, has appeared at this office and says that he is of the opinion that Leonard Coon is not living and as we have a small amount of money at this office for him I would be pleased to have you inform me if you know whether Leonard Coon is still living or not and if so where he is located. I would be pleased to have you tell me also whether you are personally acquainted with him or not.

My reason for writing you with reference to this matter is the fact that I notice in our files that in 1921 you wrote this office giving certain information with reference to Leonard Coon, and I am taking the liberty to call on you again. Thanking you for any information you may be able to give, I am

Very respectfully,

A. W. Leech,
L/Mc   Superintendent.

Shawnee Indian Agency,
Shawnee, Oklahoma,
April 29, 1924.

Mrs. Alice Wapskineh
Hominy, Oklahoma.

Dear Mrs. Wapskineh:

This is in reply to your letter of the 26th asking about some papers you signed in connection with the Joe Whipple estate. The papers you signed were application for back annuities in favor of Joseph Whipple, made by former agents at Mayetta, Kansas. Your application, with several others, was forwarded to the superintendent at Mayetta some weeks ago for his report to the Indian Office at Washington. Up to date nothing has been heard from him relative to such but in the event your application is acted upon favorably the funds which you are entitled to will come along in due course of time and they will be sent to you.

The examiner of inheritance is here now and the Franklin Wilamette case will be looked into and if it is found that you have been excluded steps will be taken for a rehearing.

Very truly yours,

A. W. Leech,

R/mc   Superintendent.

Shawnee Indian Agency,
Shawnee, Oklahoma,
May 1, 1924.

Mr. George A. Hoyo, Supt.
Ponca Indian Agency,
Whiteagle, Oklahoma.

Dear Mr. Hoyo:

There is inclosed herewith my official check No. 19907 for $103.64 payable to your order. This is drawn from the account of Richard Roubidoux and is transmitted to you for division to his heirs.

Very truly yours,

A. W. Leech,

Mc/   Superintendent.

19253-24

Shawnee Indian Agency,
Shawnee, Oklahoma,
May 2, 1924.

Mr. Leo Whistler
Hotel Lynch
Stroud, Oklahoma.

Dear Mr. Whistler:

This is in reply to your letter of the first in which you make further reference to the Marie A. Fear heirs. Previously you were informed that Mr. Charles W. Fear and Ruby Lee Carter were determined the heirs. You state in your letter that there is some doubt as to the legality of the divorce decree which was granted you and Mrs. Fear. This will be a matter for you to take up with the county courts as the same was handled by the county and not by the Department. Apparently you and Mrs. Fear would be recognized as divorced and Mrs. and Mrs. Fear as married whether the divorce complied with all legal terms or not, as you and Mrs. Fear were separated a number of years and Mr. and Mrs. Fear had lived together many years prior to her death. Under recent Departmental decisions the separation and marriage would be recognized I believe, inasmuch as Mrs. Fear was of Indian blood as well as you.

Very truly yours,

A. W. Leech,
R/Mc   Superintendent.

19253-24

Shawnee Indian Agency,
Shawnee, Oklahoma,
May 6, 1924.

The Commissioner of Indian Affairs.
Washington, D. C.

S i r:

There are transmitted herewith papers in partition of the allotments of Amanda and Thresa Turney. These allotments, it will be noted, were mentioned in a report dated April 26, 1924, in connection with drainage assessment and other matters inquired about my Congressman T. D. McKeown.

It appears that several years ago deeds were approved partitioning these two allotments and later canceled under Land-Sales 41919-16; 133278-16; 9262-17; J F L. It also appears that the deeds are recorded in deed book Inherited Indian Lands, Vol. 33, pages 140 to 144, both inclusive. Since the divisions, according to these deeds, were satisfactory to all parties concerned it is again requested that partition be made in accordance with said deeds. Inasmuch as P. A. Turney received the deed at that time without the restrictive clause it may be appropriate to issue him a patent in fee as there is no drainage assessment against the particular tract of land set aside for him. It will be noted that I. H. Tarkington deeded his interest in these two allotments to P. A. Turney and that I. H. Tarkington is a white man whose share in these allotments is therefore without restrictions.

There is inclosed, in addition to the partition papers, a letter from Mr. Lloyd LaMotte if Seger Agency, Oklahoma, requesting that this office take certain action with reference to the partition, and also the reply of this office to his letter recommending that petition for partition be attempted.

I respectfully recommend the approval of the petition.

Very respectfully,

A. W. Leech,
D/Mc   Superintendent.

Shawnee Indian Agency,
Shawnee, Oklahoma,
May 9, 1924.

Mrs. G. L. Coffman
985 East Maple
Cushing, Oklahoma.

Dear Madam:

Referring to your request for information as to the Lorenzo Dow estate, will say that this matter is now pending before the Indian Office in Washington. As soon as we hear anything of importance we will let you know.

Very respectfully,

A. W. Leech,
L-Mc   Superintendent.

———————————————————————————————

Shawnee Indian Agency,
Shawnee, Oklahoma,
May 9, 1924.

Mr. T. B. Slick
Box 1146
Oklahoma City, Oklahoma.

Dear Sir:

In compliance with the request you made over the telephone Thursday afternoon, I am inclosing herewith a copy of the Departmental findings in the heirship case of Harry Hall.

Harry Hall was Sac and Fox allottee No. 287 and was allotted the NE/4 of Section 4-17-6 East, 161.60 acres. Forty acres of this land have had the restrictions removed. The other is still held in trust and is now owned by Robert Charles Pate and Harry Samuel Pate. The Lot 1 of the NE/4 is covered by patent in fee No. 890187 issued December 11, 1922 to Robert T. Pate. Trust patent No, 892361 was issued January 6, 1923 to Robert Charles and Harry Samuel Pate for Lot 6 of the NE/4. Trust patent No. 892360 was issued January 6, 1923 to Mamie Jennings, Dollie Gokey, Lelia Bigwalker, Esther Bigwalker and Osmond Franklin for the S/2 of NE/4. The above named heirs, except Lelia Bigwalker, trust deeded the S/2 of NE/4 to Lelia Bigwalker May 10, 1923. Lelia Bigwalker sold the S/2 of NE/4 to Harry Samuel Pate and Robert Charles Pate and the transfer is covered by a restrictive deed approved November 27, 1923.

Very truly yours,

A. W. Leech,
R-Mc   Superintendent.

———————————————————————————————

Shawnee Indian Agency,
Shawnee, Oklahoma,
May 16, 1924.

Mrs, Dollie Scott
Route No. 3
Cushing, Oklahoma.

Dear Mrs. Scott:

This is to acknowledge receipt of your letter of May 14th.

Your son Benson McClellan is only 20 years of age, according to the records on file in this office. His date of birth is shown as August 8, 1904.

You peak of the interest owned by your deceased husband in the Eliza Connolly allotment and state that you have not received any money from the same for the past year or so. The lease rentals accumulating on the account of Frank Gokey have been divided and the money placed to ours and Augustine's credit in this office. The reason you have not received any money from this and other leases is because you have outstanding obligations which must be met. No money can be paid to you until these debts are paid. You will remember that you owed quite a large hospital bill on account of your son Wallace. The money that has been taken up to your credit has been applied on some of your bills. The money belonging to your child, Augustine, is held here to her credit. I do not think there is an agricultural lease on the land this year but think Mr. Connolly is living on it. You might take the matter up with Mr. Collins, who will know about it.

Very truly yours,

A. W. Leech,
Superintendent.

R-Mc

Shawnee Indian Agency,
Shawnee, Oklahoma,
May 16, 1924.

Mr. R. D. Suddath
Room 6, Eustis Building.
Henrietta, Texas.

Dear Sir:

This is to acknowledge receipt of your letter of May 3d written to Mr. Suffecool, making inquiry for the heirs of Harry Bostick, a deceased Potawatomi Indian, and asking if there were some allotments of land and money to be issued to Indians.

In reply you are informed that I know nothing of any such. The rumor is wholly unfounded. However, the Potawatomi Indians held a council at this agency May 14th for the purpose of electing a business committee to look after their affairs and selecting delegates to go to Washington in the interest of any matters that might come up concerning the tribe.

Very truly yours,

A. W. Leech,

R-Mc

Superintendent.

DEPARTMENT OF THE INTERIOR
UNITED STATES INDIAN SERVICE

Field J. V. No. __188__

JOURNAL VOUCHER (MISCELLANEOUS)

PARTICULARS	DEBIT	✓	CREDIT	✓
INDIVIDUAL INDIAN MONEY & SPECIAL DEPOSITS:				
Special Deposits			312.50	
Individual Indian Money	312.50			
CHARGE:				
Pottawatomi County Commissioners				
Tecumseh, Oklahoma----------------$312.50				
CREDIT:				
Estate of Mary Bourbonnais-----B-11--$312.50				
AUTHORITY:				
Land-Contracts				
32789-24				
M.A.P.				
17047-24 CHI				
Transfer of funds from Special Deposits to the Mary				
Bourbonnais estate, paid by the Commissioners of				

Pottawatomie County, Oklahoma, for Damages of Right-
of-way accross[sic] the Mary Bourbonnais allotment.

5-21-24
JRW

AMS.

May 21-1924.
(Date)
Shawnee Indian Agency, Shawnee, Oklahoma.
(Unit)

Shawnee Indian Agency,
Shawnee, Oklahoma,
May 26, 1924.

Dr. Jacob Breid, Supt.
Sac & Fox Sanatorium.
Toledo, Iowa.

Dear Dr. Breid:

As per request made in your letters of May 15th for copies of the
hearings in the estates of John, James and Jerome Wolf and Cora
Shaquequot I am inclosing herewith for your information and
convenience copies of the findings and trust that these will be of
assistance to you in explaining to those people there the heirship matters.

Very truly yours,

A. W. Leech,
R/Mc   Superintendent.

****

Dr. Jacob Breid
Superintendent and Physician

Department of the Interior

UNITED STATES INDIAN SERVICE
Sac & Fox Sanatorium
TOLEDO, IOWA

RECEIVED MAY 17 1924 SHAWNEE INDIAN AGENCY

May 15, 1924.

Mr. A. W. Leech, Supt.,

Shawnee, Okla.

My dear Mr. Leech:

The heirs inheriting in the estate of Cora Shaquequot have asked that I secure a decision in this case for their benefit. If one is available, I will thank you very much to forward the same to me. We have a copy of the decision of Pa phia na who inherited a part of this estate but we do not have a copy of the Cora Shaquequot decision.

Yours truly,

Jacob Breid

****

Dr. Jacob Breid
Superintendent and Physician

Department of the Interior

UNITED STATES INDIAN SERVICE
Sac & Fox Sanatorium
TOLEDO, IOWA

RECEIVED MAY 17 1924 SHAWNEE INDIAN AGENCY

May 15, 1924.

Mr. A. W. Leech, Supt.,
Shawnee, Okla.

My dear Mr. Leech:

There are so many inquiries regarding the heirship decision in the estates of John, James and Jerome Wolf that it seems advisable for me to have a copy of this decision. I am assuming that the decision is a long one and if you do not wish to make a copy of the same, please let us have your copy and we will make a copy and return the original to you. A number of the Indians of this reservation cannot understand the distribution of these estates and a copy of the decision of the Secretary of the Interior would be of benefit to us in explaining the situation to them.

Very respectfully,

Jacob Breid
JB:S.   Superintendent.

REFER IN REPLY TO THE FOLLOWING:

DEPARTMENT OF THE INTERIOR,

ADDRESS ONLY THE
COMMISSIONER OF INDIAN AFFAIRS

84146-24

OFFICE OF INDIAN AFFAIRS,

WASHINGTON,

NOV 22 1924

RECEIVED
NOV 25 1924
SHAWNEE INDIAN
AGENCY

Mr. A. W. Leech,

Supt., Shawnee Agency.

My dear Mr. Leech:

The Office is in receipt of your letter of November 14, 1924, in regard to the estate of Mary Bean, Sr., deceased Yankton Sioux allottee, stating that you are in receipt of a letter from Mary Bean, Jr., in reference to the probating of this estate.

In reply you are informed that in a decision dated November 5, 1924, the Department approved the Will of the allottee, said Mary Bean, Sr., thereby vesting the entire estate in Mary Bean, Jr., the sole beneficiary under the Will.

Very truly yours,

EB Meritt
Assistant Commissioner.

Chief Che-Ko-skuks[sic]

Last Will & Testament

Made this 8th day of
June A.D. 1889
****

Sac and Fox Agency, Ind. Ter.

June 8th 1889.

I, Che-ko-skuk, Head Chief of the Sac & Fox Nation, of sound mind, to this eight day of June, A.D. 1889, make my last will and testament, bequeathing all my property of whatsoever kind to my beloved wife, said property consisting of one (1) note, on John Whistler dated, April 1888 for the sum of Seven hundred 00/100 Dollars ($700^{00}) at the rate of 10% interest from date; one (1) lot of Ponies & Horses, twenty five, more or less; wagons, harness, agricultural & other implements; and all Buildings of whatsoever kind, and other improvements - all of said described property upon my death & bequeath to her, my beloved wife, during her natural life and upon her death to go to Aw-naw-me, my son and his heirs.

It is my desire that the US Indian Agent for the time being at Sac & Fox Agency, I.T., be the custodian of the ~~hes~~ money, herein bequeathed and to pay the same to my wife upon demand, and to protect her interest in all other property, and to be her advisor in all business transactions.

H C Jones   Che-Ko-skuk   His X Mark

D.G. Cheesman

I certify that I was present and witnessed the signature by mark to the within Will; that I fully explained to him the contents thereof, and am satisfied that he understood the same.

Sac and Fox Agency, I.T.   Alex Connolly

June 8th, 1889   Interpreter

I certify that the within Will of Che-Ko-skuk, Chief, was made and signed in my presence this 8th day of June 1889.

Sac & Fox – Shawnee Estates
1920-1924 Volume IX

Moses Neal

U.S. Indian Agent

Sac and Fox Agency, I.T.

June 8th 1889

-------W I L L -------

---------------------------oOo-----------------------------

I, John Whistler, being of sound mind and memory, do make, publish and declare this ~~day~~ to be my last will and Testament, hereby revoking all Wills by me at any time heretofore made.

Item First: -- Subject to the payment of all my just debts and funeral expenses, I Will, Devise and Bequeath to my beloved wife, Fannie Whistler, all the ~~real~~ estate of which I may die seized and possessed, both real and personal, absolutely, to do with and dispose of as she may deem fit, and I make no provision for my children at my death, or any child which may hereafter be born, knowing that my said wife, who is their mother will deal justly with them.

Item Second:--- I hereby appoint my said wife Executrix of this, my last Will and Testemant[sic], and exhonorate[sic] her from giving bond, and authorize her, without any order from the Court, to sell and dispose of such property as she may deem fit and to execute conveyances therefor.

In witness whereof, I hereto set my hand this 29th day of August 1890.

(signed)

John Whiseler[sic].

Witnesses:

J.A. Mitchell,

H.P. Farrar.

On this 29th day of August, 1890, the foregoing insturment[sic] was in our presence signed and executed by John Whistler, and by him declared to us to be his last Will and Testement[sic], and at his request and in his presence and in the presence of each other, we have subscribed our names as witnesses hereto.

Sac & Fox – Shawnee Estates
1920-1924 Volume IX

(signed)

J.A. Mitchell,

H.P. Farrar.

****

:
(
Territory of Oklahoma,   SS:
)
Logan County,   :
_____(

W.P. Hackney and Charles W. Beacom of lawful age after being first duly sworn upon their oaths in due form of law, each for himself and not for the other, upon their oaths do say:

that they have carefully examined the original Will of John Whistler now in their posession[sic], and that the above and foregoing is a true copy thereof made by the said Charles W. Beacom, and read over carefully and corrected by us and that the same is a true exact and litteral[sic] copy of said Will in substance and in fact.

<u>   WP Hackney   </u>

<u>   CW Beacom   </u>

Subscribed and sworn to before me this 16th day of December 1890.

<u>   Winfield S Smith   </u>
Notary Public

Copy of will made by William Dole, Jan. 18, 1907.

To all to whom these presents shall Come, Greeting:

I William Dole, whos[sic] residence is at Perkins, Oklahoma, and whose age is 87 years do hereby make this voluntary and unsolicited statement, to-wit:

That I am Now by reason of Old Age, and sickness, entirely unableto[sic] wait upon my self[sic], and being daily in need of some one to attend to and wait upon me, and having no house of my own nor place in which to live that I can be kept warm

248

an[sic] comfortable; Do hereby state upon my honor, that I have been living with David Tohee, and been cred[sic] for by him and his wife, when unable to care for myself, For the past Eight years, and that at this time the said David Tohee, and his wife Emma Tohee, are treating me very kindly, and tenderly careing[sic] for me and administering to my wants, for which I have never paid them anything, and whereas I realize now that I will be in the near future entirely unable to get out of my bed without being helped by some one, and whereas I have full faith and confidence in the said David Tohee and his wife Emma, continuing to care for and wait upon me until Deth[sic] relieves my sufferings. Therefore It is my request that the agent of the Iowa tribe of Indians, make provision if Posable[sic] for the said David Tohee and his Wife to be remunerated, for ther[sic] Kindness, and the trouble and expense that they have been put to in waiting on me and care ing[sic] for me as above mentioned, for the time above mentione[sic], as well as for all trouble that they may hereafter be put to in careing for me so long as I may live; out of lands allotted to me and held by me so long as I may live; out of lands allotted to me and held by me a such member of the Iowa Tribe of Indians, or accrued pension. This writing is signed by me with my own hand this 18th day of January, A.D. 1907, in the presence of the persons whose names appear as witnesses.

Signed
William Dole.

Witnesses to signature:
    A.W. Harbaugh
    John L. Burns

BUREAU OF EDUCATION.

Quinalabasa, April 9, 1908.

In the event of my death I wish all money belonging to me in the Bank of Hampton, Hampton, Va., in any trust Company or financial institution of any kind, in the Field Museum, Chicago, or any money whereever[sic] it may be, to which I am lawfully and justly entitled, the same to be paid to Miss Caroline W. Andrus or her order, or in the event of her death prior to mine, the same to be paid to Miss Cora M.

Folsam[sic], or in the event of her death prior to mine, to my father Henry Clay Jones or in the event of his death prior tomine[sic], to Harvard College, Cambridge, Massachusetts, the same to be used without any restrictions whatsoever I do not desire that any of the above names shall give bond or to be put to any trouble whatsoever but that the money be paid to the one it is to come. In witness whereof I have here unto set my hand this ninth of April, 1908.

(Signed)   Wm. Jones.

A true Copy:
HORATIO SMITH.

****

[Illegible] 27, 1908.

RECEIVED
OCT 2 1908
SAC & FOX AGENCY,
OKLAHOMA.

My dear Mr Kohlenberg:-

I am in the mountains of Northern Isabela Province of Luzon near the head waters of the River Cagayan. I am many days from the nearest post office and out of all communication with the outside world. Your letter of March 7th inclosing a check of $11.40, my share of of[sic] the spring payment was fetched me by some Filipines[sic] who strayed in her to trade with the wild people I am with. They are returning at once and I cannot write you at length about these people. I give no address of where I am because there is none. My address always while I am here is in care of Dr Paul C Freer, Bureau of Science, Manila.

I thank your kind letter and for sending the check.

Yours very truly,
William Jones

****

Sac & Fox – Shawnee Estates
1920-1924 Volume IX

Mountains of Eastern Nueva Vizcaya.
Jan 4, 1909

My dear Mr Kohlenberg:-

The check of $192.26 which you sent me last August reached me last night and I am sending this acknowledgement out tomorrow by the messenger who is carrying other mail for me & I would write more but have much mail to look over and answer.

Yours truly,

William Jones

Bureau of Science

Mr. W. C. Kohlenberg,   Manila

   Supt and Spl Dis Agent   P.I.

      Sac and Fox Agency

         Oklahoma

****

Up The Cagayan, Nueva Vizcaya P.I.
Jan. 31, 1909

My dear Mr Kohlenberg:-

The check for $44.41 which you sent me n Nov 7th of last year has just come and I am sending this acknowledgment out to day by the first messenger.

Yours truly

William Jones

****

Muskogee Oct 21 1910

My Dead Friend:

We have decided to turn over to an Attorney here Mr. J.H. [Illegible] the collection of money now in Chicago, belonging to Wm Jones deceased, and I am writing now to know if the number of checks dates and amount of each sent him in the Philippine Islands as no account

251

of his personal funds and affairs has therefore been located. Thought possibly we could trace through the Asst Treasurer [illegible] showing through which hand or hands such checks were validated, thus tracing to where he might have an account. Apparently there seems to be some mystery about this whole affair. I have no personal interest in this whole matter, except, so far as possible to prevent that Hampton Va. crowd from getting their hands on everything.

Thanking you for any information or advice in the matter, and wishing you well, I am

Very respectfully

[Illegible] W Jones

1001 East Side [Illegible]

Hon. WC Kohlenberg

Supt & Spl Disb Agent

Sac & Fox Agency Okla

****

REFER IN REPLY TO THE FOLLOWING:

Land-
Sales
33869-1909
35216-1909
C R W

DEPARTMENT OF THE INTERIOR

OFFICE OF INDIAN AFFAIRS

WASHINGTON

MAY 20 1909

RECEIVED
MAY 24 1909
SAC & FOX AGENCY,
OKLAHOMA.
Copy W.C. Jones. 5/25-09

Will of William Jones.

W. C. Kohlenberg, Esq.,

Superintendent Sac and Fox Indian School,

Sac and Fox Agency, Oklahoma.

Sir:

The Office has received your communication of May 4, 1909, relative to the will of William Jones.

No disposition will be made of the lease money until you have furnished the affidavit of heirship as requested by this Office on April 8, 1909.

The Office has received a communication from the War Department, under date of April 30, 1909, inclosing copy of a letter of April 5, 1909, written to H. C. Jones, Prague, Oklahoma, the father of Dr. Jones, who was murdered in the Philippines. The War Department says that the Field Museum of Natural History, with which Dr. Jones was connected at the time of his death, has, it is understood, sent a representative to the Philippine Islands to look after the personal effects of the deceased, and that he will doubtless write the relatives fully about the matter.

You will advise Dr. Jones' relatives hereof.

Very respectfully,
J H Dorich
Acting Chief Clerk.

ED-17
1106

REFER IN REPLY TO THE FOLLOWING:

Land
21727-1909
W R L

DEPARTMENT OF THE INTERIOR
OFFICE OF INDIAN AFFAIRS
WASHINGTON

R E C E I V E D
APR 9 1909
SAC & FOX AGENCY,
OKLAHOMA.

Will of Theresa Roubideaux.

APR -6 1909

W. C. Kohlenberg, Esq.,

Superintendent Sac and Fox Indian School,

Sac & Fox Agency, Oklahoma.

Sir:

The Office is in receipt of your letter of March 18, 1909, transmitting for Departmental consideration a will executed by Theresa Roubideaux, deceased.

In response you are informed that on February 7, 1904, the Department decided that Indians to whom lands were allotted under the allotment act of February 8, 1887 (24 Stat. L., 388), had no right to alienate their lands by will within the period during which the lands are held in trust by the United States, and that upon the death of the allottee the lands descended to the heirs according to the laws of the State or Territory in which they may be situated, and that no will purporting to make a different distribution of such lands can be recognized by the Department as conveying any title whatever.

The will is returned herewith.

Very respectfully,

John Thomas Jr
Acting Chief Clerk.

TFM-2

REGULATIONS GOVERNING THE APPROVAL OF WILLS OF INDIANS UNDER THE ACT OF CONGRESS APPROVED FEBRUARY 14, 1913.

The act of Congress approved February 14, 1913, provides (Public, No. 381):

Be it enacted by the Senate and House of Representatives of the United States of America in Congress assembled. That section two of an act entitled "An act to provide for determining the heirs of deceased Indians, for the disposition and sale of allotments of deceased Indians, for the leasing of allotments, and for other purposes," approved June twenty-fifth, nineteen hundred and ten, be amended to read as follows:

"Sec. 2." That any persons of the age of twenty-one years having any right, title, or interest in any allotment held under trust or other patent containing restrictions on alienation or individual Indian moneys or other property held in trust by the United States shall have the right prior to the expiration of the trust or restrictive period, and before the issuance of a fee simple patent or the removal of restrictions, to dispose of such property by will, in accordance with regulations to be prescribed by the Secretary of the Interior: *Provided, however,* That no will so executed shall be valid or have any force or effect unless and until it shall have been approved by the Secretary of the Interior: *Provided further,* That the Secretary of the Interior may approve or disapprove the will either before or after the death of the testator, and in case where a will has been approved and it is subsequently discovered that there has been fraud in connection with the execution or procurement of the will, the Secretary of the Interior is hereby authorized within one year after the death of the testator to cancel the approval of the will, and the property of the testator shall thereupon descend or be distributed in accordance with the laws of the State wherein the property is located: *Provided further,* That the approval of the will and the death of the testator shall not operate to terminate the trust or restrictive period, but the Secretary of the Interior may, in his discretion, cause the lands to be sold and the money derived therefrom, or so much thereof as may be necessary, used for the benefit of the heir or heirs entitled thereto, remove the restrictions or cause patent in fee to be issued to the devisee or devisees, and pay the moneys to the legatee or legatees either in whole or in part from time to time as he may deem advisable, or use it for their benefit: *Provided also,* That sections one and two of this act shall not apply to the Five Civilized Tribes or the Osage Indians."

The will of any Indian filed for approval under this act shall be forwarded through the superintendent or other officer in charge of the agency having supervision over the property disposed of, and he will lend all necessary assistance to the Indian, aiding him as far as possible in the drawing of his will, informing and advising him as to the law and his rights, but under no circumstance endeavoring to influence the manner of testamentary disposition. It is not necessary, however, that the will be drawn by, or in the presence of, such superintendent or other officer.

It shall be the duty of such superintendent or other officer, before submitting such will, to inquire fully into the mental competency of the Indian; the circumstances attending the execution of the will; the influences which induced its execution; and the names of those entitled to share in the estate under the State law of descent; and, where the distribution proposed by the will has cut off natural heirs and disposed of all the estate to persons who would not otherwise inherit, there should be obtained from the testator, if living, an affidavit setting forth the reasons for so disinheriting such natural heirs. In case the testator is dead, endeavor should be made to ascertain from the most reliable sources the reasons for making such disposition. The competency of all devisees and legatees to manage their own affairs should be investigated.

The will, together with the execution thereof, should conform to the laws of the State in which the testator is domiciled, where personal property is bequeathed, and to the laws of the State where the real estate is located, when such property is devised, and the will should be submitted in duplicate.

In case the will is filed and approved before the death of the testator, it will be returned to the superintendent or other officer for safe-keeping, and, after the death of the testator, should again be forwarded for record in the Office of the Commissioner of Indian Affairs.

The Indian should be advised that the filing and approval of his will will not prevent its subsequent modification or revocation by the testator, but any such modification or revocation can be made only with departmental approval. The report of the superintendent or other officer submitting the will should contain in full detail all the information required by these regulations and a specific recommendation respecting its approval.

The will should describe specifically the trust property attempted to be disposed of in order that examination may be made in the Indian Office by reference to its records to determine whether the land is actually allotted or inherited by the testator, whether a patent in fee has previously issued therefore, or whether the land has been sold under any law applicable thereto. A certificate of the appraised value of the land must be furnished.

In cases where a will had been made and the testator has died before submitting the will for the consideration of the department, a hearing shall be held to determine his or her legal heirs, and, where the distribution made in the will differs from that which would otherwise be made under the State law of descent, if the testator had died intestate, the legal heirs shall be notifies of the existence of the will and its provisions and be given full opportunity to object to its approval.

F. H. ABBOTT,
Acting Commissioner of Indian Affairs.

Approved June 18, 1913.

LEWIS C. LAYLIN,
Assistant Secretary of the Interior.

DEPARTMENT OF THE INTERIOR
R E C E I V E D

UNITED STATES INDIAN SERVICE

JAN 4 1916

Round Valley School.   SAC & FOX AGENCY, OKLAHOMA.

Covelo, Cal., Dec. 29, 1915.

Supt. Horace J. Johnson,
  Sac and Fox Reservation,
    Stroud, Oklahoma.

Dear Sir:

It has been brought to my attention that a will was written for Delia Wright, Round Valley allottee #340 by Charles Dorman, who was the farmer at this Agency at that time, and signed by two witnesses and then same was turned over to you.

Notices of hearing to determine the heirs of Delia Wright have been issued, to be held the 29th day of January, 1916 and if you have this will or any information concerning it, will you please forward same to me at your earliest convenience.

Very respectfully,

EA Hutchinson

MEG/RL.   Superintendent.

By Michael E. Gorman

    Clerk. in Inheritance.

****

Sac & Fox Indian School,
  Stroud, Okla., Jan. 8, 1916.

Supt. E. A. Hutchison,
  Round Valley School,
    Covelo, Cal.

Dear Sir:

257

I acknowledge receipt of your letter of December 29th with reference to the will of Delia Wright, Round Valley allottee #340. I have to advise that I have an indistinct recollection that such a will was filed with me while I was superintendent, and I do not think though that I had anything to do [sic] its preparation and believe that I stated to the parties that it was my opinion that it was of no force or effect. I do not remember where it was filed, but think it was placed in the safe in the office. At any rate I can give you no definite information, and I do not have the will.

Very respectfully,

Supt. & S. D. A.

HJJ/L

Shawnee Indian Agency,
Shawnee, Oklahoma,
Dec. 6, 1921.

Mrs. Annie Perry Tohee,
Red Rock, Oklahoma.

Dear Madam:

When you were in this office that last time you left a statement to the effect that you wished to make a will to your son and grandson, namely, Farron Roubidoux and Harrison Whitehorn.

You are informed that it is the desire of this office at all times to carry out the wishes of the Indians under its jurisdiction whenever it can reasonably do so. Therefore, you may come to this office or the Agency nearest you for the purpose of making the will mentioned by you. In the event you take up this matter with an Agency nearest you the papers should [sic] mailed to this office for transmittal to the Indian Office for approval.

Should you conclude to come to this office for transaction of this matter you should write us as to the date you will be here.

Very truly yours,

12 od 6,   J. L. Suffecool,
                                                                      Superintendent.

Shawnee Indian Agency
Shawnee, Oklahoma
December 27, 1921

W. L. Chapman
Attorney
Shawnee, Oklahoma

Dear Sir:

Replying to your letter of December 21, concerning your request for a copy of the will left by Cinda Switch, (La ko nah ha), you are advised that this will, as approved by the Department covers her trust allotment, which the heirs are agreeable to, and under the regulations of the Department, the will concerns the trust property held in trust for the Indians, by the United States, and is no applicable to other property, hence, no copy of the will is deemed advisable to be given to other than the interested parties.

Very truly yours,

J. L. Suffecool
Superintendent

JJ/JC

Shawnee Indian Agency,
Shawnee, Oklahoma,
January 2, 1923.

Mr. Thomas Lincoln,
    Perkins, Oklahoma.

Dear Sir:-

        There is inclosed herewith the will you had Mr. Dushane prepare for you according to your wishes with perhaps one exception--

259

the paragraph relative to Jack Lincoln's share in this will which covers the John Moses allotment instead of the Joseph Enabler allotment. This was done for two reasons; first, the Joseph Enabler allotment is not susceptible to an equal division whereas the Moses allotment is. The second reason is that the Moses allotment is almost in the same section as the land now owned by Jack Lincoln. I trust this will meet with your approval.

There is perhaps another deviation from you wish as to the matter of payment of debts. Your wish written to Mr. Dushane that all debts made after date of this will should be considered only could not be complied with without destroying the purpose of your will, as the State law particularly states that all [illegible] assume just debts of the deceased.

On January 19th representatives from this office will be in Cushing, Oklahoma, and it is directed that you make your visit there for the purpose of executing this will, if the will is satisfactory to yourself and wife. If the will is not satisfactory to you and wife, please return the same with instructions for such changes as you consider proper.

Very respectfully,

J. L. Suffecool
Superintendent

CD:EV. ENCL.

Shawnee Indian Agency,
Shawnee, Oklahoma,
January 27, 1923.

Mr. John Thompson,
 R#4, Cushing, Okla.

Dear Sir:-

Referring to my conversation with you with reference to a will you desire to make in favor of your daughter, Grace Thompson; I have to advise that I am going to give this matter consideration, and just as soon as the time can be found to attend to the same.

I will be pleased to confer with you further with reference to the matter.

Very respectfully,

J. L. Suffecool
Superintendent.

JLS
EV

Shawnee Indian Agency,
Shawnee, Oklahoma,
February 8, 1923

Mrs. Julia Vieux,
  Konawa, Oklahoma,
  R #2, Box 58.

Dear Madam:-

There is inclosed herewith a deed conveying your inherited interest in the allotment of Pete Ship-she-wano, allottee No. 548 to your children Frank Wano, Isaac Wano, Stella Wano, and Benjamin Wano; also heirs of the deceased allottee.

You will notice that this deed has the necessary restrictive clause with the condition that you will retain a lifetime use therein. You understand that the purpose of this deed is as a will giving your share of this allotment to your several children.

Immediately after you have completed the execution of this deed, return it to this office for submittal to the Department. You will notice that it will be necessary to have two witnesses sign the deed with you in the space provided for their names. Also you should have it acknowledged before some Notary Public.

Very respectfully,

J. L. Suffecool
Superintendent.

Shawnee Indian Agency,
Shawnee, Oklahoma,
February 24, 1923.

Mrs. Mary Kent Pettit,
Redrock, Oklahoma.

Dear Madam:-

This replies to your letter of the 10th inst. relative to a will that you say was made by your father, Frank Kent of Redrock, Oklahoma.

You are advised that there has been no will made by Frank Kent but there has been a deed made in favor of two of his youngest daughters. You understand that this property belongs solely to Frank Kent and that the Government recognizes his right to dispose of this property by will or deed as he chooses with its approval. This deed has been submitted to the Indian Office for appropriate action and if approved you will have no recourse for the reason that Frank Kent has the right to dispose of this property in this manner.

If this had been made in the form of a will you would have a right to protest within a certain period after the death of your father, but since this has been done by deed it appears to this office that there is nothing further to be done.

Very respectfully,

J. L. Suffecool
Superintendent.

CD:EV.

Shawnee Indian Agency,
Shawnee, Oklahoma,
April 4, 1923.

The Honorable,
The Commissioner
    of Indian Affairs,
        Washington, D. C.

My dear Mr. Commissioner:-

Information is requested as follows:

Harriett Pratt, Pottawatomie Indian, died many years ago. She was allotted 330 acres of land. She was survived by a husband and eight children and the heirs have been determined by the Secretary of the Interior. The husband is a white man and he received according to this determination one-third of the entire estate. The other being divided equally among the eight children.

A year ago last July the husband of Harriett Pratt, deceased, executed a will. In this will he willed to his youngest son, Charley Pratt his undivided one-third interest in the wife's estate. The father died the fifth day of July, 1922. Shortly after his death this will was brought to this office and kept on file here.

During October, 1922 there was a hearing held to determine the heirs but the papers in the case were never fully completed. Now one of the heirs comes and declares that he is of the opinion that his father being a white man could not under the law of the Federal Government execute a will and information is desired as to whether he could or could not execute this will under existing Federal law.

Very respectfully,

J. L. Suffecool,
Superintendent.

JLS:EV.

Shawnee Indian Agency,
Shawnee, Oklahoma,
April 9, 1923.

Mr. Leo Wilmot,
R#3, Mayetta, Kansas.

Dear Sir;-

I have your letter of March 8, 1923 with regard ti the estate of Frank Wilmette, wherein you inquire concerning certain will made by, for, or in connection with the estate of Frank Wilmette. You are advised that this office has no knowledge whatever of said will which you say was forced by Superintendent A. R Snyder and Mrs. Anna May Linscum. Information concerning said will should be requested of Supt. A. R. Snyder.

Anything concerning the allotment of said Frank
Wilmette will be given you at your request.

Very respectfully,

CD:EV.

J. L. Suffecool,
Superintendent.

Shawnee Indian Agency,
Shawnee, Oklahoma,
Oct. 17th, 1923.

The Commissioner
of Indian Affairs,
Washington, D. C.

Dear Mr. Commissioner:-

Inclosed herewith are two deeds covering the
allotment of Benjamin Harrison, Sac & Fox allottee No. 424, described
as the SW/4 of 29-17-6. These two deeds were made in favor of Ione
C. Bass and Lee Bass with the proper restrictive clause and with the
further condition that a lifetime use thereof be retained by the grantor.

The purpose of these deeds is to take the place of a
will, in as much as Ione C. Bass and Lee Bass are the grandchildren of
Jane Bentley, the grantor.

Ione C. Bass has on deposit to her credit something
like $1,000. Lee Bass has no funds to his credit but is a patent in fee
Indian and fairly competent.

I would respectfully recommend approval of the deeds
for the purpose for which they are made.

Very truly yours,

J. L. Suffecool,
Superintendent.

CD:EV.
encls.

Shawnee Indian Agency,
Shawnee, Oklahoma,
February 19, 1924.

The Honorable
    The Commissioner of Indian Affairs,
        Washington, D. C.

My dear Mr. Commissioner:

        There is submitted herewith Indian Deed covering the
allotment of Peter Ship-she-wano, allottee #648 of the Citizen
Pottawatomie tribe.

        This deed is in the nature of a will conveyed by Julia
Wano, now Vieux, in the favor of her five children wherein she retains
a lifetime use.

        I respectfully recommend that the deed be approved.

                Very respectfully,

incl.   J. L. Suffecool,
CD-Mc   Superintendent.

Shawnee Indian Agency,
Shawnee, Oklahoma,
March 22, 1924.

The Commissioner of Indian Affairs,
        Washington, D. C.

My dear Mr. Commissioner:

        There is transmitted herewith Indian Deed Inherited Lands
covering the allotment of Sophia Embler or Kish-tah-che-un, of the
Iowa tribe, from Thomas Lincoln, sole heir, to his son Thomas Lincoln
Jr., age 9 months.

        This deed is in the nature of a will and I respectfully recommend
its approval.

Very respectfully,

D/Mc

J. L. Suffecool,
Superintendent.

Index

www.ingramcontent.com/pod-product-compliance
Lightning Source LLC
Chambersburg PA
CBHW020247030426
42336CB00010B/653

Other Books and Series by Jeff Bowen

Compilation of History of the Cherokee Indians and Early History of the Cherokees by Emmet Starr with Combined Full Name Index
(Hardbound & Softbound)

1901-1907 Native American Census Seneca, Eastern Shawnee, Miami, Modoc, Ottawa, Peoria, Quapaw, and Wyandotte Indians (Under Seneca School, Indian Territory)

1932 Census of The Standing Rock Sioux Reservation with Births And Deaths 1924-1932

Census of The Blackfeet, Montana, 1897- 1901 Expanded Edition

Eastern Cherokee by Blood, 1906-1910, Volumes I thru XIII

Choctaw of Mississippi Indian Census 1929-1932 with Births and Deaths 1924-1931   Volume I
Choctaw of Mississippi Indian Census 1933, 1934 & 1937, Supplemental Rolls to 1934 & 1935 with Births and Deaths 1932-1938, and Marriages 1936-1938 Volume II

Eastern Cherokee Census Cherokee, North Carolina 1930-1939
Census 1930-1931 with Births And Deaths 1924-1931 Taken By Agent L. W. Page Volume I
Eastern Cherokee Census Cherokee, North Carolina 1930-1939
Census 1932-1933 with Births And Deaths 1930-1932 Taken By Agent R. L. Spalsbury   Volume II
Eastern Cherokee Census Cherokee, North Carolina 1930-1939
Census 1934-1937 with Births and Deaths 1925-1938 and Marriages 1936 & 1938 Taken by Agents R. L. Spalsbury And Harold W. Foght Volume III

Seminole of Florida Indian Census, 1930-1940 with Birth and Death Records, 1930-1938

Texas Cherokees 1820-1839 A Document For Litigation 1921

Starr Roll 1894   (Cherokee Payment Rolls) Districts: Canadian, Cooweescoowee, and Delaware Volume One
Starr Roll 1894 (Cherokee Payment Rolls) Districts: Flint, Going Snake, and Illinois   Volume Two
Starr Roll 1894 (Cherokee Payment Rolls) Districts: Saline, Sequoyah, and Tahlequah; Including Orphan Roll   Volume Three

Cherokee Intruder Cases Dockets of Hearings 1901-1909 Volumes I & II

Indian Wills, 1911-1921 Records of the Bureau of Indian Affairs
Books One thru Seven

Other Books and Series by Jeff Bowen

Native American Wills & Probate Records 1911-1921

Turtle Mountain Reservation Chippewa Indians 1932 Census with Births & Deaths, 1924-1932

Chickasaw By Blood Enrollment Cards 1898-1914 Volume I thru V

Cherokee Descendants East An Index to the Guion Miller Applications Volume I
Cherokee Descendants West An Index to the Guion Miller Applications Volume II (A-M)
Cherokee Descendants West An Index to the Guion Miller Applications Volume III (N-Z)

Applications for Enrollment of Seminole Newborn Freedmen, Act of 1905

Eastern Cherokee Census, Cherokee, North Carolina, 1915-1922, Taken by Agent James E. Henderson   Volume I (1915-1916)
Volume II (1917-1918)
Volume III (1919-1920)
Volume IV (1921-1922)

Complete Delaware Roll of 1898

Eastern Cherokee Census, Cherokee, North Carolina, 1923-1929, Taken by Agent James E. Henderson   Volume I (1923-1924)
Volume II (1925-1926)
Volume III (1927-1929)

Applications for Enrollment of Seminole Newborn Act of 1905 Volumes I & II

North Carolina Eastern Cherokee Indian Census 1898-1899, 1904, 1906, 1909-1912, 1914   Revised and Expanded Edition

1932 Hopi and Navajo Native American Census with Birth & Death Rolls (1925-1931) Volume 1 - Hopi
1932 Hopi and Navajo Native American Census with Birth & Death Rolls (1930-1932) Volume 2 - Navajo

Western Navajo Reservation Navajo, Hopi and Paiute 1933 Census with Birth & Death Rolls 1925-1933

Cherokee Citizenship Commission Dockets 1880-1884 and 1887-1889 Volumes I thru V

Applications for Enrollment of Chickasaw Newborn Act of 1905 Volumes I thru VII